ZAGATSURVEY®

2000 UPDATE

PHILADELPHIA RESTAURANTS

**Edited and Updated by Michael Klein
and Norma Gottlieb**

Coordinated by Mark Brown

Published and distributed by
ZAGAT SURVEY, LLC
4 Columbus Circle
New York, New York 10019
Tel: 212 977 6000
E-mail: zagat@zagatsurvey.com
Web site: www.zagat.com

Acknowledgments

Our warmest thanks to our spouses and to the following individuals: Fran and Joe Alberstadt, Charlotte Ann Albertson, Claudia Archer, Bunny and Richard Bortel, Heidi Bortner, Greg Boyer, Jane Buffam, Don Camera, Mary Di Stanislao, Sherley Hollos, Tim Hunter, Rachel and Lindsay Klein, Marcie Meritz, Sarah Sweeney Denham, Pat Tabibian; and to the following organizations and businesses: American Institute of Wine and Food, Assouline and Ting, Borders Books, Chadds Ford Winery, Chef's Market, Cherry Hill Fine Wines and Liquors, The Cookery Ware Shop, Fantes, Feast Your Eyes, Foster's, Grandpa Hicks, Greenfield Grocer, Jill's Vorspeise, Kitchen Kapers, La Chaine des Rotisseurs, Les Dames d'Escoffier, Mr. Yummy, The Pennsylvania General Store, The Philadelphia Women's Culinary Guild, Rizzoli Bookstore and Triangle Liquors; without your help, this *Survey* would not have been possible.

Contents

Starters

This is not an all-new *Survey*. It is an *Update* reflecting significant developments since our last *Philadelphia Restaurant Survey* was published. We have included a section of "2000 Additions" (see pages 19–26), covering over 32 key places that were not in the previous *Survey*. We also have made changes throughout the book (excluding indexes) to show new addresses, phone numbers, chef changes, closings, etc.

As a whole, this *Update* covers more than 913 restaurants in the Philadelphia area, including Atlantic City, Cape May, Lancaster/Berks County, Wilmington and nearby Delaware, with input from nearly 3,300 people. We sincerely thank each participant. This book is really "theirs." By surveying large numbers of regular restaurant-goers, we think we have achieved a uniquely reliable guide. We hope you agree.

To help guide our readers to Philadelphia's best meals and best buys, we have prepared a number of lists. See, for example, Philadelphia's Most Popular Restaurants (page 11), Top Ratings (pages 12–16) and Best Buys (pages 17–18). On the assumption that most people want a "quick fix" on the places at which they are considering eating, we have tried to be concise and to provide handy indexes.

We are particularly grateful to our editors, Michael Klein, an editor and columnist at the *Philadelphia Inquirer,* and Norma Gottlieb, a cooking and art instructor at the Delaware Valley Friends School, and to our coordinator, Mark Brown, a marketing specialist to the gourmet and gift industries.

We invite you to be a reviewer in our next *Survey*. To do so, simply send a stamped, self-addressed, business-size envelope to ZAGAT SURVEY, 4 Columbus Circle, New York, NY 10019, so that we will be able to contact you. Each participant will receive a free copy of the next *Philadelphia Restaurant Survey* when it is published.

Your comments, suggestions and even criticisms of this *Survey* are also solicited. There is always room for improvement with your help!

New York, New York   Nina and Tim Zagat
June 16, 1999

What's New

"I once went to Philadelphia and it was closed."

W.C. Fields – who made our city a punch line – must be rolling in his grave. Closed? Hah! 11 PM and they're three-deep at chic watering holes along Walnut Street. At 2 AM, the streets in the Old City section of town are jammed with revelers who reluctantly wind down shortly before dawn after breakfast at an all-night eatery.

Philadelphia is open. Very open. For years, we've quietly enjoyed a dynamic dining scene that was a best-kept secret. Now our chefs are bringing home national awards: Marc Vetri of the brand new rustic Italian Vetri, recently named one of *Food & Wine* magazine's best new toques, is our latest honoree. And he's just one factor in the gastronomic windfall that began with restaurants popping up all over town to serve the increasingly booked Convention Center. The recent announcement by the Republican National Convention that they will convene here in 2000 to choose their Presidential nominee has turned the heat up even higher.

Ground zero of the current boom is the hot-hot-hot Old City area where the latest newsmakers include Buddakan, a jam-packed Pan-Asian catering to beautiful people; DiPalma, a plush, chef-owned Italian; Lena, a sleek, family-run Eclectic; Marmont, a smart Asian fusion salon; Oberon, a boisterous Mediterranean bistro and Sabooor!, a festive little Latin BYO.

South Street, whose fortunes and demographics tend to wax and wane, seems to be on an upswing. Bill Beck has retooled his Pompano Grille into a successful Euro lounge fittingly named Bohemian Bistro. Amara Cafe, the Center City Thai gem, has sprouted a branch called East of Amara in the former digs of Sala Thai.

Restaurant Row in Center City saw the opening of the Sheraton Rittenhouse Square Hotel in early 1999, with three well-received eateries under the direction of chef Tony Clark, who had left his eponymous Broad Street venue in 1998. Though Clark already has announced his intentions to move on (and one restaurant has already closed), the remaining Potcheen, a casual pub, and Square Bar, an arty Italian, are doing quite nicely. Center City's other notable arrivals include Pasion!, a sizzling Latin starring Guillermo Pernot (ex Vega Grill) and Michael Dombkoski (ex Susanna Foo).

Other solid rookies include Il Cantuccio, a postage stamp–sized trattoria in Northern Liberties and Kristian's, a dazzling, chef-run Italian in South Philadelphia. In other late-breaking news, Mia's, the superb Mediterranean in the Warwick Hotel, is closing for a summer renovation and due back in the fall with a new name and concept. Morton's of Chicago, the Logan Square steakhouse, is planning a move to new digs on Walnut Street. Striped Bass snagged a new chef

(Terence Feury of NYC's Le Bernardin) and the posh sea-fooder is even better than before. The Italian stalwart DiLullo has resurfaced after being renovated and renamed Toto.

Yet even as the scene continues to percolate, some closings are inevitable. Noteworthy departures include Jake & Oliver's House of Brews, La Cocotte, Loose Ends, Mademoiselle de Paris and Purple Sage, but there are plenty of contenders preparing to take their place. The revival of the Cajun-Creole favorite Cafe Nola should be open by fall, along with Davio's, the Boston-based Italian seafooder that's readying a space at 17th and Chestnut. Another splashy entry, a big-budget International called Kaleidoscope Kafe, is on track for a mid-1999 debut. At press time, Joseph Varalli was about to unveil Sotto, a global seafooder, tucked beneath his long-running hit Upstares at Varalli. And, within two years, a DisneyQuest entertainment center is coming to Market Street, between the Convention Center and the Liberty Bell. A slew of upscale eateries are sure to follow.

And elsewhere in the extended area, this *Survey* covers the Pennsylvania suburbs, where the Big River Fish Co., with branches in Jenkintown and Bryn Mawr, has just added grilled meats to their seafood menu and changed their name to the Lewis & Clark Grill & Bar. Bala Cynwyd's Montgomery Grill is drawing Main Liners with prime steakhouse fare, while the busiest newcomer in Huntingdon Valley is Stefano's, a cozy Italian BYO. In Radnor, Carlo deMarco (ex Bridget Foy's on South Street) is prepping 333 Belrose, a straightforward American. And the Valley Forge Brewing Co. is mastermind-ing a pub in Center Square's former Tiffany Dining Place.

Happening New Jersey newcomers include Olive, a Cherry Hill Mediterranean; Daniel's on Broadway, a New American in West Cape May; and the revived Knife & Fork, a Continental in Atlantic City. In Wilmington, Black Trumpet Bistro, a chef-owned New American, is generating a favorable buzz.

The average cost for a meal in this *Survey* is $26.54, which compares quite favorably to New York City ($31.68), though it's somewhat pricier than other East Coast hubs like Washington, D.C. ($25.46) and Boston ($21.76). Still, your dining dollar covers a lot of ground here – and we trust that this guide will steer you to some fine meals, whether they be quick, after-work fixes or leisurely repasts by the sea.

And we're holding a table for W.C. Fields, wherever he may be.

Philadelphia, PA   Michael Klein
June 16, 1999

Key to Ratings/Symbols

This sample entry identifies the various types of
information contained in your Zagat Survey.

(1) Restaurant Name, Address & Phone Number

(2) Hours & Credit Cards

(3) ZAGAT Ratings

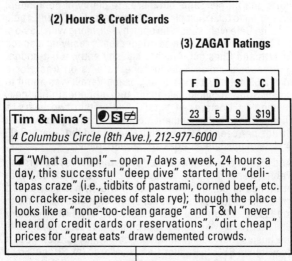

F	D	S	C
23	5	9	$19

Tim & Nina's ◖ S ≠

4 Columbus Circle (8th Ave.), 212-977-6000

◪ "What a dump!" – open 7 days a week, 24 hours a
day, this successful "deep dive" started the "deli-
tapas craze" (i.e., tidbits of pastrami, corned beef, etc.
on cracker-size pieces of stale rye); though the place
looks like a "none-too-clean garage" and T & N "never
heard of credit cards or reservations", "dirt cheap"
prices for "great eats" draw demented crowds.

(4) Surveyors' Commentary

The names of restaurants with the highest overall ratings,
greatest popularity and importance are printed in **CAPITAL
LETTERS**. Address and phone numbers are printed in *italics*.

(2) Hours & Credit Cards

After each restaurant name you will find the following
courtesy information:

◖ .... *serving after 11 PM*

S .... *open on Sunday*

≠ .... *no credit cards accepted*

(3) ZAGAT Ratings

Food, **Decor** and **Service** are each rated on a scale of **0** to **30**:

F	D	S	C

F .... *Food*
D .... *Decor*
S .... *Service*
C .... *Cost*

23	5	9	$19

0 - 9	.... *poor to fair*
10 - 15	.... *fair to good*
16 - 19	.... *good to very good*
20 - 25	.... *very good to excellent*
26 - 30	.... *extraordinary to perfection*

▽ 23	5	9	$19

▽ .... *Low number of votes/less reliable*

The **Cost (C)** column reflects the estimated price of a dinner with one drink and tip. Lunch usually costs 25% less.

A restaurant listed without ratings is either an important **newcomer** or a popular **write-in**. The estimated cost, with one drink and tip, is indicated by the following symbols.

–	–	–	VE

I	.... *$15 and below*
M	.... *$16 to $30*
E	.... *$31 to $50*
VE	.... *$51 or more*

(4) Surveyors' Commentary

Surveyors' comments are summarized, with literal comments shown in quotation marks. The following symbols indicate whether responses were mixed or uniform.

◪ .... *mixed*
◼ .... *uniform*

9

Most Popular Restaurants

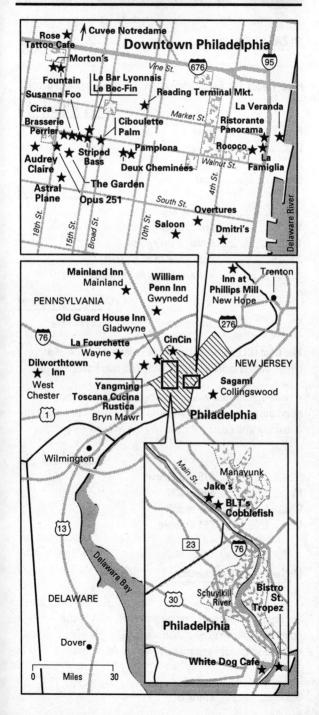

Downtown Philadelphia

Cuvee Notredame
Rose Tattoo Cafe ★
Morton's
Fountain
Le Bar Lyonnais
Le Bec-Fin
Susanna Foo
Reading Terminal Mkt.
Circa
La Veranda
Brasserie Perrier
Ristorante Panorama
Ciboulette
Palm
Rococo
La Famiglia
Pamplona
Striped Bass
Audrey Claire
Deux Cheminées
Astral Plane
The Garden
Opus 251
Overtures
Saloon
Dmitri's

Vine St. 676 95
Market St.
Walnut St.
South St.
18th St. 15th St. Broad St. 10th St. 4th St.
Delaware River

Mainland Inn
Mainland
William Penn Inn
Gwynedd
Inn at Phillips Mill
New Hope
Trenton

PENNSYLVANIA
Old Guard House Inn
Gladwyne
La Fourchette
Wayne
CinCin
Dilworthtown Inn
West Chester
Yangming
Toscana Cucina Rustica
Bryn Mawr
NEW JERSEY
Sagami
Collingswood
Philadelphia

Wilmington

76 276 1 13 30

Manayunk
Jake's
BLT's
Cobblefish
Main St.
23 76

Delaware Bay
DELAWARE
Schuylkill River
Bistro St. Tropez

Dover

0 Miles 30

White Dog Cafe

Philadelphia

Most Popular Restaurants

Each of our reviewers has been asked to name his or her five favorite restaurants. The 40 spots most frequently named, in order of their popularity, are:

1. Le Bec-Fin	21. Le Bar Lyonnais
2. Fountain	22. Toscana Cucina Rustica
3. Susanna Foo	23. Palm
4. Brasserie Perrier	24. Ristorante Panorama
5. Striped Bass	25. Old Guard House Inn
6. Jake's	26. Rococo
7. White Dog Cafe	27. Pamplona
8. Dmitri's	28. Overtures
9. Ciboulette	29. Astral Plane
10. Dilworthtown Inn	30. CinCin
11. Yangming	31. Inn at Phillips Mill
12. Saloon	32. Morton's of Chicago
13. Deux Cheminées	33. William Penn Inn
14. Mainland Inn	34. BLT's Cobblefish
15. Bistro St. Tropez	35. La Famiglia
16. Sagami	36. Audrey Claire
17. Rose Tattoo Cafe	37. La Veranda
18. Garden, The	38. Opus 251
19. Reading Terminal Mkt.	39. La Fourchette
20. Circa	40. Cuvee Notredame

It's obvious that many of the restaurants on the above list are among the most expensive, but Philadelphians also love a bargain. Were popularity calibrated to price, we suspect that a number of other restaurants would join the above ranks. Thus, we have listed over 100 Best Buys on pages 17–18.

Top Ratings*

Top 40 Food Ranking

29 Le Bec-Fin
Fountain
Le Bar Lyonnais
27 Sagami
Brasserie Perrier
Susanna Foo
Deux Cheminées
Mainland Inn
Isabella's
Swann Lounge
Jake's
Dmitri's
Dilworthtown Inn
26 Ciboulette
Striped Bass
Coventry Forge Inn
Morton's of Chicago
Tacconelli's Pizza
Overtures
Monte Carlo Liv. Rm.

Evermay/Delaware
La Famiglia
La Campagne
25 Saloon
Catelli
Founders
La Fourchette
Jean Pierre's
Inn at Phillips Mill
Spiga d'Oro
Savona
Umbria
Beau Rivage
Alisa Cafe
Diamond's
24 Black Walnut
La Bonne Auberge
Yangming
Fork
Vietnam Restaurant

Top Spots by Cuisine

Additions
Buddakan
Pasion!
Philippe's on Locust
Pompeii
Vetri

American (New)
27 Mainland Inn
Jake's
Dilworthtown Inn
26 Evermay/Delaware
25 Founders

American (Regional)
23 Opus 251
Roscoe's Kodiak Cafe
22 Kimberton Inn
21 California Cafe
King George II Inn

American (Traditional)
23 Old Guard House Inn
Meil's
22 Braddock's Tavern
Joseph Ambler Inn
Century House

Breakfast**
24 Reading Terminal Mkt.
23 Shank's & Evelyn's
Meil's
22 Blue in Green
19 Carman's Country Kitchen

Brunch
29 Fountain
27 Swann Lounge
26 La Campagne
25 Founders
La Fourchette

---

* Excluding top Lancaster/Berks County, Atlantic City/Cape May/
Shore and Wilmington and nearby Delaware restaurants, which
start on pages 128, 133 and 151, and restaurants with low voting.
** Other than hotels.

Chinese
27 Susanna Foo
24 Yangming
   CinCin
23 Lee How Fook
   Charles Plaza

Continental
29 Fountain
27 Swann Lounge
23 Rose Tree Inn
   Duling-Kurtz House
   Vickers Tavern

Dessert
27 Swann Lounge
24 Pink Rose Pastry Shop
   Roselena's Coffee Bar
23 Cassatt Tea Room
21 Main-ly Desserts

Dining with Kids
24 Reading Terminal Mkt.
19 Le Bus
   El Mariachi
18 Joy Tsin Lau
17 City Tavern

Eclectic
25 Umbria
24 A Little Cafe
   General Warren Inne
   Roselena's Coffee Bar
23 Marker, The

French
29 Le Bec-Fin
27 Deux Cheminées
26 Coventry Forge Inn
25 La Fourchette
   Jean Pierre's

French Bistros
29 Le Bar Lyonnais
26 La Campagne
25 Inn at Phillips Mill
24 Frenchtown Inn
   Bistro St. Tropez

French New
27 Brasserie Perrier
26 Ciboulette
24 Black Walnut
   Siri's Thai French
   Taquet

Hotel Dining
29 Fountain
   Four Seasons
27 Swann Lounge
   Four Seasons
25 Founders
   Park Hyatt/Bellevue
24 Ritz-Carlton Grill
   Ritz-Carlton Hotel
   Marker
   Adam's Mark

Indian
23 Palace of Asia
21 Tandoor India
20 Passage to India
   Minar Palace
19 Sitar India

International
24 Reading Terminal Mkt.
23 Totaro's Ristorante
21 Spring Mill Café
   Knave of Hearts
20 Paradigm

Italian/N&S
27 Isabella's
26 Monte Carlo Liv. Rm.
   La Famiglia
25 Catelli
   Spiga d'Oro

Italian/Northern
25 Saloon
24 Giumarello's Ristorante
   La Locanda del Ghiottone
22 Il Portico
   Gourmet's Table

Italian/Southern
25 Savona
23 Shank's & Evelyn's
22 D'Angelo's
   Ristorante Positano
21 Ristorante Primavera

Japanese
27 Sagami
23 Genji
   Shiroi Hana
20 Meiji-En
   Hikaru

Mediterranean
27 Dmitri's
26 Overtures
24 Ritz-Carlton Grill
23 Hamilton's Grill Room
22 Mirna's Cafe

Mexican/SW
23 Tequila's
22 Zocalo
19 Mexican Food Factory
   El Mariachi
18 Santa Fe Burrito Co.

Mideastern/Moroccan
23 Bitar's
21 Persian Grill
19 Maccabeam
   Alyan's
18 Al Khimah

People-Watching
27 Brasserie Perrier
26 Striped Bass
25 Savona
24 Fork
   White Dog Cafe

Pizza
26 Tacconelli's Pizza
23 DeLorenzo's Tomato Pies
22 Arpeggio
20 Celebre's Pizzeria
19 La Cipolla Torta

Power Lunch
29 Le Bec-Fin
   Fountain
27 Brasserie Perrier
26 Striped Bass
   Morton's of Chicago

Seafood
27 Dmitri's
26 Striped Bass
23 Ristorante La Buca
   Roscoe's Kodiak Cafe
   La Veranda

Steakhouses
26 Morton's of Chicago
24 Kansas City Prime
23 Palm
   Ruth's Chris
21 Seven Stars Inn

Thai
22 Siam Cuisine
   Amara Cafe
   Pattaya Grill
   Thai Singha House
21 My Thai

Trips to Bucks County
26 Evermay/Delaware
25 Jean Pierre's
   Inn at Phillips Mill
24 Black Walnut
   La Bonne Auberge

Trips to Chester County
27 Dilworthtown Inn
26 Coventry Forge Inn
24 General Warren Inne
23 America Bar & Grill
   Duling-Kurtz House

Trips to New Jersey
27 Sagami
26 La Campagne
25 Catelli
   Beau Rivage
24 Frenchtown Inn

Vietnamese
24 Vietnam Restaurant
22 Saigon
21 Capital Vietnam
   Pho 75
   Vietnam Palace

Yearlings/Rated
27 Brasserie Perrier
25 Savona
24 A Little Cafe
23 Opus 251
   Siggie's L'Auberge

Yearlings/Unrated
   Beaujolais
   Beau Monde
   Le Colonial
   Penang
   Rouge 99

Top 40 Decor Ranking

29 Le Bec-Fin
Fountain
28 Deux Cheminées
Founders
Striped Bass
27 Barrymore Room
Swann Lounge
Dilworthtown Inn
Savona
Brasserie Perrier
Kennedy-Supplee
Roselena's Coffee Bar
26 Inn at Phillips Mill
Cassatt Tea Room
Evermay/Delaware
La Bonne Auberge
Rococo
Susanna Foo
25 Passerelle
Nicholas Nickolas

Fork
Beau Rivage
Duling-Kurtz House
Coventry Forge Inn
DiLullo Centro
Mainland Inn
Moshulu
Catelli
24 Ciboulette
General Warren Inne
Garden, The
La Campagne
Treetops
Monte Carlo Liv. Rm.
Azalea Room
Overtures
Ritz-Carlton Grill
Le Bar Lyonnais
Yellow Springs Inn
Vickers Tavern

Top Outdoor

Arroyo Grille
City Tavern
Dilworthtown Inn
Garden, The
Inn at Phillips Mill

Inn Philadelphia
Katmandu
La Terrasse
Pompano Grille
Rock Lobster

Top Romantic

Ciboulette
Deux Cheminées
Inn at Phillips Mill
Inn Philadelphia
La Campagne

Le Bec-Fin
Meritage
Opus 251
Roselena's Coffee Bar
Vetri

Top Views

Black Bass Hotel
Chart House
Evermay/Delaware
Hamilton's Grill Room

Hartefeld National
Meiji-En
Treetops
Upstares at Varalli

Top 40 Service Ranking

29	Le Bec-Fin	23	Beau Rivage
28	Fountain		Overtures
26	Swann Lounge		Isabella's
	Dilworthtown Inn		Barrymore Room
	Mainland Inn		Savona
	Deux Cheminées		La Famiglia
	Evermay/Delaware		La Campagne
25	Founders		La Bonne Auberge
	Le Bar Lyonnais		Old Guard House Inn
	Brasserie Perrier		Inn at Phillips Mill
	Susanna Foo		Cassatt Tea Room
	Ritz-Carlton Grill		Morton's of Chicago
24	Monte Carlo Liv. Rm.		Passerelle
	Striped Bass		Saloon
	Ciboulette		A Little Cafe
	Coventry Forge Inn		Diamond's
	Spiga d'Oro		Nicholas Nickolas
	La Fourchette		General Warren Inne
	Jean Pierre's		Kimberton Inn
	Jake's		Mendenhall Inn

Best Buys*

80 Top Bangs For The Buck

This list reflects the best dining values in our *Survey*. It is produced by dividing the cost of a meal into the combined ratings for food, decor and service.

1. Old City Coffee
2. Pink Rose Pastry Shop
3. Hot Tamales Cafe
4. Dalessandro's Steaks
5. Jim's Steaks
6. Geno's Steaks
7. Pho 75
8. Reading Terminal Mkt.
9. Nifty Fifty's
10. Bitar's
11. Tony Luke's
12. Blue in Green
13. Carman's Country Kit.
14. Pat's King of Steaks
15. Santa Fe Burrito Co.
16. Xando Coffee & Bar
17. Samosa
18. Best of British
19. More Than Ice Cream
20. 30th St. Station Mkt.
21. Roselena's Coffee Bar
22. Silk City
23. Manayunk Farmer's Mkt.
24. Dahlak
25. Tenth St. Pour House
26. La Cipolla Torta
27. Fergie's Pub
28. Hank's Place
29. Rachael's Nosheri
30. Capriccio Cafe
31. Celebre's Pizzeria
32. New Corned Beef Acad.
33. Ruby's
34. Taco House
35. Cafette
36. Shank's & Evelyn's
37. Day by Day
38. Alyan's
39. Marathon Grill
40. Main-ly Desserts
41. Melrose Diner
42. Mayfair Diner
43. 1521 Café Gallery
44. ZuZu
45. Cherry Street
46. Beijing
47. Tacconelli's Pizza
48. McGillin's Olde Ale Hse.
49. Rizzo's
50. Minar Palace
51. Charles Plaza
52. El Azteca
53. Down Home Diner
54. Vietnam Restaurant
55. Maccabeam
56. Jamaican Jerk Hut
57. Famous 4th St. Deli
58. Singapore Kosher
59. Effie's
60. Saigon
61. H.K. Golden Phoenix
62. Ben & Irv Deli
63. Tandoor India
64. New Delhi
65. Abacus
66. Ray's Cafe
67. Capital Vietnam
68. Sitar India
69. Cassatt Tea Room
70. Arpeggio
71. Rangoon
72. Cedars
73. Sugar Mom's
74. Little Pete's
75. Peking Restaurant
76. Harmony Vegetarian
77. Golden Pond
78. California Pizza Kit.
79. Pattaya Grill
80. Little Saigon

---

* Excluding top Lancaster/Berks County, Atlantic City/Cape May/ Shore and Wilmington and nearby Delaware restaurants, which start on pages 128, 133 and 151, and restaurants with low voting.

Additional Good Values
(A bit more expensive, but worth every penny)

Athens Cafe

Bertucci's

Bomb Bomb Bar-B-Q

Cafe Michaelangelo

Champps Americana

Chestnut Grill

Chung Hing

Copa-Too!

East Side Mario's

El Sombrero

Hymie's Merion Deli

Imperial Inn

Joy Tsin Lau

La Pergola

Le Bus

Lee How Fook

Mexican Post

Moriarty's

Murray's Deli

Painted Parrot Cafe

Pietro's Coal Oven Pizzeria

Ron's Ribs

Sage Diner

Sang Kee

South St. Souvlaki

Tang Yean

Vietnam Palace

2000 Additions

Philadelphia

R | C

Brew Moon S ††† | M
Plaza at King of Prussia, 1001 Mall Blvd. (Gulph Rd.),
King of Prussia, PA, 610-337-7737
Out-of-this-world eats send diners into orbit at this lunar-themed brewpub at the edge of the Plaza at King of Prussia; while blithe spirits perched at the streamlined bar can't get enough of the made-on-premises beers, foodies savor the inventive New American menu (which includes savory smoked chicken nachos and sesame-seared tuna); the Sunday jazz brunch adds a lyrical note.

Buddakan S †††† | E
325 Chestnut St. (bet. 3rd & 4th Sts.), 215-574-9440
A chic, sleek setting that's as stylish as a movie set – complete with a glass-enclosed waterfall – dominates this Old City Asian-Eclectic, which opened with one of the biggest splashes in years; owner Stephen Starr (The Continental) has installed chef Scott Swiderski (ex Miami's China Grill) whose contemporary cooking is playful yet not too daunting for unsophisticated palates; the staff is arguably the best-looking and tallest in the city, with a level of competence that's equally high.

DiPalma †††† | VE
114 Market St. (bet. Front & 2nd Sts.), 215-733-0545
This handsome Old City Northern Italian is named for chef-owner Salvatore DiPalma, an alum of both the Ritz-Carlton and Roscoe's Kodiak Cafe, who's known for his skill with grilled meats and fish; power types and celebrating couples alike are deftly dealt with by a polished yet unassuming staff, and the slick downstairs bar and winning wine cellar are already hits.

Il Cantuccio ⊘ †††† | M
701 N. Third St. (Fairmount Ave.), 215-925-1572
Minuscule BYO trattoria in otherwise-lackluster Northern Liberties that's well worth seeking out, as it's backed by the irascible Giuseppe Roselli (of La Locanda del Ghiottone fame); you can count on outstanding, bold-flavored Italian dishes served with a sassy attitude amidst artsy furnishings.

Iron Hill Brewery & Restaurant [S] — 🍴🍴🍴 M

3 W. Gay St. (High St.), West Chester, PA, 610-738-9600
Something special is brewing at this former Woolworth's in Downtown West Chester, where a barrel-shaped ceiling and woodsy touches lend a wine-cellarish feel; the exceptional beers (stored in gleaming casks) complement the American menu, accented with German, Mexican and New Orleans touches; don't miss the beer-based porter cake.

Kristian's [S] — 🍴🍴🍴🍴 M

1100 Federal St. (11th St.), 215-468-0104
Despite being in a South Philly neighborhood location that's already known for outstanding Mediterranean fare, this Italian neophyte stands out due to the efforts of chef Kristian Leuzzi (ex DiLullo's), who pays homage to his row house roots in a nuanced and sophisticated manner; welcoming service is extended to all, but particularly to the pols, power brokers and sports sorts who pop in to wheel and deal over their risotto.

Lena [S] — 🍴🍴🍴 E

246 Market St. (bet. 2nd & 3rd Sts.), 215-625-4888
Thanks to its cool, ultramodern design and an expansive picture window facing Market Street, this family-owned Old City Eclectic looks like a million bucks (and it should, 'cause that's what it cost); the menu leans toward updates of classic specialties like duck and filet mignon – a chef change shortly after opening was for the better – and the under-$30 wine list is pleasing to both palate and wallet.

Marathon on the Square ◐ [S] — 🍴🍴🍴 M

1839 Spruce St. (19th St.), 215-731-0800
Where the funky Diner on the Square once held court, now sits a spiffy yet comfortable New American diner, courtesy of the Borish family (owners of the Marathon Grill minichain); though some Rittenhouse Square types are content to hang at the bar (the former lunch counter), others perch at teeny tables to sample the hearty, upscale grub; late-night breakfasts lure insomniacs.

Marmont ◐ [S] — 🍴🍴🍴 M

222 Market St. (bet. 2nd & 3rd Sts.), 215-923-1100
Trendies are talking about this plush minigem in Old City that's fast developing into a hopping late-night watering hole for the under-35 set, yet this Asian-Mediterranean is also a solid dinner destination with some dandy small plates and outstanding desserts; welcoming service from owners who care is a bonus; N.B. dinner only, Wednesday–Sunday.

Melange Cafe S   ††† E

1601 Chapel Ave. (bet. Haddonfield Rd. & Rte. 38), Cherry Hill, NJ, 856-663-7339
Scenemakers jam chef-owner Joe Brown's packed Cherry Hill BYO for robust, flavorful New Orleans–inspired dishes with a few Italian items thrown in for good measure; the staff is skillful, the decor is pleasant if not fancy, and smoke won't get in your eyes, as lighting up is verboten.

Meritage S   ††† E

116 E. Gay St. (High St.), West Chester, PA, 610-431-1981
Formerly Clemente's, this romantic Eclectic Eurobistro in restaurant-rich Downtown West Chester is one of the most gorgeous new spots in Chester County – and the beauty extends to the plates, which showcase extraordinarily presented cuisine drawn from the far-reaching corners of the globe; early visitors suggest you exercise some restraint and leave room for one of the luscious desserts.

Montgomery Grill S   ††† VE

261 Montgomery Ave. (Tregaron Rd.), Bala Cynwyd, PA, 610-664-3000
Adam Simon, whose résumé includes stints with the Palm as well as the Main Street Restaurant Group, has arrived on the Main Line with a stylishly simple steakhouse that's already a popular see-and-be-seen scene for an affluent doctor-and-lawyer crowd; though chef Edwin Hepner's straightforward cooking is the star here, owner Simon's presence is inescapable – he even lists his home phone number on the menu.

Oberon S   †† M

126 Chestnut St. (bet. Front & 2nd Sts.), 215-629-8337
The owners of Rococo have refashioned the former Middle East in Old City into a hip, slick Mediterranean bistro that just might be the noisiest place in town during prime time; its youngish following digs into earthy, well-priced fare (cassoulet, rabbit, lamb shank), while late-night revelry revolves around the raw bar.

Olive S   ††† VE

Short Hills Farm, 482 Evesham Rd. (Springdale Rd.), Cherry Hill, NJ, 856-428-4999
Fun-seeking South Jerseyites populate this posh, multilevel newcomer set on a Cherry Hill hilltop; while the bar hops with older singles, more settled types sit down to enjoy hearty, if steeply priced, Mediterranean food via chef Ed Doherty, formerly of La Campagne; service can be spotty, but it's always well-meaning.

Pasion! ◐ S ††††| E

211 S. 15th St. (bet. Locust & Walnut Sts.), 215-875-9895
Chef Guillermo Pernot, who set palates ablazin' at Vega Grill, partners with Michael Dombkoski (ex Susanna Foo) at this lush Center City South American that's one of the city's hottest newcomers in every sense of the word; foodies are packing the seviche bar and the richly appointed dining room where they're rewarded with bold tastes and superior presentations (not to mention dazzling Latin desserts); the bilingual staff excels at explaining the unfamiliar and is especially helpful with wine pairings.

Philippe's on Locust ††††| VE

1614 Locust St. (bet. 16th & 17th Sts.), 215-735-7551
Philippe Chin, the talented French toque who made his mark at Chanterelles, has moved his operation into larger quarters at the once-private Locust Club, with extraordinary results: a scintillating fusion of Classic French and Contemporary Asian cooking that's enhanced by formal though personable service and an atmosphere that reeks of class – right down to the silver domes covering the plates; N.B. lunch is available only in the bar area.

Pompeii Cucina d'Italia S †††| E

121 S. Broad St. (Sansom St.), 215-735-8400
Back on Broad Street, South Philly–bred chef Joseph Tucker has taken over Tony Clark's former space to excellent notice; expect gutsy Italian dishes made with passionate creativity, along with not-to-be-believed desserts, all served by handsome, earnest neighborhood joes ('you'se ok?'); the room retains the power vibe and sheer metal screens of its predecessor.

Potcheen ◐ S ††| M

Sheraton Rittenhouse Square, 227 S. 18th St. (Locust St.), 215-546-9400
Hearty American pub grub from chef Tony Clark and a convivial, smoke-free bar scene make for a winning combination at this new spot in the Sheraton Rittenhouse Square Hotel; think thin before digging into big-portioned, bellyfilling dishes like meat loaf and dumplings.

Sabooor! S ⊄ †††| M

213 Chestnut St. (bet. 2nd & 3rd Sts.), 215-351-3915
Yes, the name is spelled with three o's – as in 'ooohh' – and this miniature Caribbean BYO in Old City owes its success to a festive, sunny atmosphere, unpretentious staff and modest prices; charismatic chef Rudy Wu validates his Chinese-Dominican roots with a constantly changing menu that has won over both expats and locals alike.

San Marzano [S] | †† | I

1509 Walnut St. (15th St.), 215-564-3562
Upscale pizza partisans have a yen for this homey, bi-level storefront smack in the middle of Philly's Restaurant Row; it's already established itself as late-night hang for Gen Xers who relish its thin crusts and satisfactory selection of wines and beers.

Scargo on Main [S] | ††† | E

65 E. Main St. (Locust St.), Marlton, NJ, 856-985-5585
Marlton's quaint Main Street is a throwback to a more elegant era, and this top-drawer Continental follows suit, situated in an appealing Victorian that once housed Clayton's; chef Eric McGrath turns out a well-executed menu with Contemporary French touches, and while the formal service can veer toward hovering, it's clear that the staff cares.

Shula's Steak 2 [S] | †† | M

Sheraton University City, 36th St. (Chestnut St.), 215-387-8000
University City meat eaters are sated by the mammoth steaks and sports-bar grub at this lively, midpriced outpost of the chain fronted by the legendary Miami Dolphins coach; even when the televised games are unreeling, the staff somehow manages to transcend the din.

Square Bar ◐ [S] | ††† | E

Sheraton Rittenhouse Square, 227 S. 18th St. (Locust St.), 215-546-9400
Thrill seekers sample a contemporary, small-plate Italian menu at this Sheraton Rittenhouse Square spot set in arty, understated surroundings; granted, the prices can add up, but the park view is agreeable and the service equally so.

Station, The [S] | ††† | E

4401 Cresson St. (Gay St.), 215-482-6030
The Manayunk SEPTA station (a block off the Main Street drag) is the backdrop for this handsome Italian seafooder that's now the playground for chef Frankie Chiavaroli (of Frankie's Seafood Italiano fame), who's having fun in the kitchen – and it shows; his homey South Philly–style dishes and the overall buoyant mood make this a safe bet for special occasion celebrators.

Stefano's [S] | †††† | M

2519 Huntingdon Pike (Red Lion Rd.), Huntingdon Valley, PA, 215-914-1224
Alas, the Montco pack has already discovered this casual, reasonably priced Italian BYO in restaurant-poor Huntingdon Valley; if you manage to snag a table, you'll feast on traditional specialties in a cozy atmosphere, though you might encounter some occasional service lapses.

Venus and the Cowboy ttt E
1700 Ben Franklin Pkwy. (17th St.), 215-568-3770
Striped Bass founding chef Alison Barshak has thrust herself back into the scene with this hyped-to-the-hilt Mediterranean seafooder on the Parkway, and her menu cleverly offers several portion sizes; the bar cooks too (especially at night), while the separate, low-ceilinged dining room oozes class.

Vetri tttt VE
1312 Spruce St. (bet. Broad & 13th Sts.), 215-732-3478
Seldom has a newcomer hit its stride (and become booked solid) as quickly as this romantic Italian in the Center City space that once housed early incarnations of Chanterelles, Ciboulette and Le Bec-Fin; it's clear that chef Marc Vetri and his dedicated staff are up to the challenge, and although portions aren't huge, each course incorporates rare ingredients and shows serious thought; bonus points go to the winsome wine list.

White Rose Cafe [S] ttt E
Meadows Edge Mktpl., 515 Rte. 73 S. (bet. Brick & Evesham Rds.), Marlton, NJ, 856-810-2000
This family-run Marlton BYO survived an early change of chefs and is succeeding admirably under the guidance of new toque Stephen Delaney, whose ever-changing, Eclectic-American menu shows some decidedly Asian influences; its sophisticated ambiance nicely offsets the polished cooking.

Atlantic City/Cape May

Cabanas on the Beach ◐[S] ttt M
429 Beach Ave. (Decatur Ave.), Cape May, NJ, 609-884-4800
Cape May now boasts two complementary operations sharing one roof at this bi-level French-Eclectic that offers fine dining with a South Beach air upstairs and a high-energy blues club with a lighter menu below; the food comes courtesy of a Johnson & Wales–trained chef brought in from the Berkshires and the early word is overwhelmingly positive; the kind of following it will attract as it enters its first season remains to be seen.

Daniel's on Broadway [S] tttt E
416 S. Broadway (bet. Eldredge & Emerald Aves.), West Cape May, NJ, 609-898-8770
Set in a restored Victorian in West Cape May, this family-run New American BYO is a stunning mix of elegant dining rooms, flawless service and exquisitely prepared, Asian-accented fare via chef Harry Gleason; it's easily one of the best finds in Cape May County, if not the entire region.

Knife and Fork, The [S] tttt VE

Albany & Pacific Aves., Atlantic City, NJ, 609-344-1133
Both nostalgics and first-timers alike are dazzled by this well-conceived reincarnation of an AC landmark by the previous owner's son; the pricey Continental menu is predominantly filled with retro steaks and seafood, but the tried-and-true is enlivened by inventive touches; although there are many gambles in this town, you really can't lose here.

Wilmington/Nearby Delaware

Black Trumpet Bistro ttt M

1828 W. 11th St. (bet. Lincoln & Scott Sts.), Wilmington, DE, 302-777-0454
Newly ensconced in a spacious setting that's all exposed brick and soft lighting, this charming, family-operated New American in Downtown Wilmington celebrates the mushroom as an art form; CIA-trained chef Karen Boyd interprets it both in classic and contemporary dishes with excellent results.

Alphabetical Directory of Restaurants

Philadelphia

Directory of
Restaurants

F	D	S	C

Abacus 🅂   22 | 19 | 22 | $20
N. Penn Mktpl., 1551 Valley Forge Rd. (Sumneytown Pike), Lansdale, 215-362-2010
■ "Charming" host Joe Chen is a "card" (if a little "pushy with the specials") and the staff is "friendly" at this "well-run", "upscale", BYO Chinese in Lansdale; it's "mobbed on weekends" with fans who count on it for "great", "fresh", "innovative" dishes.

Abbey Grill ◖🅂   14 | 16 | 16 | $26
Radnor Hotel, 591 E. Lancaster Ave. (Radnor-Chester Rd.), St. Davids, 610-341-3165
◪ A Radnor Hotel American that's a "quiet", "comfortable" "place to relax" thanks to "cozy booths" and a "nice fireplace"; but while the "good but pricey" Sunday brunch earns applause, and local boosters say it would be "abbey-normal to not like" this "old standby", nonbelievers swear the food's just "ordinary" and condemn "slow service."

Abilene ◖🅂   14 | 13 | 16 | $19
429 South St. (bet. 4th & 5th Sts.), 215-922-2583
◪ Despite the allure of alligator pizza, most go to this "noisy" Southwestern-Cajun on South Street "for the music" rather than the "glorified bar food" and "plain-Jane" decor; but a "friendly" staff , "can't go wrong tricolor nachos" and "good drink specials" make it a "great place to hang out and listen to a cool band."

Acacia 🅂   – | – | – | M
2637 Main St. (bet. Craven Ln. & Gordon Ave.), Lawrenceville, NJ, 609-895-9885
This BYO, trompe l'oeil jewel, set in the former Lawrenceville post office on Route 206, is always packed thanks to "artistically presented", "outstanding" Contemporary American cuisine and "accommodating" service.

Academy Cafe 🅂   14 | 16 | 15 | $24
Doubletree Hotel, Broad St. (Locust St.), 215-893-1667
◪ With the city's hotel restaurant boom in full swing, it's possible that the new chef will turn around what most call "pedestrian" fare at this Doubletree American-Continental; it wins praise nonetheless for its "warm space" and "well-meaning" staff, not to mention its "convenience" to, and "great view" of, the Academy of Music across the street.

Adobe Cafe S
15 | 12 | 15 | $20

4550 Mitchell St. (Leverington Ave.), 215-483-3947

☑ A "cheerful", "funky", "family" Southwestern "away from
the Manayunk madness"; amigos call the food "decent for
the price" and the atmosphere "pleasant outdoors during
warm weather", but grouches cite a "limited menu" with
"no pizzazz", "long waits" and a "too dark" interior.

Alaina's Fine Food (CLOSED)
20 | 18 | 19 | $21

*236 Egypt Rd. (bet. Main St. & Rte. 363), Jeffersonville,
610-630-2300*

☑ A newly enlarged, "low-key" French-American BYO in an
"off the beaten track" neighborhood outside of Norristown;
suburbanites say the "less it's known, the better", labeling it
a "gem" with "original presentations" of "consistently
good food" and "friendly" service; a few city slickers say
it stands out because it's in an area that's "starved for good
restaurants"; sooner or Alaina we'll get a consensus.

Alberto's Newtown Squire S
18 | 19 | 18 | $32

*191 S. Newtown St. Rd. (½ mi. south of Rte. 3), Newtown
Square, 610-356-9700*

☑ Comments on this Delco Northern Italian are all over
the table; although it strikes advocates as a place for
"surburban haute cuisine served with flair", and many
applaud the "romantic", "homey" decor ("try the wine
cellar for atmosphere"), just as many critics claim the
kitchen is "capable of fine food but doesn't always deliver"
and that prices are "too high" for the quality.

Al Dar S
15 | 13 | 14 | $21

*281 Montgomery Ave. (bet. 54th St. & Levering Mill Rd.),
Bala Cynwyd, 610-667-1245*

☑ This "convivial but noisy" Mediterranean is packed nightly
with young, hip Main Liners unwinding "at the end of a long
day"; a "creative menu" and "nice portions" win points
though there are mutterings that "quality has gone down"
and service is "uneven"; lunch is more quiet.

Alexander's Cafe S
∇ 16 | 17 | 17 | $21

*Valley Forge Hilton, 251 W. DeKalb Pike (Rte. 202), King of
Prussia, 610-337-1200*

■ A "pretty" but "predictable" Traditional American in the
Valley Forge Hilton that's "full of mall shoppers" and trade-
show goers; the "terrific" brunch is the main attraction.

Alfio's Restaurant S
16 | 13 | 18 | $22

*15 Limekiln Pike (bet. Mt. Carmel Ave. & Willow Grove Ave.),
Glenside, 215-885-3787*

☑ Owner "Alfio is a magician" who "tosses tableside
Caesars" and performs "cute" tricks that "charm" many
visitors to his Glenside Italian; but the shtick is "old hat"
to some veterans who say the "typical" "food has lost its
magic"; still, it's a "decent neighborhood place."

Alisa Cafe　　　　25 | 14 | 22 | $31
109 Fairfield Ave. (bet. Garrett Rd. & Terminal Sq.), Upper Darby, 610-352-4402
■ "What's this doing near 69th Street?" ask incredulous newcomers to this chef-owned, "high-quality" BYO French-Asian in Upper Darby, where the atmosphere is so "friendly" and "intimate" that "you feel like you're visiting your best friend"; although "every bite is a treat", a few grit their teeth at the neighborhood ("watch the police cars go by") and "cramped seating" at this "diamond in the rough."

A Little Cafe S　　　24 | 19 | 23 | $28
Plaza Shoppes, 118 White Horse Rd. (Burnt Mill Rd.), Voorhees, NJ, 856-784-3344
■ This "tiny", "quaint" Eclectic BYO, "well-hidden" in a Voorhees strip mall, draws raves for "creative", "delicious" and "beautifully presented" food, plus an "accommodating" staff and early-bird special that's a "steal"; "tight tables" are the only negative – "if only it were twice as big."

Al Khimah S　　　18 | 20 | 18 | $24
Pinetree Plaza, 1426 E. Marlton Pike (bet. Rtes. 70 & 295), Cherry Hill, NJ, 856-427-0888
■ "It's a party" so "be sure you're comfortable with anyone" you bring to this strip mall Moroccan BYO where belly dancers inspire "an evening of indulgence"; even naysayers who grouse that the seating is "uncomfortable" and there's "too much reliance on theatrical aspects" agree that it's "great one time."

Allie's American Grill S　　▽ 13 | 14 | 16 | $18
Convention Ctr. Marriott, 1201 Market St. (bet. 12th & 13th Sts.), 215-625-6726
■ Most are not impressed with this "average" American inside the Convention Center Marriott, though it's "pretty" and "convenient", especially for the brunch buffet.

Alyan's S　　　19 | 8 | 14 | $11
603 S. Fourth St. (South St.), 215-922-3553
■ This "terrific", "authentic" Middle Eastern BYO off South Street may be "kind of a dive" but "who cares?"; the "cheap", "tasty" food, including "the best fries in Philly", makes it perfect for a "quick pick-me-up", but beware – "service can be slow."

Amara Cafe S　　　22 | 14 | 20 | $21
165 S. 22nd St. (bet. Chestnut & Sansom Sts.), 215-564-6976
East of Amara
700 S. Fifth St. (Bainbridge St.), 215-627-4200
■ "The mix-and-match menu" of "delightful" Thai choices at this Center City BYO allows you to "choose exactly what you want", earning it a following that calls it "the best Thai in the city"; early reports say East of Amara, a new offshoot near South Street, is just as good.

America Bar & Grill [S] | 23 | 22 | 21 | $33 |

Shops at Lionville Station, 499 E. Uwchlan Ave. (bet. Lionville Station Rd. & Rte. 113), Chester Springs, 610-280-0800

■ "Exciting" Contemporary American food from an open kitchen, "beautiful", "airy" decor and a "nice selection" of wines and drafts make this "trendy", "out-of-the-way", strip mall Chester bistro "worth the trip"; quibblers warn of "cigar smoke from the bar" and suggest it's a "little expensive for the location", but overall it's "needed and appreciated."

Andreotti's Viennese Cafe [S] | 20 | 16 | 17 | $26 |

Pine Tree Plaza, 1442 E. Rte. 70 (bet. Covered Bridge Rd. & Kings Hwy.), Cherry Hill, NJ, 856-795-0172

◪ The "freebies are a nice touch" ("unbelievable spoiling of diners") at this "cozy" Cherry Hill Italian-Mediterranean that's a hit among the "over-40 lounge crowd"; "reasonable prices" and "after-dinner dancing" add to its appeal; those who can't pack the food away grumble "quantity not quality here."

Anthony's Italian Coffee House [S]⊄ ▽ | 18 | 19 | 18 | $8 |

Italian Mkt., 903 S. Ninth St. (Christian St.), 215-627-2586

■ "Life is wonderful, listening to people gossip" while nibbling on "homemade treats" and sipping "some of the best espresso in the city" croon admirers of this glam Italian Market coffee-and-dessertery with a "pleasant" "family feeling"; N.B. it's "always a pleasure" but hours are limited: Saturday 8 AM–6 PM, Sunday 8 AM–3 PM.

Anton's at the Swan [S] | 21 | 21 | 20 | $44 |

43 S. Main St. (Swan St.), Lambertville, NJ, 609-397-1960

◪ A "romantic", "hip" Lambertville American where some prefer to dine in the "cozy bar by the Franklin stove" – it's "the best place to be on a cold winter's day"; though most think the "limited menu" is "too pricey", diners usually get a "very good meal."

Aoi [S] | 19 | 14 | 16 | $24 |

1210 Walnut St. (bet. 12th & 13th Sts.), 215-985-1838

◪ The "solid", "all-you-can-eat sushi" is an "excellent value" at this Center City Japanese, but "dark" decor that has the "feel of someone's rec room" and service that can be "a little slow" put a cap on ratings.

Arpeggio [S] | 22 | 11 | 20 | $18 |

Springhouse Village Ctr., 542 Springhouse Village Ctr. (bet. Bethlehem Pike & Norristown Rd.), Spring House, 215-646-5055

■ A Montco Mediterranean-Eclectic "charmer" with "marvelous pasta", "great, interesting pizzas" and "warm", "gracious" service; you can "forget the decor", have to eat "elbow-to-elbow with neighbors" and there's often a "wait for a table", but the "high-quality" kitchen gets it right.

Arroyo Grille [S] 15 | 20 | 16 | $25

Leverington & Main Sts., 215-487-1400

◪ This "super trendy" Southwestern yuppeteria on its own little island in Manayunk is prized for its "attractive" clientele, "funky", "colorful" interior, "great deck" and "spacious parking lot"; a seriously high decibel level, "mediocre" food and "slow service" from the "young and the careless" only slightly diminish its appeal, especially for "good margaritas" "on a sultry summer night."

Artful Dodger [S] 12 | 14 | 15 | $17

Second & Pine Sts. (Arch St.), 215-922-7880

■ A "cozy", "congenial" Society Hill "neighborhood" pub with "unambitious" but "decent" American-English "pub grub" (e.g. shepherd's pie, wings – "bland" goes with the territory) and a "friendly" staff; the "young, loud kids" find it just right for downing pints while playing darts and watching football.

Arugula! [S] 13 | 11 | 15 | $20

2895 Pine Rd. (Philmont Ave.), Huntingdon Valley, 215-938-6626

◪ Although most agree this "just ok" "neighborhood" American in a tough location in Huntingdon Valley is "not good enough to warrant a trip", a "diversified" menu, "decent prices" and early-bird "bargains" earn points with some locals who find it "good for after-work relaxing."

Asakura [S] 19 | 11 | 18 | $22

339 N. Lansdowne Ave. (Garrett Rd.), Lansdowne, 610-259-4052

◪ While ratings have slipped a little for this Delco BYO Japanese, diehards still cite "fantastic sushi" and solid "presentation", though even they concede there's "not much atmosphere."

Assaggi Italiani [S] 17 | 15 | 17 | $28

935 Ellsworth St. (bet. 9th & 10th Sts.), 215-339-0700

◪ While a few praise this "friendly" South Philadelphia Italian (in the former home of Osteria Romana) as the source for the "Madonna of antipasti", others consider it a "disappointing successor" that "doesn't live up to the hype", citing "overpriced" "small portions" of "ordinary food."

ASTRAL PLANE [S] 21 | 22 | 20 | $28

1708 Lombard St. (17th St.), 215-546-6230

■ "Like entering a time warp", this "funky", "romantic" New American "date place" on the edge of Center City "still holds up" among "aging hippies", who savor the "creative" menu and "campy", "bohemian" decor that's a little like a "crazy grandmother's living room"; though it strikes a few Gen Xers as a "dusty attic" ("get these people a calendar"), many with "'60s memories" "love this eccentric restaurant."

Athena [S] ≠ | 17 | 12 | 16 | $19 |
264 N. Keswick Ave. (Easton Rd.), Glenside, 215-884-1777
◪ "You get your money's worth" from the "epic portions" of "all the Greek basics" at this smoke-free, Athenian BYO near the Keswick in Glenside; comments about "attitude" and a staff that "seems confused" are the main drawbacks.

Athens Cafe [S] | 19 | 9 | 19 | $17 |
1030 W. Marlton Pike (Rte. 70), Cherry Hill, NJ, 856-429-1061
■ "The tables are too close together" and "it's nothing to look at", but this Cherry Hill strip mall Greek is an "authentic" ("real Greeks eat here") experience "at a reasonable price" (and it's BYO); the "ample-portioned" food has that "home-cooked" flavor and the staff is "friendly."

Audrey Claire [S] ≠ | 22 | 17 | 20 | $26 |
276 S. 20th St. (Spruce St.), 215-731-1222
■ "Spartan", "light and breezy" atmospherics, "innovative" Mediterranean cooking and a "young and hip" Center City crowd ("it feels like the TV show *Friends*") make this BYO the "new in-spot"; a no-reservations policy and "long waits" mean "get there early."

August Moon [S] | 23 | 17 | 20 | $24 |
300 E. Main St. (Arch St.), Norristown, 610-277-4008
■ If you can overlook the "unsavory location", this "unpretentious" Japanese-Korean "surprise" is "worth the trip" into Downtown Norristown; the food is "delectable" ("garlic lovers, unite!") and the "superfriendly, helpful waitresses point the way."

Azafran [S] | – | – | – | M |
617 S. Third St. (bet. Bainbridge & South Sts.), 215-928-4019
Queen Villagers say it's "worth the wait on weekends" for this "funky" BYO "find" off South Street; "eclectic Latin" cuisine is the main appeal, but you can't overlook the "colorful", rustic atmosphere.

Azalea Room [S] | 21 | 24 | 22 | $40 |
Omni Hotel, 401 Chestnut St. (bet. 4th & 5th Sts.), 215-931-4260
■ A "pleasant", "unsung" American in the Historic District's Omni Hotel that's a "dignified", "elegant" place to "take your future in-laws" for a "spectacular Sunday brunch" overlooking the park; while the kitchen's had its "ups and downs", a recent chef change may deliver more consistency.

Bangkok City [S] ▽ | 20 | 16 | 18 | $18 |
Eagle Plaza, 700 Haddonfield-Berlin Rd. (Evesham Rd.), Voorhees, NJ, 856-309-0459
■ This BYO Thai bistro with "chatty servers" seems to have "improved" since moving to its new Voorhees digs; there's a "lot to choose from", especially "great appetizers."

Bards, The S   17 | 18 | 18 | $20
2013 Walnut St. (bet. 20th & 21st Sts.), 215-569-9585
◪ Sure it "needs a real fireplace", but "after a long day at
the office" this "homey", "convivial" (at times "too loud")
Irish pub makes an ideal stop for "the best draft Guinness
in Philly"; while responses to the menu range from "bland"
to "surprisingly tasty", everyone agrees that the live music
on Sundays completes the "trip back to the Auld Sod."

Barnacle Ben's S   19 | 11 | 16 | $20
Kingsway Plaza Shopping Ctr., Kings Hwy. & Lenola Rd.,
Maple Shade, NJ, 856-235-5808
◪ "Adored by the older set", this "noisy", "crowded family
seafood house" in Maple Shade has "excellent" "fresh fish"
("the best crab cakes") but a "no-frills", "teal and purple"
setting you'll "need sunglasses to tone down"; service "can
be a problem" but a few think "it's gotten better."

Barnacle Ben's West S   16 | 15 | 16 | $25
14 Balligomingo Rd. (Rte. 23 W.), West Conshohocken,
610-940-3900
◪ Not yet as popular as its older sibling, this West Conshy
seafooder "has possibilities" – a "pretty view" and an
"extensive menu", including the ever-popular "A +" crab
cakes among them – but while the fish is "fresh", some find
the preparation "pedestrian" and service "so-so"; "horrible
acoustics" seem to run in the family.

BARRYMORE ROOM S   21 | 27 | 23 | $38
Park Hyatt at the Bellevue, 200 S. Broad St. (Walnut St.),
215-790-2814
■ "A gorgeous setting for afternoon tea" or the "dazzling
Sunday brunch", this Classic French "room with a view"
overlooking the city is "Philadelphia's answer to New York's
Plaza" and, to some visionaries, "a preview of dining in
heaven"; psst, "whispering is an art" here – otherwise
the "high-powered gossip" echoes off the lofty ceiling.

Bay Pony Inn S   20 | 22 | 21 | $30
508 Old Skippack Rd. (bet. Rte. 113 & Salfordville Rd.),
Lederach, 215-256-6565
◪ It's a "long ride" to get to this "charming" Lederach
country inn (and its "adorable attached train sidecar"),
but most feel the "accommodating" staff and "pleasant"
atmosphere make it "worth the trip"; while responses to the
American-Continental fare range from "solid" to "not quite
there yet", the "good value" prix fixe clinches the deal.

Beaujolais S   – | – | – | M
261 S. 20th St. (bet. Locust & Spruce Sts.), 215-732-8000
By day, sunlight pours into this pleasing French bistro off
Rittenhouse Square; by night, the entire neighborhood
seems to flow into the bar; the food is toothsome and
consistent, but a better value at lunch than at dinner.

Beau Monde S
– | – | – | M |

624 S. Sixth St. (Bainbridge St.), 215-592-0656
Philadelphia's first crêperie in years is a clever concept:
luscious, inexpensive Breton crêpes in a corner location
near South Street coupled with artsy decor that makes you
feel as if you're dining in a glowing lantern; flip-out windows
near the kitchen allow for excellent people-watching –
inside and out.

Beau Rivage S
25 | 25 | 23 | $48 |

128 Taunton Blvd. (Tuckerton Rd.), Medford, NJ,
856-983-1999
☑ "Exquisite" food, "the best wine list around", "classy"
(some say "snooty") service and an "elegant", "formal"
setting are still the stock in trade of this long-running,
"special occasion" Classic French in a "hard-to-find"
Burlington County locale; while a few insist it's "declined in
recent years", ratings are actually up from our last *Survey*;
N.B. regulars warn "prices of off-menu items will shock you."

Beijing S
17 | 8 | 17 | $13 |

3714 Spruce St. (bet. 37th & 38th Sts.), 215-222-5242
■ Hungry Penn students flock to this "no-nonsense"
University City "institution" for "cheap", "decent" Chinese
and "friendly", "very quick" (if "rushed") service that allows
you to "eat dinner in 10 minutes"; those more interested in
flavor than getting to class on time recommend "taking
the subway to Chinatown."

Bella Trattoria S
16 | 14 | 15 | $20 |

4258 Main St. (Cotton St.), 215-482-5556
☑ During warm weather you can sit in the "charming
outdoor cafe and watch the world go by" at this "simple"
Manayunk Italian known for its "good pizzas"; although a
few naysayers gripe that the food is "average at best", the
majority is satisfied that it's "decent" and "affordable."

Ben & Irv Deli Restaurant S
16 | 9 | 15 | $13 |

1962 County Line Rd. (Davisville Rd.), Huntingdon Valley,
215-355-2000
■ This Huntingdon Valley "yenta's meeting place" draws
"big crowds" "before or after the movies" for "hearty
portions" of "standard" but "reliable" Jewish-style deli fare
at "reasonable prices"; while the decor is "typical" of the
genre, the "uncharacteristically friendly" service is not.

Benkady S⌿
– | – | – | I |

4519 Baltimore Ave. (45th St.), 215-386-2226
There's "no atmosphere" (aside from being "a bit dark")
and the neighborhood can be chancy, but this small West
African BYO in West Philadelphia is a "quaint" spot for an
"authentic" dining experience.

Bentley's Five S
−|−|−| M
(fka American Grill)
*Cherry Hill Hilton, 2349 Marlton Pike W. (Cuthbert Blvd.),
Cherry Hill, NJ, 856-665-6666*
They bill this Italian/Asian/barbecue/seafooder/steakhouse
in the Cherry Hill Hilton as five restaurants in one; the early
word is that it's similar to its predecessor American Grill:
that is, decent food from a varied menu and brisk service.

Berlengas Island S
21 | 12 | 17 | $24
4926 N. Fifth St. (west of Roosevelt Blvd.), 215-324-3240
■ "What the neighborhood lacks in safety the owner makes
up for in effort" at this "splendid" "basement" Portuguese
off Roosevelt Boulevard; reviewers recommend "going with
friends" to sample the full variety of "homestyle", "stick-
to-your-ribs" treats including "wonderful seafood platters."

Bertolini's Authentic Trattoria S
17 | 17 | 16 | $21
*King of Prussia Plaza, 160 N. Gulph Rd. (Mall Blvd.), King
of Prussia, 610-265-2965*
☑ Shoppers "renew their energy" at this King of Prussia
Plaza Italian sporting a "cool" "California look" and "above-
average mall food"; although some find it "noisy" and "too
much like a chain", "friendly" service, "good pizza" and
paper tablecloths and crayons make it "great for kids."

Bertucci's S
16 | 14 | 14 | $15
1515 Locust St. (bet. 15th & 16th Sts.), 215-731-1400
*Market Pl. Shopping Ctr., 2190 County Line Rd. (Davisville Rd.),
Huntingdon Valley, 215-322-2200*
Eastgate Sq. Mall, 1220 Nixon Dr., Mt. Laurel, NJ, 856-273-0400
523 W. Lancaster Ave. (Conestoga Rd.), Wayne, 610-293-1700
☑ While the "novelty has worn off" of this "casual" pizza
chain, it's still "dependable" for a "light bite" when you don't
want to cook; but you may need to "bring a lasso" for
roping in both "unpredictable" service and youngsters
amidst the "noisy" "preschool" ambiance.

Best of British S
17 | 18 | 18 | $13
*8513 Germantown Ave. (bet. Evergreen & Highland Sts.),
215-242-8848*
■ "To experience a bit of England", try this "reliable",
"lovely" Chestnut Hill tearoom; the veddy "charming" decor
brings to mind "lunch at your maiden aunt's house", though a
few stiff-upper-lippers say it's "not like Fortnum & Mason."

Between Friends S
19 | 19 | 20 | $29
Wyndham Franklin Plaza Hotel, 17th & Race Sts., 215-448-2000
☑ Hotel guests and office workers populate this Continental
in the Franklin Plaza that dishes up "surprisingly good"
vittles, especially during the "superb" lunch buffet and
Sunday brunch; the unconverted point to service that "varies
on the day you're there" and a "too reserved" ambiance,
enlivened only by those "dangerous desserts."

Big Fish 🅂   16 ⏐ 17 ⏐ 16 ⏐ $27 ⏐
140 Moorehead Ave. (Rte. 23), West Conshohocken, 610-834-7224
587 DeKalb Pike (Rte. 63), North Wales, 215-616-0940
◪ There are two schools of thought on this West Conshy seafooder (the North Wales sibling opened post-*Survey*); one dubs it "reasonably priced" for "simply prepared" fish and "wonderful desserts"; the other carps about "bland" preparations, a "hokey" feel and "inconsistent" service.

Big River Fish Co. 🅂   17 ⏐ 18 ⏐ 16 ⏐ $26 ⏐
(nka Lewis & Clark Grill & Bar)
39 Morris Ave. (Lancaster Ave.), Bryn Mawr, 610-527-1400
505 Old York Rd. (Fairway), Jenkintown, 215-886-3474
◪ The jury is still out on these "bustling" seafooders (one in Jenkintown, the other in Bryn Mawr); some focus on the "excellent value" for "fresh", "tasty" fish, but others frown at "underwhelming" fare, "noise" and "unpredictable service"; your call.

Bistro Romano 🅂   17 ⏐ 17 ⏐ 18 ⏐ $25 ⏐
120 Lombard St. (bet. Front & 2nd Sts.), 215-925-8880
◪ "Ask for the wine cellar room" when visiting this "casual" Society Hill Italian famed for its "great tableside Caesar" – "worth it for this alone"; while many view the "dark", "candlelit" "grotto" setting as "cozy" and "romantic", a few modernists find it too "catacomb"-like and add that other than the signature salad, "the rest is average."

BISTRO ST. TROPEZ   24 ⏐ 20 ⏐ 20 ⏐ $31 ⏐
2400 Market St., 4th fl. (23rd St.), 215-569-9269
■ An "artsy", "offbeat" location in the Marketplace Design Center sets the stage for this "authentic" French bistro, a "hip"place for "excellent food" at "reasonable prices for the quality"; toss in "great views" overlooking the Schuylkill, "cute waiters whose suggestions you should always take", jazz on Thursday nights and it all adds up to a "hidden jewel."

Bitar's   23 ⏐ 8 ⏐ 19 ⏐ $10 ⏐
947 Federal St. (10th St.), 215-755-1121
■ Perfect for takeout (though it does have a few tables), this "friendly", lunch-only South Philly Middle Eastern grocery with "bargain basement prices" is "falafel heaven"; "garlic lovers" savor what could be the "best Middle Eastern food in the city" and assert "the brothers Bitar rule."

Black Bass Hotel 🅂   20 ⏐ 22 ⏐ 19 ⏐ $37 ⏐
Black Bass Hotel, 3774 River Rd. (Rte. 263), Lumberville,
215-297-5770
■ "Anglophiles" and "history buffs" in search of "lots of English royalty memorabilia" flock to this New American "institution", "beautifully set" in a New Hope inn overlooking the Delaware; yes, the interior strikes some as "musty" and the food is "outclassed" by the view, but it's "still enjoyable" and "far enough away" to qualify as a "a two-hour vacation."

Black Walnut, The 🅂   24 | 19 | 21 | $36
80 W. State St. (bet. Clinton & Hamilton Sts.), Doylestown, 215-348-0708
■ "For a touch of Manhattan in Doylestown", reviewers suggest a visit to this "suburban surprise", a "small", "cozy", "elegantly formal" Contemporary American–French with a "creative chef" ("the guy's food is good") and an "accommodating staff."

BLT's Cobblefish 🅂   21 | 14 | 17 | $28
443 Shurs Ln. (bet. Main St. & Ridge Ave.), 215-483-5478
■ A "poor man's Striped Bass" is the consensus on this muraled, "dark", "warehouse"-like BYO seafooder up the hill in Manayunk; while gripers complain about the potluck service, "incredibly noisy" and "rushed environment" and find the $2 parking fee "absurd", hundreds of fin-atics rave about the "creative" preparation of "excellent" "fish Cousteau never heard of."

Blue Bell Inn   21 | 18 | 19 | $33
601 Skippack Pike (Penllyn-Blue Bell Pike), Blue Bell, 215-646-2010
🅩 Defensive senior citizens "don't care who knocks" this Montco American with a well-established reputation for "dependably good" food (especially "excellent steaks"), and an "extensive wine list priced to suit every occasion"; insolent whippersnappers ("at 57 I brought the average age down") say the place "hasn't changed in 35 years" and "needs new blood."

Blue in Green 🅂⊠   22 | 16 | 16 | $12
7 N. Third St. (bet. Church & Market Sts.), 215-928-5880
■ "Gen Xers" and other members of the "cool crowd" know the "amazing" homestyle eats are "worth the wait" at this "hip", "avant-garde" Old City breakfast-and-luncher; the pancakes, magazine selection and "friendly" service also receive kudos, though one diner fears "finding a nose ring in my omelet."

Blüe Ox Brauhaus 🅂   21 | 20 | 20 | $27
7980 Oxford Ave. (Pine Rd. & Rhawn St.), 215-728-9440
■ Even though there's a "new, lighter menu" at this "first-class" Northwest German, it still offers "potato pancakes to die for"; a "great beer list", "friendly service" and "attractive", "authentic decor" add to the appeal.

Bobby's Seafood 🅂   15 | 13 | 15 | $25
5492 W. Chester Pike (Plumsock Rd.), Newtown Square, 610-296-4430
■ The happy hour half-price raw bar and lobster bisque are the main attractions at this Delco seafooder; otherwise, preparations lean toward the "uncreative" and the decor "needs a facelift", reflected in the drop in ratings since our last *Survey*.

Bomb Bomb Bar-B-Q Grill ⊄　　19 | 9 | 18 | $17
1026 Wolf St. (Warnock St.), 215-463-1311
■ Those looking for "some real ethnic warmth" and "the true South Philly experience" should head to this "spartan" Italian-barbecue tavern with "excellent" ribs and "AYCE mussels served by staff in muscle shirts"; but "don't tell your cardiologist you ate here."

Bonaparte S (CLOSED)　　– | – | – | M
260 S. Broad St. (Spruce St.), 215-735-2800
At press time, the crew from the now-closed Napoleon was taking over at the short-lived Joseph's on the Avenue, adding touches of whimsy and serving a moderately priced International menu; desserts, a specialty at Napoleon, are where dieters can expect to meet their Waterloo.

Bookbinders Seafood House S　18 | 15 | 17 | $32
215 S. 15th St. (Walnut St.), 215-545-1137
◪ This Center City "institution", not to be confused with Old Original Bookbinders in Society Hill, is a "touristy" "old standby" serving "large portions" of "decent" but "pricey" seafood; some disenchanted locals sneer that it's still "getting ready to enter the 20th century" and call for an "updating" of both food and decor.

Braddock's Tavern S　　22 | 23 | 21 | $34
39 S. Main St. (Coates St.), Medford, NJ, 609-654-1604
■ There are "romantic fireplaces" galore at this "very colonial", "Williamsburgish" country inn "nestled in Medford", NJ; the usually "delicious" Traditional American fare can be "rich", but overall, a trip is a safe bet "for out-of-town guests" or a "holiday dinner."

Brasil's Restaurant & Night Club S　18 | 16 | 18 | $26
112 Chestnut St. (Front St.), 215-413-1700
◪ The rodizio-style meats "show off the great service" at this "festive" Brazilian in Old City, "an interesting" "change of pace", dressed up in decor that's "trendy and masculine, like *Esquire*"; on a more samba note, some think the "great dancing" in the club upstairs "is better than the food."

BRASSERIE PERRIER S　　27 | 27 | 25 | $50
1619 Walnut St. (bet. 16th & 17th Sts.), 215-568-3000
■ "Another Georges Perrier masterpiece" rave legions of admirers blown away by this "suave", "art deco" Contemporary French, a "great new addition" to Restaurant Row at "more reasonable prices" than its older sibling, Le Bec-Fin; expect "wonderful presentations" and "complex tastes" from chef Francesco Martorella and a "superbly trained" staff; a few grumblers scoff at the 'brasserie' tag and "pricey wine", but overall – "believe the hype."

Bravo Bistro   19 | 17 | 18 | $27
175 King of Prussia Rd. (Lancaster Ave.), Radnor, 610-293-9521
☑ Respondents recommend visiting this Main Line French bistro (that shares its kitchen with Passarelle) in the spring or summer when you can "sit outside by the pond" and watch the swans; it's especially "good for a quiet lunch" with a "creative" if "limited" menu, and although service can be "slow", the "trendy" crowd doesn't seem to mind.

Bridget Foy's S   18 | 15 | 18 | $24
200 South St. (2nd St.), 215-922-1813
■ There's "great" warm weather people-watching and a "nice view" from the outdoor patio of this South Street New American; however, "surprisingly good", "mildly inventive" dishes can be marred by "Jekyll and Hyde" "inconsistency."

Bridgid Restaurant ◑ S   20 | 14 | 18 | $23
726 N. 24th St. (Meredith St.), 215-232-3232
■ Respondents love the "stick-to-your-ribs", "bargain" Continental food and "top five" beer selection at this "dark", "cozy" Fairmount "hideaway"; the only negative – a "cramped" dining room – is now positively smoke free.

Broad Axe Tavern S   15 | 14 | 16 | $20
Butler Pike (Rte. 73), Broad Axe, 215-646-0477
■ "Marvelous ribs" and "superb crab cakes" keep this "casual" Montco Traditional American "always busy" (and "noisy"); many admit that other items are only "average", but the "friendly staff" and "reasonable prices" are more reasons why it's a "good family place"; a remodeling and expansion should ease complaints about "close tables."

Bugaboo Creek Steak House S   14 | 17 | 16 | $20
Franklin Mills Mall, 601 Franklin Mills Circle, 215-281-3700
☑ This "Outback wanna-be" chain steakhouse in Franklin Mills amuses tykes with its "Disney-like" "talking animals", but the atmosphere might seem "annoying on a date"; otherwise, the food's "average" and the waits can be long.

Bunha Faun S   – | – | – | M
152 Lancaster Ave. (¼ mi. from Rte. 29), Malvern, 610-651-2836
Main Liners say the "friendly staff" serves an "interesting blend" of "good value" Thai and French at this "cozy" BYO "gem" in a former Dairy Queen "hidden" off Lancaster Avenue in Malvern.

Cafe Arielle S   23 | 22 | 21 | $40
100 S. Main St. (Ashland Ave.), Doylestown, 215-345-5930
☑ "For a romantic Saturday night", amorous types endorse this "lovely", "pricey" Classic French in an "old agricultural work building" in Doylestown; though a few label it "a bit pretentious" and reactions to the service vary ("gracious" vs. "need training"), any minor flaws are forgiven since "Jacques Colmaire is an outstanding chef."

Cafe Espresso [S] ▽ 21 | 14 | 17 | $24
Adams & Tabor Shopping Ctr., 718 Adams Ave. (Tabor Rd.), 215-533-0141
■ "Copious portions" of "authentic" Iberian dishes ("yummy paella", "great seafood"), plus an "earnest", "native" staff, make a visit to this "Portuguese haven" in the "middle of nowhere" (actually the Northeast) a "pleasant" experience.

Cafe Flower Shop [S] 18 | 17 | 16 | $21
2501 Meredith St. (25th St.), 215-232-1076
◪ "Buy a plant after eating" at this "charmer" in a Fairmount flower shop offering an "imaginative" Eclectic menu and "great brunches" "before or after the Art Museum"; fans find it "delightful inside or outside", but critics note that "somewhat cramped" seating and "disorganized" service can wilt the experience.

Cafe Gallery [S] 20 | 22 | 20 | $32
219 High St. (Delaware River), Burlington, NJ, 609-386-6150
■ "Between the artwork [in the upstairs gallery] and [the view of] the Delaware" this New French–Continental is "a feast for the senses", with "charming ambiance", "light yet indulgent fare" and "dependable" service; the "delightful" Sunday brunch is "worth the trip."

Cafe Giuseppe [S] **(CLOSED)** 16 | 12 | 17 | $25
473 Leverington Ave. (Ridge Ave.), 215-482-1422
◪ Some regulars like the "good, solid" cooking and "free parking" at this Roxborough Italian, but there are gripes that the decor is "tacky" and "prices have gone up."

Cafe Michaelangelo [S] 16 | 12 | 15 | $17
CJC Shopping Ctr., 11901 Bustleton Ave. (Byberry Rd.), 215-698-2233
◪ In "an area loaded with choices", this "no-frills" Italian in the Northeast wins votes for the "best brick-oven pizza" ("a slice of authenticity"), but many say other items are only "so-so."

Cafe Noelle [S] – | – | – | M
20 S. Main St. (Rte. 70), Medford, NJ, 609-953-1155
This simple downtown Medford BYO yearling – the former La Trattoria – dazzles with sophisticated Eclectic food in an understated setting; service is "caring."

Cafe Preeya [S] 19 | 14 | 18 | $26
2651 Huntingdon Pike (Red Lion Rd.), Huntingdon Valley, 215-947-6195
■ An International BYO in Huntingdon Valley that's a "quiet haven" for "delicious", "unconventional", Thai-influenced dishes at "reasonable prices"; the "friendly" staff "really tries hard to please", and those who've noticed appreciate the "timely new decor" (no more Quonset huts).

Cafette S ⇄   19 | 12 | 16 | $13
8136 Ardleigh St. (Hartwell Ln.), 215-242-4220
☑ Chestnut Hillers appreciate this "funky, colorful"
neighborhood "bargainville" that's popular with families
and the "eat-and-run" crowd for "innovative", "healthy"
Eclectic dishes and its "unpretentious" "homey" ambiance
("snobs eat elsewhere"); the few naysayers bemoan "slow"
service and "uncomfortable" seats.

Cafe Zesty S   18 | 15 | 16 | $26
4382 Main St. (Levering St.), 215-483-6226
☑ The "good food" ("the name says it all") at this "lively"
Greco-Roman in "the heart of Manayunk" compensates
for "cramped seating" ("even the sardines complain"),
"uneven" service and "long waits" on weekends; N.B.
the Greek dishes are favored.

Caffé Aldo Lamberti S   20 | 18 | 19 | $29
2011 Rte. 70 W. (Haddonfield), Cherry Hill, NJ, 856-663-1747
☑ "The best of the Lamberti chain", this Italian directly
across from the racetrack offers "dependable, "high-
quality" food in "huge portions"; but reactions to the
decor run the gamut from "elegant" to "gaudy" ("the only
thing missing was a pink flamingo on the lawn"); P.S. the
outdoor patio is "lovely with friends in summer."

Caffe La Bella S   17 | 13 | 17 | $22
61 E. Main St. (bet. Chester Ave. & Church St.),
Moorestown, NJ, 856-234-7755
■ A "cozy", "neighborhood" Northern Italian BYO in
Moorestown known for its "wonderful" harpist (Tuesday,
Wednesday and Sunday nights); "big portions" of "homey"
food are "ok", too.

California Cafe S   21 | 20 | 19 | $26
King of Prussia Plaza, 160 N. Gulph Rd. (bet. Mall Blvd. &
Rte. 202), King of Prussia, 610-354-8686
■ It's a "major surprise" to run into this "sleek", "high-tech"
Californian in the King of Prussia Plaza; it "sure beats the
food court" thanks to "very tasty", "creative combinations",
an "attentive" staff and an "ambitious", "fabulous" wine
list; "it may be a chain, but the quality is always there."

California Pizza Kitchen S   18 | 15 | 17 | $17
Court at King of Prussia, 470 Mall Blvd., King of Prussia,
610-337-1500
■ "Purists may frown at toppings like pineapple", but
this Italian chain in the food court at King of Prussia is
a "welcome newcomer" to adventurous souls who crave
"creative pizzas" and "interesting" pastas.

Capital Vietnam S
21 | 8 | 18 | $15
1008 Race St. (bet. 10th & 11th Sts.), 215-925-2477
■ "Let them tell you what to order" and "you can't go wrong" say return visitors to this "*Cheers* of Vietnamese restaurants" in Chinatown, where everyone raves about the "charismatic owner" and his "fabulous soups", and overlooks the "no-atmosphere" storefront setting.

Capriccio Cafe S⊄
15 | 13 | 13 | $11
Warwick Hotel, 1701 Locust St. (17th St.), 215-735-9797
◪ While it's "one of Philly's first coffee shops", this "hangout" in the Warwick Hotel "doesn't particularly stand out" among its competitors; most say it's "consistent but uninspired" and laud the desserts and "fun late snacks."

Carambola S
∇ 25 | 19 | 22 | $23
1650 Limekiln Pike (Dreshertown Rd.), Dresher, 215-542-0900
■ "Wow" – "a hit" sums up reactions to this "fabulous", "frenetic", Italian-American BYO with a "creative" menu, "interesting" high-tech decor and a "strolling chef"; delighted locals say it's "the best thing to ever come to Dresher"; try one of the "great shrimp dishes."

Caribou Cafe S
19 | 19 | 16 | $21
1126 Walnut St. (bet. 11th & 12th Sts.), 215-625-9535
■ A "comfortable place to talk", this "cozy", "hip" Center City French bistro is like "being in Paris", complete with "stylish" food, a "great selection of beers", "magnificent desserts", "artsy" decor and "uneven" staff that can be both "charming and annoying"; fans say it's an "excellent" lunch or pre-theater choice.

Carman's Country Kitchen S⊄
19 | 15 | 20 | $12
1301 S. 11th St. (Wharton St.), 215-339-9613
◪ "An experience in and of itself", this "offbeat" Eclectic breakfast-and-luncher in South Philly is called "Carman's kitsch" by one surveyor because it "seems just like your family's kitchen"; most enjoy the "down-home" brunch and "friendly" service, though a few feel "crowded" and call the food combinations "bizarre."

Carversville Inn S
24 | 22 | 21 | $38
6205 Fleecydale Rd. (bet. Aquetong & Carversville Rds.), Carversville, 215-297-0900
■ The "food is always out of this world" at this "excellent" New American that's like an "1800s time capsule" in a "beautiful" country setting in Upper Bucks; the "laid-back" atmosphere is fueled by the "nicest fireplace on a cold winter night" and a "friendly" staff that makes diners feel "warm" and welcome.

Cary Restaurant Bar (CLOSED)   19   15   16 $30
211 S. 15th St. (bet. Locust & Walnut Sts.), 215-735-9100
◪ A "loud" Center City Eclectic with a new "cool",
"metallic" interior; some give points to a kitchen that's
"trying hard" and turning out "occasionally excellent"
"creative" food, but others, supported by a drop in the
food rating, find it "more hype than substance" and are
turned off by "indifferent service."

Cassano Italian Cafe & Bar S   19   16   18 $26
(nka Jac Daddy's)
1334 Brace Rd. (bet. Kresson Rd. & Rte. 70), Cherry Hill,
NJ, 856-354-1199
■ "You can smell the aroma from the parking lot" at this
"relaxing" Cherry Hill Italian where everything comes in
"generous portions" ("be sure to bring a friend" "in the
same mood"); it's a "great neighborhood place", though a
little "too garlicky" for a few.

CASSATT TEA ROOM S   23   26   23 $24
Rittenhouse Hotel, 210 W. Rittenhouse Sq. (19th St., bet.
Locust & Walnut Sts.), 215-546-9000
■ For a "charming" "rainy day treat", anglophiles
recommend "taking a niece or granddaughter" to the
Rittenhouse's "beautifully done" afternoon tea; there's a
"superb three-tiered" offering of "addictive sandwiches
and petit fours" and plenty of "people-watching" amid the
"restful", "très chic" setting complete with "exquisite
beveled-glass French doors and a Tuscan terrace."

Casselli's Ristorante S ⌿   –   –   –   M
7620 Ridge Ave. (Minerva St.), 215-483-6969
"Old Italy comes to Roxborough" at this "cozy", cash-only,
"family-style" joint; the Southern Italian food is so "authentic
it comes with a lounge singer" (Wednesday–Saturday
evenings) and the staff is warm and friendly.

CATELLI S   25   25   23 $35
1000 Main St. (bet. Evesham & Kresson Rds.), Voorhees, NJ,
856-751-6069
■ "Fine dining in Voorhees – who'd have thought it?"; but
this "popular" "special occasion" Italian in the Main Street
complex gets glowing reviews for its "unusual combinations
of delicious food", "elegant" (though "noisy") interior and
"nice outdoor tables"; the "veal dishes are outstanding."

Cedars S   20   11   17 $16
616 S. Second St. (bet. Bainbridge & South Sts.), 215-925-4950
◪ While "there is really no decor", this "informal"
Mediterranean off South Street is still a "fine" outpost for
"well-seasoned" "Lebanese comfort food", such as "yummy
hummus", "delicious garlic chicken" and (sprinkled with
a dash of hyperbole) "the best stuffed grape leaves in the
world"; now "if only the waiters would smile."

Celebre's Pizzeria ◐ [S] ≠ — 20 | 8 | 15 | $12

Packer Park Shopping Ctr., 1536 Packer Ave. (Broad St.), 215-467-3255

■ Sports fans cheer this "crowded" pizzeria across from the stadiums in South Philly for its "great" "thin crust" pies that are "an antidote to doughy chain pizza" ("what's a Flyers game without it?"); a minority of disgruntled fans call the "strip mall" setting "cheesy"; N.B. it was redecorated post-*Survey*.

Cent'Anni [S] — 19 | 15 | 18 | $28

770 S. Seventh St. (bet. Catharine & Fitzwater Sts.), 215-925-5558

■ Sit "cheek to cheek" with a "big group" at this "better than your average red gravy" South Philadelphia Italian ("the only things missing are Sinatra and Pacino"); regulars praise "peasant" cooking and a "warm" staff that moves "like pigeons on bread crumbs."

Centre Bridge Inn [S] — 19 | 22 | 19 | $38

Centre Bridge Inn, 2998 N. River Rd. (Rtes. 32 & 263), New Hope, 215-862-9139

◪ This "rustic" New Hope Continental, with a "lovely view" of the Delaware, may be "cozy on a winter's night" and a "charming" choice for alfresco romantics, but atmosphere aside, critics assert that the fare's "disappointing" and the service "indifferent"; perhaps the new chef can turn around "slipping" food ratings since the last *Survey*.

Century House [S] — 22 | 16 | 21 | $29

Rte. 309 (north of Unionville Pike), Hatfield, 215-822-0139

■ "Always reliable", "first-class" "comfort food" draws a loyal clientele to this "quiet" Montco American "standby" with "excellent" early-bird deals; although a few trendies "yawn" and call for "new decor", it's ideal "when your group is not adventuresome"; the "attentive" staff's motto: "nobody leaves hungry."

Chadds Ford Inn [S] — 20 | 22 | 20 | $32

Chadds Ford Inn, Rtes. 1 & 100, Chadds Ford, 610-388-7361

◪ "The Wyeth prints make the decor" at this "classy", "history-drenched" Traditional American in Brandywine Valley, a favorite of Longwood Garden–goers and "Main Line grandmas"; while ratings are holding steady, many wish the "solid" food were less "predictable."

Chambers [S] — 16 | 13 | 16 | $20

19 N. Main St. (State St.), Doylestown, 215-348-1940

■ There's an "upbeat" atmosphere and "interesting food at inexpensive prices" at this International "neighborhood joint" "near the courthouse" in Doylestown, though a few who wince at the "*Where's Waldo* wallpaper" suggest "an overhaul" in decor.

Champion's Sports Bar ◗🆂   11   14   14 $16
Convention Ctr. Marriott, 1201 Market St. (12th St.), 215-625-2900
◪ A "noisy" sports bar in the Convention Center Marriott
that's a "good place to catch a game"; foodies sniff at the
"bland everything" pub grub, but wanna-be linemen find it
"acceptable" and like the "enormous" portions.

Champps Americana 🆂   15   16   16 $19
*Marlton Crossing, 25 S. Rte. 73 (Marlton Circle), Marlton, NJ,
856-985-9333*
■ A Marlton "sports watcher's paradise" that's a "sensory
overload", from the big screen TVs showing "every game
imaginable", to the "loud music", to the "pick-up" match of
"beautiful babes" and "single jocks"; despite "big portions"
of "good bar food" some ask: "wait on line to get in – why?"

CHANTERELLES (CLOSED)   26   20   24 $53
1312 Spruce St. (bet. Broad & 13th Sts.), 215-735-7551
◪ "It feels like they're cooking just for you" at Philippe Chin's
"innovative" Center City French-Asian, "one of Philly's
gems" for a prix fixe dinner that's a "terrific buy", with the
added pleasure of "knowledgeable" service; on the down
side, it's "so cramped you want to eat off the next table."

Charles Plaza 🆂   23   16   22 $18
234-236 N. 10th St. (Vine St.), 215-829-4383
■ Impressed reviewers say that "gracious" owner Charles
"makes everyone feel at home" at his Chinatown stop
known for "phenomenal", "fresh, light" Chinese "without
that thick cloying sauce"; "they do fantastic banquets."

Chart House 🆂   18   21   19 $32
*Penn's Landing, 555 S. Columbus Blvd. (Lombard Circle),
215-625-8383*
◪ "You can always count on" this "touristy" Penn's Landing
American chain for a "dynamite salad bar", "fabulous" view
and "friendly" staff; foes carp about an "overpriced" menu
filled with "boring staples", but it "works" for the majority.

Chateau Silvana 🆂   22   22   20 $38
*324 Main St./Rte. 541 N. (2 mi. north of Medford intersection),
Medford, NJ, 609-654-1706*
■ "Romantic on a snowy night", this "cozy" Southern
French–Northern Italian in a 200-year-old farmhouse
makes a "lovely setting" for "excellent" food; but what's
"very good" service to some feels "snobby" to others.

Chef Charin 🆂   20   11   20 $24
*126 Bala Ave. (bet. City Line & Montgomery Aves.), Bala
Cynwyd, 610-667-8680*
■ "Still a sleeper" rave insiders about this chef-owned BYO
across from the Bala Theatre; its "imaginative" "mix of
French and Thai" is matched by "courteous", "personal"
service and "fair prices"; while "tiny" and "claustrophobic",
admirers urge "try it, you'll like it."

Chef Tell's Manor House S   20 | 19 | 19 | $37
1800 River Rd. (4 mi. south of Rte. 611), Upper Black Eddy, 610-982-0212

◪ There's a "lovely view of the Delaware" from Chef Tell's sole venture in Upper Bucks, but reviewers are divided on his Eclectic ("Euro-island") cuisine, with some labeling it "innovative" and others calling it "hyped"; a slipping food rating backs up the critics.

Cherry Street Chinese Vegetarian S   20 | 15 | 20 | $16
1010 Cherry St. (bet. 10th & 11th Sts.), 215-923-3663

■ This "no-frills" BYO kosher Chinese-Vegetarian ("a strange yet compelling concept") has "excellent", "always hot and fresh" food and "solid" service; "ask owner Anita Fung what to have, and you'll love it", even though the consensus is that the "dynasty [mock] chicken rules."

Chestnut Grill & Sidewalk Cafe S   15 | 15 | 17 | $17
Chestnut Hill Hotel, 8229 Germantown Ave. (Southampton St.), 215-247-7570

■ The food at this "friendly", "informal" American in the Chestnut Hill Hotel is a "great improvement from when it was Winberrie's"; however, many suggest "sit upstairs" or "eat outside in warm weather" – otherwise "you're still eating in a basement" that gets "noisy."

China Castle ◑S   ▽ 16 | 8 | 14 | $16
939 Race St. (bet. 9th & 10th Sts.), 215-925-7072

■ A "good value", "very consistent" Chinatown "old-timer" serving "comforting Cantonese" to the masses out of a "dingy", "uncomfortable" space on Race Street; amateur decorators say "spend some money to fix the place up."

Christopher's S   15 | 13 | 16 | $20
1211 S. Bethlehem Pike (1 block south of Butler), Ambler, 215-646-8500

◪ Brick-oven crust mavens say "stick with the pizza, which can be very good", at this "spartan" Ambler Italian; others say "just average" food and "snooty service."

Chung Hing S   19 | 11 | 17 | $17
Pathmark Shopping Ctr., 4160 Monument Rd. (City Line Ave.), 215-879-6270

■ Offering "consistently good" Chinese behind the Adam's Mark, this "family-friendly" "neighborhood favorite" is run by "sweet people who remember their regular customers"; it's "as close to Chinatown as you can get in the 'burbs."

Church Street Bistro S   ▽ 21 | 16 | 20 | $33
11½ Church St. (Main St.), Lambertville, NJ, 609-397-4383

■ Surveyors familiar with this "attractive", "hard-to-find" Lambertville bistro consider it "a gem", with an "interesting menu" of "well-presented", "generously portioned" "flavorful dishes" served by a "friendly, professional" staff; this "great value" certainly seems worth a try.

Cibo S (CLOSED) − | − | − | M

603 S. Third St. (bet. Bainbridge & South Sts.), 215-625-3700
There's a positive buzz on this warm Euro bistro off South
Street, run by the team from Ciboulette; the hearty dishes
embrace Italy, France and Spain and the atmosphere is
subdued enough to satisfy romantics as well as celebrants.

CIBOULETTE S 26 | 24 | 24 | $52

Bellevue Bldg., 200 S. Broad St. (Walnut St.), 215-790-1210
■ Acolytes gush that Bruce Lim's "heavenly" New French
in a "lovely" room in the Bellevue "lives up to its reputation";
and while his "appetizer portion" concept "adds up quickly",
it also "allows for a taste of many wonderful selections"
including "foie gras to quack about"; save room for the
"fabulous dessert cart."

CINCIN S 24 | 21 | 22 | $27

7838 Germantown Ave. (Springfield Ave.), 215-242-8800
■ "This terrific addition to Chestnut Hill" is a French-Chinese
fusion from the owner of Yangming; reviewers are gaga
over the "cin-fully delicious" tastes including "delicate"
sauces and "outstanding Peking duck carved tableside";
"elegant" surroundings and an "eager to accommodate"
staff are more pluses; it's "a bit noisy, but that's easily
forgotten after the first bite."

CIRCA S 22 | 24 | 20 | $35

1518 Walnut St. (bet. 15th & 16th Sts.), 215-545-6800
■ Be sure to "wear black" and "request the vault" room
when dining at this restored bank, a "noisy" "favorite"
Restaurant Row scene; chef Eric Hall's New American
food is "fabulous" to many, merely "interesting" to others,
but even those who think the waiters have "terminal
baditude" concede they sure look "hot" (and "cool"); "fun
late-night dancing" adds appeal.

City Tavern S 17 | 23 | 19 | $33

138 S. Second St. (Walnut St.), 215-413-1443
◪ "Even if you're not a tourist" this 1776-themed Society
Hill tavern with "costumed waiters" is "enjoyable",
especially on the "great deck"; to charges of "slow" service
and "bland" cuisine, defenders respond the "food has
improved greatly" and anyway, a visit "makes you want to
sign the *Declaration of Independence*."

Clayton's Fine Dining (CLOSED) 20 | 21 | 19 | $36

65 E. Main St. (Locust St.), Marlton, NJ, 856-985-5585
■ A "pleasant", "quiet" New American in Marlton that's
"reliable" for "good local fare" and "attentive" service in
a "nicely redone old home" on Main Street.

Cock 'n Bull ▣   15 | 18 | 17 | $24
Peddler's Village, Rtes. 202 & 263, Lahaska, 215-794-4010
☑ Defenders of this Peddler's Village colonial American like the "quaint", "country" atmosphere and find it "convenient while shopping", especially during the "winter holidays" when "superb decorations" "put me in the spirit"; grinches say it's "average", "touristy" and "over the hill"; your call.

Coco Pazzo   17 | 18 | 16 | $28
One Liberty Pl., 1650 Market St. (bet. 16th & 17th Sts.),
215-851-8888
☑ The "business crowd" can't agree on whether this "corporate Italian" that replaced Sfuzzi in Liberty Place is an "improvement", "was better" before, or shows "not much change"; but it's clear that while "good", it "rarely inspires", and rush-rush regulars find it's "not Tuscan enough except for leisurely service."

Concordville Inn ▣   17 | 17 | 18 | $27
780 Baltimore Pike/Rte. 1 (Rte. 322), Concordville, 610-459-2230
■ Yes, it's "a time trip back to the '70s", but this Delco American has "thankfully predictable", if "unexciting" food (the "best" crab cakes), delivered by "pleasant young servers"; the decor may "need refurbishing", but the "geriatric set" doesn't seem to mind.

Continental, The ▣   20 | 20 | 16 | $25
138 Market St. (2nd St.), 215-923-6069
■ This "cosmopolitan" tapas joint in a former Old City diner exudes "NYC" "hipness", from the "cool" olive and toothpick light fixtures to the "trendy" staff; but while poseur-loathers growl it's "too chic for its own good" and "unfriendly to the masses", many others say Bradlee Bartram's "creative" food is "surprisingly delicious" and the "wide variety of martinis" is "great."

Copabanana ◑▣   15 | 10 | 11 | $16
344 South St. (bet. 3rd & 4th Sts.), 215-923-6180
☑ Service runs from "spacey" to "rude" and the setting is "shabby", but this "raucous", "always fun", South Street "hangout" still packs 'em in, with boosters trumpeting the "best burgers" in the city and "unbelievably good" margaritas that are "worth the hangover."

Copa-Too! ◑▣   15 | 11 | 13 | $15
263 S. 15th St. (bet. Locust & Spruce Sts.), 215-735-0848
☑ This "casual" Center City sibling to the Copa on South Street has the same "awesome" Spanish fries, legendary burgers and "deadly" margaritas; too bad most agree that the "rude" service and "smoky" surroundings are also on a par, although this one may be a tad "quieter."

Coppermill Harvest [S] ▽ 19 | 17 | 18 | $24

Park Ridge Hotel, 480 N. Gulph Rd. (opp. Valley Forge Golf Course), King of Prussia, 610-878-1400

■ "When the grandparents come to town", bring them to this New American in King of Prussia's Park Ridge Hotel for the Saturday night "high-quality seafood buffet"; it's also a popular choice for breakfast.

Cotton Club [S] – | – | – | E

Cotton & Cresson St. (1 block off Main St.), 215-508-1800

The glitz of the old-time supper club has come to Manayunk in the form of this swank, three-level joint off Main Street; the ambitious menu of 'nouvelle international bistro cuisine with an Italian flair' has won early praise, and there's dancing upstairs to work it off.

Country Club [S] 16 | 11 | 16 | $15

1717 Cottman Ave. (Algon St.), 215-722-4880

◪ A "glorified diner" in Northeast Philly that's "still going strong" thanks to "home-cooked" Jewish "comfort" specialties ("great chicken soup") served by "old school" waitresses who "still call you hon"; dissenters say desserts from the on-premises bakery are still "wonderful" ("the best cheesecake") but otherwise it's "living on reputation."

COVENTRY FORGE INN 26 | 25 | 24 | $45

3360 Coventryville Rd. (1½ mi. west of Rte. 100), Pottstown, 610-469-6222

■ Even after 44 years, the Callahans' "long-standing favorite" in Pottstown "hasn't lost its touch" for "excellent" "traditional" French fare in a "warm", "serene" country setting that even city folk don't mind driving to; "attentive" servers have "all the right moves" and the Saturday night prix fixe is an "excellent value."

Coyote Crossing [S] 17 | 18 | 17 | $22

800 Spring Mill Ave. (8th Ave.), Conshohocken, 610-825-3000

◪ Surveyors are on different sides of the coyote crossing regarding this Mexican "tucked away" in Conshohocken; amigos say it's a "warm, friendly place" that's "more authentic than most" with "sophisticated" dishes and an "outstanding" mole sauce; foes howl over "incredibly noisy" crowds, "slow service" and food that's "very average."

Cresheim Cottage Cafe [S] 16 | 19 | 18 | $25

7402 Germantown Ave. (bet. Allens Ln. & Cresheim Valley Rd.), 215-248-4365

■ For now, the "charmingly restored", "historic" 1748 cottage with "delightful" summer patio dining is "more exciting" than the "predictable", "limited" menu at this "pleasant" American newcomer on the Chestnut Hill–Mount Airy border; but recent chef changes and a "friendly and welcoming" staff give locals hope, particularly since the "area lacks restaurants."

Crier in the Country ◧   21 | 22 | 21 | $37 |
Rte. 1 (Rte. 261), Glen Mills, 610-358-2411
◪ The "new owners have a tough act to follow", but they seem to be "coming along" admirably at this "nouvelle" Continental in Glen Mills, set in a "beautiful" historic building known for its "haunted house" mystique ("ask to see Lydia's room").

Cuisines   ▽ 20 | 16 | 19 | $28 |
200 Rte. 202 (Rte. 491), Chadds Ford, 610-459-3390
▪ There's a "great range" of dishes to choose from at this International in Chadds Ford that's "pleasantly surprising" to first-timers and "always good" to regulars who dine here "at least a dozen times a year"; try the "super" rack of lamb.

Cuttalossa Inn   16 | 22 | 17 | $34 |
River Rd. (Cuttalossa Rd.), Lumberville, 215-297-5082
▪ The "enchanting" "waterfall view" is the selling point at this otherwise "nothing special" Upper Bucks Traditional American, popular among "romantics" oblivious to the "dull" food; eating outside is "great if the weather's nice", though dining "by the fire" in winter is also appealing.

Cutters   20 | 22 | 19 | $30 |
2005 Market St. (bet. 20th & 21st Sts.), 215-851-6262
▪ "The best salmon in the city" attracts a crowd of "professionals" to this "sleek", "modern" Center City New American; it's a "solid choice" for business lunching and "festive" Friday happy hours at the "beautiful bar", where "young attorneys look at each other" and strive to appeal.

Cuvee Notredame ◑◧   21 | 18 | 18 | $28 |
1701 Green St. (17th St.), 215-765-2777
◪ "The lunchtime $5 bar menu is a great deal" at Michel Notredame's "charming" Belgian on the edge of Fairmount, home of "awesome mussels" and pommes frites; apostates cite "spotty" service and caution that "they get you" with the beer prices.

Dahlak ◧   23 | 14 | 17 | $14 |
4708 Baltimore Ave. (bet. 47th & 48th Sts.), 215-726-6464
▪ "Finger food at its finest" is the consensus on this "affordable" Ethiopian BYO that's "probably the best of its kind" in town ("worth the venture into West Philly"); the food is "exotic" and "flavorful" and the staff "delightful"; though service can be "slow", the "communal" "fun" makes it "worth the wait."

Dalessandro's Steaks ◑⌿   23 | 7 | 16 | $9 |
600 Wendover St. (bet. Henry Ave. & Walnut Ln.), 215-482-5407
▪ There are "lines out the door" at this "friendly", "world-class" Roxborough steak-and-hoagie joint serving "juicy", "melt-in-your-mouth" cheese steaks; the decor may be "dismal", but this joint is the top-rated cheese steakery in the *Philadelphia Survey.*

D'Angelo's ◐ 22 17 19 $34

256 S. 20th St. (bet. Locust & Spruce Sts.), 215-546-3935

■ "Don't miss the veal chop" when dining at this "well-kept secret off Rittenhouse Square", an "excellent" red gravy Italian known among cognoscenti for "large portions", "upscale prices" and the "strolling troubadour" ("please tell the guy to stop singing").

Dante & Luigi's [S] 18 12 17 $22

762 S. 10th St. (Catharine St.), 215-922-9501

◪ An "old-world" South Philly Italian where you still get "good, solid", "traditional" basics (ravioli, meatballs, lasagna) and "never leave hungry"; as always, a few upstarts claim it's "seen better days."

Dave & Buster's ◐ [S] 12 16 13 $18

Pier 19 N., 325 N. Columbus Blvd. (bet. Callowhill & Race Sts.), 215-413-1951

◪ While no one goes to this Penn's Landing "Chuck E. Cheese for grown-ups" arcade for the "virtual" American food, it's a "fun", if "ear-splitting", carnival of games "for kids of all ages."

David's Yellow Brick Toad [S] 19 20 20 $33

1495 Hwy. 179 (1 mi. north of Lambertville), Lambertville, NJ, 609-397-3100

◪ "The personal attention of David" and "lovely view" are the strong suits of this "plant-filled", long-running New American, a "quiet" favorite of "romantics"; detractors sigh "if only the food matched the setting."

Day by Day 19 13 17 $14

2101 Sansom St. (21st St.), 215-564-5540

■ A "variety" of "unusual food" served up by a "theatrical yet attentive" staff makes this "charming" Center City Eclectic lunchery "popular with residents and businessmen" alike; "excellent prices" and consistency ("never had a bad meal here") make up for "tight quarters."

Deetrick's Cafe & Jazz Bar [S] (CLOSED) 18 18 18 $27

211 Old York Rd. (West Ave.), Jenkintown, 215-576-7690

◪ Admirers note that the "very good" American food "matches the outstanding music" at this "sexy" Jenkintown jazz club that gets mighty "smoky" and "crowded on weekends"; detractors dis the "uptight" staff and say the cover charge for dinner patrons (on weekends) is a "great way to turn away customers."

DeLorenzo's Tomato Pies [S] ⊘ 23 12 18 $26

530 Hudson St. (Swann St.), Trenton, NJ, 609-695-9534

■ "You'll never see pizza the same" after trying this Trenton tomato pie shop's "incomparable" version; they've been in business for half a century, but there's "no atmosphere" and still "no bathroom – a minus."

DEUX CHEMINÉES 27 | 28 | 26 | $65

1221 Locust St. (bet. 12th & 13th Sts.), 215-790-0200

■ If you "forgot what it was like to have your senses exhilarated", Fritz Blank's "romantic" Classic French in an "elegant" Center City townhouse will remind you; "rich" dishes are "so amazing you'd swear they came from heaven" and service is "unobtrusive", though a few contend that at these prices "I want to eat on Limoges, not buy it."

Diamond's ◐ [S] 25 | 19 | 23 | $40

132 Kent St. (bet. Anderson & Division Sts.), Trenton, NJ, 609-393-1000

■ This "classic", "not your typical Chambersburg" Italian features "great" pastas and breads and "superb service"; some say "upstairs is more refined" and "quiet."

Dick Clark's American Bandstand Grille [S] 13 | 19 | 15 | $17

211 Mall Blvd., King of Prussia, 610-337-9096

■ "A new theme but the same old food" is the consensus on this "fun" stroll down "memory lane", a "Hard Rock wanna-be" with "loads of" "fascinating" artifacts ("you can even see Madonna's bra") and TV "clips from 25 years of *Bandstand*"; P.S. get ready to shake it, 'cause there's a dance floor.

Dickens Inn [S] 16 | 20 | 17 | $26

421 S. Second St. (bet. Lombard & Pine Sts.), 215-928-9307

■ A favorite watering hole for ex-pats, "anglophiles and college kids" looking to "drink ale and shoot darts", this "cozy" Head House Square pub also offers genuine, if "unexciting", Brit fare (which in most minds is one and the same).

D'Ignazio's Towne House [S] 16 | 17 | 18 | $27

117 Veterans Sq. (Baltimore Pike), Media, 610-566-6141

◪ "You could get lost in the maze of rooms" at this "Old Delaware County standby" that "stands the test of time" thanks to "decent", "homestyle" American-Italian food in "large portions" and a "reliable" staff; a few find the "unique" "antique decor" a bit "cluttered" and reminiscent of "Fred Sanford's" place.

DiLullo Centro 21 | 25 | 21 | $41

(nka Toto)

1407 Locust St. (bet. Broad & 15th Sts.), 215-546-2000

◪ "Spectacular", "lush", "over-the-top" decor (mirrors, "Gaugin-like paintings") is the hallmark of this "sexy" but "often overlooked" Italian across from the Academy of Music; although even admirers concede that the "glitz" "overshadows" the "good" food and "smooth" service, and a few grumble that it's "all smoke and mirrors", ratings suggest there's substance as well as style; N.B. lower prices accompanied the name change.

DILWORTHTOWN INN, THE 🅢   27 | 27 | 26 | $44

1390 Old Wilmington Pike (Brinton Bridge Rd.), West Chester, 610-399-1390

■ "What a romantic treat" sigh reviewers lovestruck by this West Chester country inn ("the prettiest of them all") that has "come back strong" after a fire; as the "Le Bec-Fin of the 'burbs", expect "wonderful " Classic French–American cooking, an "outstanding" wine list, "impeccable" service and an "incredible attention to detail" overall – the "goblets and silver glisten."

DiNardo's Famous Seafood 🅢   19 | 12 | 16 | $24

312 Race St. (bet. 3rd & 4th Sts.), 215-925-5115

■ A "quintessential" Old City seafooder serving up a "messy", "three-napkin" meal of "great hard-shell crabs and fries" ("but only" these items); the "grungy" dining room has "just the right feel."

Dinon's   ▽ 23 | 16 | 21 | $29

133 E. Gay St. (bet. Matlack & Walnut Sts.), West Chester, 610-430-3600

■ This "romantic", chef-owned BYO in West Chester is a "pleasant surprise" with "imaginative", "wholesome" Italian dishes and a "cozy", "candlelit" room that's "like eating in someone's home."

DMITRI'S 🅢⊄   27 | 13 | 19 | $23

795 S. Third St. (Catharine St.), 215-625-0556

■ It may be a "claustrophobic's nightmare", but this "fabulous" Mediterranean BYO in Queen Village is an "all-time favorite" for "consistently fresh" seafood ("the best octopus on the planet"); regulars recommend you "arrive at 5 PM" (with cash) or be prepared to "camp out for the evening"; P.S. "sit at the counter" to watch how "two cooks feed 40 people."

Dock Street 🅢   16 | 17 | 16 | $22

2 Logan Sq. (18th St., bet. Arch & Cherry Sts.), 215-496-0413

▨ While excited suds-heads foam at the mouth over the "luscious", "full-bodied" beers at this "French brasserie meets brewhouse" in Logan Square, the reaction to the "hearty", ever-changing menu is less favorable; some say they'll return "now that the trio fries are back", but the disenchanted say "it used to be great."

Downey's ◑🅢   15 | 17 | 16 | $26

526 S. Front St. (South St.), 215-625-9500

▨ A "touristy" Irish-American pub at Front and South that's "the place to be on St. Patrick's Day"; the lobster special (in season) can be "good", but overall the food quality is "so-so"; N.B. the addition of a new chef has improved the quality of the food.

Down Home Diner ⊘ | 18 | 12 | 14 | $14
Reading Terminal Mkt., 51 N. 12th St., 215-627-1955
◪ "Homestyle", "belly-filling" breakfasts "like your mom should have made" are the specialty of Jack McDavid's "appropriately named" "clean greasy spoon" in the "frenetic" Reading Terminal Market; "sporadic" service and a "hokey, faux-country setting" are drawbacks to some.

Doylestown Inn [S] | 16 | 17 | 16 | $25
18 W. State St. (Main St.), Doylestown, 215-345-6610
◪ It's best to sample this Doylestown Eclectic "in summer" when the outdoor tables are fine "for a drink" or "casual dining"; though a few boosters say "it's getting better", more suggest it's "just average."

Duling-Kurtz House [S] | 23 | 25 | 22 | $40
146 S. Whitford Rd. (Rte. 30), Exton, 610-524-1830
■ A "beautiful country inn" in Exton with "period decor" and "epicurean pleasures" from a Continental menu; the younger set finds it a little "stuffy", but the "gray-hair" crowd likes the fact that they're "pampered."

East Side Mario's [S] | 14 | 16 | 16 | $17
1760 Swede Rd. (1½ blocks north of Rte. 202), Blue Bell, 610-277-1711
1370 Blackwood-Clementon Rd. (Rte. 534), Clementon, NJ, 856-782-1969 ◐
180 E. Lincoln Hwy. (Rtes. 30 & 100), Exton, 610-363-0444
◪ "Little Italy meets Wendy's" at this "noisy", "bright" family-style Italian chain that most agree is "comfortable for young families" ("our screaming kids love it") but "miserable for adults" not toting tots; the "average" food is "very affordable" and the staff is "friendly", making it, all in all, not "authentic" but "not bad."

Ebenezer's Olde World Cafe [S] | – | – | – | M
Marlton Crossing, Rte. 73 (Rte. 70), Marlton, NJ, 856-983-7477
United Jersey Bank Plaza, 3131 Rte. 38 (Larchmont Blvd.), Mt. Laurel, NJ, 856-866-1001
This stunning Euro-American BYO in Marlton Crossing is winning adherents thanks to fabulously presented, creative dishes, an open kitchen and friendly, attentive service; the Larchmont location, a coffeehouse, is a must-try.

Edge ◐[S] | – | – | – | M
4100 Main St. (Shurs Ln.), 215-483-4100
The former downscale River Deck Cafe has been turned upside down by new owners and a $2 million renovation: there's multilevel dining, interior waterfalls and a hip and hot South Beach–style nightclub aimed at an older crowd; tasty appetizers dominate the American menu, available from midday to late at night.

Effie's [S]⊄ | 21 | 16 | 20 | $18

1127 Pine St. (Quince St.), 215-592-8333

■ "Homespun" Greek cuisine from a "caring" family charms local "garlic lovers" at this BYO in Center City; fans predict "you'll want to linger" over the "fresh", "lovingly prepared" dishes, especially in the less-crowded courtyard.

El Azteca [S] | 15 | 11 | 15 | $13

1710 Grant Ave. (Bustleton Ave.), 215-969-3422

◩ "No-frills" Mexican cantina in the Northeast gets mixed marks; some say it's "muy bueno" with the "best cheap food this side of the Mississippi", but others insist it's only "better than Taco Bell, barely."

Elena Wu [S] | ▽ 19 | 13 | 19 | $18

Plaza 70 E., Rte. 70 (¼ mi. east of Marlton Circle), Marlton, NJ, 856-596-5599

■ "Elena is a charmer" and the kitchen "will modify a dish if requested" at this Chinese BYO in Marlton, a "local favorite" for its "carefully prepared" meals using "fresh ingredients"; some quibble that the food's "not spicy enough", but fans say "such nice people deserve good ratings."

Elephant & Castle ◐[S] | 8 | 13 | 12 | $18

Holiday Inn Select, 1800 Market St. (18th St.), 215-751-9977
Franklin Mills Mall, 1141 Franklin Mills Circle (Woodhaven Rd. near I-95), 215-281-9801

■ Even though most already agree "the English aren't exactly known for great cuisine", many suggest that this "pseudo-Brit pub" in the Holiday Inn Select "gives new meaning to the term 'bad English food'"; still, the "great selection" of "good beer" is enough to make it "a fave for after-work socializing"; N.B. the Franklin Mills Mall branch is new and unrated.

El Mariachi | 19 | 16 | 20 | $24

Bourse Bldg., 21 S. 5th St. (entrance on 4th St., bet. Chestnut & Market Sts.), 215-625-4835 [S]
135 S. 24th St. (Sansom St.), 215-567-6060
Whitpain Shopping Ctr., 1510 DeKalb Pike (Rte. 73), Blue Bell, 610-239-7773 [S]

◩ Surveyors are of dos minds about these "festive" Mexicans (two Downtown and one in the 'burbs) with "loud" mariachi bands; most hail the "exceptional" "authentic" food, "cordial" staff and "lively" atmosphere, but naysayers protest that the tab's "too much for too little."

El Sombrero [S] | 15 | 11 | 16 | $17

295 Buck Rd. (bet. Holland & Rocksville Rds.), Holland, 215-357-3337

◩ "A step above fast-food Mexican" sizes up this "friendly", family-run Bucks BYO, now up the road "in a smaller location with no liquor license" in Holland; loyalists swear it's "still the best around" and a "bargain."

Emerald Fish – – – M

Barclay Farms Shopping Ctr., Rte. 70 E. (bet. Rtes. 41 & 295), Cherry Hill, NJ, 856-616-9192

This smoke-free, BYO seafooder in Barclay Farms is building a following for its simple grilled dishes with contemporary flair; the colorful, playful decor features an open kitchen and service is accommodating.

Engine 46 Steakhouse ◐ [S] 13 16 14 $21

10 Reed St. (Columbus Blvd.), 215-462-4646

◪ Although the "funky" firehouse motif is "really cool for the kids" and prices are "very reasonable", many say the "food department needs work" at this "noisy-as-a-fire-alarm" steakhouse next to the Riverview cineplex in South Philadelphia; purists spotted amid the dalmatians decor tend to skip the "fair", "cheaper cuts" of meat and "visit just to enjoy the building and bar."

Epicurean, The [S] 22 19 20 $26

902-8 Village at Eland, Rte. 113 (Dawson Dr.), Phoenixville, 610-933-1336

■ A "cozy", "relaxing" Chester County New American that actually lives up to its highfalutin name, turning out "creative" "California-style" fare amid "exceptionally clean", "modernist" surroundings; the "bright", "pleasant" staff is another reason it's "a permanent favorite."

Euro Cafe [S] – – – M

414 S. Second St. (bet. Lombard & Pine Sts.), 215-574-1687

The former Cafe Elana on Head House Square has been renovated into an intimate, clubby hangout for over-35s; though the focus is on the bar, the ambitious Northern Italian menu by Nick Ventura is not to be ignored.

EVERMAY ON THE DELAWARE [S] 26 26 26 $54

River Rd. (Headquarters Rd.), Erwinna, 610-294-9100

■ A "best bet for romance", this "most impressive" New American "hidden charmer" north of New Hope is prized for "well-prepared" "three-hour dinners" with "impeccable" service in a "classic setting"; though a few workaholics growl about the "limited" menu and hours ("any chef who serves three meals a week is on vacation"), the sybaritic majority dubs it "definitely a go"; the attached B&B gets high marks as well.

Evviva 19 21 19 $36

1236 Montgomery Ave. (bet. Old Gulph & Wynnewood Sts.), Narberth, 610-667-1900

◪ Although this "classy" Continental with "Main Line atmosphere" serves à la carte, it's favored mainly as "an elegant setting for that special affair" (especially the wedding kind – "they did a great job"); while the food rating is "decent", a few suggest the "owners should try to raise the level" to match the decor.

Famous 4th Street Delicatessen S   19 | 9 | 13 | $13
700 S. Fourth St. (Bainbridge St.), 215-922-3274
☑ While the "great" corned beef sandwiches and "dynamite" chocolate chip cookies ensure that this Queen Village Jewish-style deli "landmark" remains "famous after all these years", surveyors warn that "the chips are on the shoulders as well as in the cookies" and that the "mildly depressing", "retro" digs need sprucing up.

Fat Jack's ◑S   ▽ 17 | 11 | 15 | $18
1146 S. Delsea Dr. (1 mi. south of Landis Ave.), Vineland, NJ, 856-563-0001
☑ Some connoisseurs say the "fat, juicy ribs", "great sides" and live blues at this South Jersey "real barbecue" joint make it "worth a drive" when starved ("you can't under-eat"); hard-to-please displaced Southerners sniff "average."

Felicia's S   23 | 16 | 20 | $32
1148 S. 11th St. (Ellsworth St.), 215-755-9656
■ An "outstanding" South Philly Italian with "consistently" good fare ("terrific veal chop") and "friendly" service from a "staff that almost reads your mind"; a few say it's "good midweek" but "not on Saturday night" when it's "very noisy."

Fergie's Pub ◑S   16 | 16 | 18 | $13
1214 Sansom St. (12th St.), 215-928-8118
☑ This "fun" Center City Irish "watering hole" has "fairly priced" "stick-to-your-ribs" food, frequent quiz nights and a "warm" staff; though many feel "at home" here, some revelers find the food "so-so."

Fez Moroccan Cuisine S   21 | 22 | 22 | $25
620 S. Second St. (bet. Bainbridge & South Sts.), 215-925-5362
■ "Eat with your fingers and sit on the floor" at this "surprisingly delicious" South Street Moroccan that's a "fun dining experience" especially "with a group"; the "entertaining" belly dancer is a plus on Friday and Saturday, but "bring a flashlight" because it's "dark."

1521 Café Gallery S   19 | 17 | 18 | $16
1521 Spruce St. (bet. 15th & 16th Sts.), 215-546-1521
☑ To many artsy types, this "cozy", "down-to-earth" Center City Northern Italian cafe is the "vanguard of low-cost chic" ("like a corner of Greenwich Village") with "art-filled walls", "friendly" (if "at times inattentive") service and a "limited" but "high-quality" menu; a few negativists find the food "bland" and many "regret the return of smokers."

Filomena Cucina Italiana S   ▽ 21 | 16 | 20 | $25
Commerce Plaza, 1245 Blackwood-Clementon Rd., Clementon, NJ, 856-784-6166
■ "Head and shoulders above most shopping center restaurants", this Clementon Italian is a "special place" for locals who "don't want to travel far" for "tons of" "well-prepared" "homemade" dishes.

Filomena Cucina Rustica 🄢　　▽ 22 | 22 | 19 | $29
13 Milford Crosskeys Rd. (Berlin Circle), Berlin, NJ, 856-753-3540
■ This "beautiful" newcomer from the Filomena Cucina
Italiana people is dazzling diners with both "delicious" "old
favorites" and "innovations never seen in Berlin"; the style is
"casual but elegant" and service is "accommodating."

Finnigan's Wake 🄢　　▽ 13 | 13 | 14 | $15
537 N. Third St. (Spring Garden St.), 215-574-9240
☑ The mood is the main thing at this "spacious", "always
crowded" bar off the beaten path in Northern Liberties;
there's no denying the "friendly service with Irish flair",
and despite so-so ratings a few even find the food "good."

Fireside Room at　　▽ 21 | 23 | 18 | $24
Ashbourne, The 🄢
Ashbourne Country Club, Ashbourne Rd. & Oak Ln.,
Cheltenham, 215-635-2546
■ Now here's a surprise: the "gorgeous", "once private
dining room" at the Ashbourne Country Club has gone à la
carte as a "relaxing" American; while service isn't quite up
to the decor and food, it's clear management is "trying hard."

Fisher's 🄢　　– | – | – | M
7312 Castor Ave. (Cottman Ave.), 215-725-6201
There's a new lease on life at this longtime Northeast
standby which has reinvented itself as lively sports bar
serving pub grub and familiar if unspectacular seafood;
though oldsters still show up (especially for early dinner), the
median age of the clientele has been effectively cut in half.

Fisher's Tudor House 🄢　　15 | 16 | 16 | $24
1858 Street Rd. (Hulmeville Rd.), Bensalem, 215-244-9777
■ This "faux Tudor" Bucks seafooder is "a slightly better
version" of the Northeast original, which makes it an
"ok" choice to "take your aunt" for lunch; "good banquet
facilities" can handle parties up to 500.

Five Spot, The ⬤🄢　　17 | 22 | 16 | $22
5 Bank St. (Market St.), 215-574-0070
■ "Yo, Daddy-O!" – this Old City Eclectic is "one of the few
dinner-and-dancing spots in the city", a "hip" place to
"forget the '90s", and, depending on the night's theme (swing,
big band, lounge or Latin), groove to another era; those who
pause to chow down say the food's "good for a nightclub."

Flowing Springs 🄢　　16 | 20 | 17 | $31
Flowing Springs Rd. & Rte. 100, Spring City, 610-469-0899
☑ At this "pretty", "romantic", long-running International
in Chester County, they seem to "make an effort", but
those who insist "only the setting and friendly servers
save the place" are backed up by a drop in the food rating
since the last *Survey.*

Flying Fish　　　21　16　18　$28
8142 Germantown Ave. (Hartwell Ln.), 215-247-0707
☑ "Creatively prepared", "healthy", "savory" fish dishes offset the "tight squeeze for seating" and "Ikea"-like oak decor ("lacks soul") at this "frenetic" but "friendly" Chestnut Hill seafooder.

Foggia 🇸 (CLOSED)　　　–　–　–　M
1418 Rodman St. (bet. Lombard & South Sts.), 215-735-2900
Chef Frank DeCotis has moved his homey, affordable, Fitler Square Italian into the former Rodz Cafe, a handsome townhouse near Broad and South; so far, results have been good: the service is delightful and the cooking has a light approach.

Food for Thought　　　23　23　22　$36
Marlton Crossing Shopping Ctr., 129 Marlton Crossing (Rte. 73), Marlton, NJ, 856-797-1126
■ "South Jersey gone Center City" is the line on this "leading edge", California-style BYO bistro, an "unexpected gem" in a Marlton shopping center; a jump in the decor rating supports the majority that praises the "elegant", "cozy Victorian" setting, but a few lone voices find it "pretentious" compared to the former Haddonfield site; while "pricey", it's "the best restaurant in the area."

Forager Restaurant 🇸 (CLOSED)　　21　19　19　$33
1600 River Rd. (Lurgan Rd.), New Hope, 215-862-9477
■ Lots of surveyors consider this New American on "a lonely stretch of road" in New Hope the "quintessential Bucks County" restaurant; there's a "friendly staff that makes you feel like a regular", a "rustic", "sparse, yet homey" interior and "imaginative", "very good" food – in other words, a find.

Fork 🇸　　　24　25　22　$31
306 Market St. (bet. 3rd & 4th Sts.), 215-625-9425
■ "My new favorite restaurant" sums up reactions to this "casual", "low pressure" New American in Old City that oozes style, from its "cool chandeliers", "way hip" plates and "imaginative cutlery" to a clientele that's "as well-dressed as the decor"; toss in "fabulous food" and "so far, so good."

FOUNDERS 🇸　　　25　28　25　$51
Park Hyatt at the Bellevue, 200 S. Broad St. (Walnut St.), 215-790-2814
■ "A journey back to a finer past" can still be found at this "quiet", "elegant" main room at the Bellevue, perhaps "the most classic dining space in the city" ("where I want to be proposed to"); expect "top-drawer" New American food, a dazzling Downtown view, "old-fashioned" service and "great music" and dancing on weekends; an appreciative "older crowd" says "thank the Lord for tradition."

FOUNTAIN RESTAURANT Ⓢ 29 | 29 | 28 | $60
Four Seasons Hotel, 1 Logan Sq. (Benjamin Franklin Pkwy. & 18th St.), 215-963-1500
■ For "the most sophisticated dining in Philadelphia", it would be hard to top Jean-Marie Lacroix and company (and their ratings) at this "consistently fabulous" Continental-French in the Four Seasons; business people tout it as a "super meeting place" for a power lunch, and the brunch-and-dinner crowd says it's a "wow" for "imaginative", "sublime" food and "flawless" service in a room that's "elegance personified"; it "keeps Le Bec-Fin on its toes."

Four Dogs Tavern Ⓢ – | – | – | M
1300 W. Strasbury Rd. (Rte. 162), Marshallton, 610-692-4367
This cozy American-Continental, set in the former barn of the Marshalton Inn, is a fine choice at brunch or dinner when a variety of music is also dished up.

Frangelica Ⓢ 23 | 21 | 22 | $31
200 S. 12th St. (bet. Locust & Walnut Sts.), 215-731-9930
■ An "undiscovered" Eclectic bistro down the way from the Convention Center that's tagged as an "excellent", "unpretentious" "date restaurant" with "innovative" food, "caring" service and "Gothic decor", all at a "great value."

Frankie's at Night/Eclipse Cafe Ⓢ 23 | 10 | 19 | $25
932 S. 10th St. (Carpenter St.), 215-629-1093
■ "Shhh, don't tell anyone" beg devotees of this second-story, dinner-only BYO over Shank's & Evelyn's, where Frank Perri dishes out "giant portions" of "always tasty", salt-of-the-earth Southern Italian classics; converts swear his "sublime sauces" prove he "has a knack for seasoning."

Frankie's Seafood Italiano Ⓢ 20 | 13 | 14 | $28
1100 Tasker St. (11th St.), 215-468-9989
☑ "You'd never expect to find food like this in a place like this" "authentic" South Philly Italian with the obligatory "large portions" of "great, homey" fare; but diners warn that "you can't see through the smoke", the decor is "*Gilligan's Island*-esque" and service is "slow."

Frederick's Ⓢ 22 | 23 | 19 | $38
757 S. Front St. (Fitzwater St.), 215-271-3733
☑ "You'll leave your four-hour meal plump" but satisfied at this "engagingly pretentious" South Street Italian; the "Roman" decor might be "a tad tacky" and "waits are interminable", but the food is "superb" and "everyone is made to feel welcome"; big bands are also a draw.

Frenchtown Inn Ⓢ 24 | 22 | 21 | $45
7 Bridge St. (Rte. 29), Frenchtown, NJ, 908-996-3300
■ The new chef-owners of this "dark and romantic" Classic French bistro along "scenic" Route 29 (above Lambertville) continue to make it "worth a drive", turning out "innovative" "meals to remember" with "splendid" service as a bonus.

Friday, Saturday, Sunday [S] 22 | 19 | 20 | $30

261 S. 21st St. (bet. Locust & Spruce Sts.), 215-546-4232

■ "The '70s live" at this "quirky", "oldie but goodie" in Center City, a "cozy spot" with a "great" "upstairs tank bar"; while "there's nothing understated" about the "flamboyant" American-Continental food, it's always "reliable", as are the "career waiters who really make a difference"; tables "too close together" is the main complaint.

Fuji Mountain [S] 19 | 14 | 19 | $24

2030 Chestnut St. (bet. 20th & 21st Sts.), 215-751-0939
801 Montgomery Ave. (S. Woodbine Rd.), Narberth, 610-668-9959

◪ Reviewers of these "quick" Japanese twins in Center City and Main Line praise the "huge portions" of "good", "basic" sushi, but the staff's attitude is a "very pleasant" vs. "nasty" *Rashomon* tale; those with long memories say Narberth "still looks like a gas station."

Full Moon [S] ⊄ 20 | 15 | 18 | $22

23 Bridge St. (west of Union), Lambertville, NJ, 609-397-1096

■ The Lambertville "bohemian" crowd waxes enthusiastic about this "funky", "consistently good" BYO French-accented American that packs 'em in for Sunday brunch ("great omelets"); the "reasonably priced" menu has "healthy" choices for a "quick, casual bite" "after antiquing."

GARDEN, THE 24 | 24 | 22 | $45

1617 Spruce St. (bet. 16th & 17th Sts.), 215-546-4455

■ The "Energizer Bunny of restaurants" "keeps going and going" in Center City with a "first-rate" American menu, an "unstuffy staff" and "a nice, quiet" atmosphere that "oozes old money"; and, of course, in "the spring and summer" it's "wonderful" to dine outside in the garden.

Garnian Wa [S] ▽ 19 | 13 | 19 | $16

Paoli Plaza, 1776 E. Lancaster Ave. (bet. Rtes. 30 & 252), Paoli, 610-889-1761

■ "Exceptional Chinese in a no-frills atmosphere" is the line on this "consistent" Main Line BYO, a "neighborhood favorite" for "bargain lunches" and "big portions."

General Lafayette Inn & Brewery ◐[S] 16 | 17 | 17 | $25

646 Germantown Pike (Church Rd.), Lafayette Hill, 610-941-0600

◪ The "excellent beer made on premises" is a hit for the new owners of this Lafayette Hill landmark that received a "nice face-lift"; the colonial interior is consistent with the "hearty" American fare that's still working itself out.

General Warren Inne 24 | 24 | 23 | $40

W. Old Lancaster Hwy. (Rte. 29), Malvern, 610-296-3637

■ "Take your best significant other" or "out-of-town guests" to this "well-run", "historic" (1745) "country inn" in Malvern for a "romantic" meal of "excellent" Eclectic food by the fireplace "on a cold winter night."

Genji I S   23 | 16 | 19 | $28
4002 Spruce St. (40th St.), 215-387-1583

Genji II S
1720 Sansom St. (bet. 17th & 18th Sts.), 215-564-1720
■ The "ultrafresh", "excellent" sushi and "wide variety of nonsushi dishes" at these "restful", "cool, clean" Japanese twins (in Center City and University City) have many musing that they "might be the best in town."

Geno's Steaks ●S⚄   18 | 8 | 13 | $7
Italian Mkt., 1219 S. Ninth St. (bet. Federal St. & Passyunk Ave.), no phone
☑ A "classic" for "artery-clogging", "wickedly delicious" cheese steaks "at 3 AM", this "quick", "no-frills" South Philly "landmark" across the street from arch rival Pat's is deemed "cleaner" than its competitors; disgruntled diners (a minority) say "bring Rolaids."

Gianna's S   ▽ 17 | 14 | 17 | $26
721 Wharton St. (bet. 7th & 8th Sts.), 215-468-4605
☑ For those who seek "solid" Italian specialties such as "wonderful veal" in "plentiful" portions, this "nothing exotic" dinner-only spot in South Philly might fill the bill.

Girasole Ristorante S   21 | 18 | 17 | $31
1305 Locust St. (Broad St.), 215-985-4659
☑ "Sunflowery" decor, "perfect lighting" and "superb" food ("stylish, good pizzas") make this Center City Italian a "romantic" date and "pre-theater" choice, even if some find the staff a bit "snotty."

Giumarello's Ristorante   24 | 16 | 21 | $29
512 Station Ave. (White Horse Pike), Haddon Heights, NJ, 856-547-9393
■ Adherents of this "low-key", "chichi", Haddon Heights Northern Italian BYO say it's a "word-of-mouth favorite" thanks to "enormous portions" of "great food" (the garlic bread is "the best in four states") at a "wide range of prices"; P.S. "reserve early for the weekend" and don't leave without trying the signature veal chop stuffed with lobster.

Goat Hollow S   18 | 14 | 18 | $22
300 W. Mt. Pleasant Ave. (Lincoln Dr.), 215-242-4710
■ This Mount Airy New American is an "artsy", "funky" "neighborhood place" with a "welcoming" air, a "wonderful mix of people" and "curiously good food", though "smoke and noise" from the bar ("sit upstairs") gets the goat of some.

Golden Pheasant Inn S   21 | 22 | 20 | $46
763 River Rd. (14 mi. north of New Hope), Erwinna, 610-294-9595
■ There's "fine country dining" at this "charming", "romantic" Classic French inn by the river north of New Hope; acolytes appreciate the "well-presented", "gourmet dishes" and "charming" "greenhouse decor", though the economical warn of "high prices."

Golden Pond 🅂
22 | 16 | 21 | $20

1006 Race St. (10th St.), 215-923-0303

■ A "white tablecloth" Chinese BYO that's "the only Chinatown destination" for those who rave over "exquisite", "healthful" dishes, "civil" service and "clean, bright" surroundings; the yin-yang soup is a "must."

Golden Sea 🅂
▽ 23 | 18 | 20 | $17

Center Sq. Shopping Ctr., 1301 Skippack Pike, Blue Bell, 610-292-8881

■ "A sleeper in the 'burbs" ("never had a bad meal there"), this "first-class", BYO Chinese in a Montco strip mall has an "excellent", "sooo nice" staff, "consistently good" food and a "clean and pretty" atmosphere; and finally, a place where "the hot and sour soup is really hot and sour."

Gourley's 🅂⊘
– | – | – | M

2624 Brown St. (Tancy St.), 215-235-4341

This Victorian BYO in Fairmount, designed and built by John Gourley, is winning raves for its "sophisticated" American-Continental cuisine, easy-on-the-eyes decor and welcoming staff.

Gourmet Restaurant 🅂
23 | 16 | 21 | $32

3520 Cottman Ave. (Frankford Ave.), 215-331-7174

■ This French-Asian storefront is a "real surprise" that "draws a crowd" despite a "strange location" in the Northeast; expect "consistently very good" food that's definitely a cut "above most neighborhood places."

Gourmet's Table, The 🅂
22 | 15 | 20 | $28

2 Waterview Rd. (1 mi. west of Rte. 352 on West Chester Pike), East Goshen, 610-696-2211

☑ They're "trying hard to make the big time" at this Contemporary French–Italian BYO near West Chester where a "creative, energetic, young chef" prepares "serious food" ("excellent mussel bisque") in a "casual ambiance"; detractors wish they would "stop running out of food" and think the interior's a bit "spartan."

Grasshopper
21 | 17 | 20 | $31

4427 Main St. (Carson St.), 215-483-1888

☑ "On slow nights" this "cozy" French with Asian accents in Manayunk "is a place to be savored" thanks to a "pleasant" atmosphere (get a "window seat and people-watch") and "very good food and service"; but many think it's a "pity they're no longer a BYO."

Graziella's 🅂
19 | 15 | 20 | $37

90 Haddon Ave. (Cuthbert Rd.), Westmont, NJ, 856-854-4816

■ "Retreat into operatic Italy" at this Westmont (of all places) spot where opera is sung on weekends between courses of "good" Italian; it makes for a "very entertaining" experience, especially "with a group."

Gullifty's ◑🕃 13 12 14 $17
Rosemont Sq., 1149 Lancaster Ave. (bet. Franklin & Montrose), Rosemont, 610-525-1851
☑ This "crowded", collegian-friendly Rosemont "watering hole" is "a step ahead of Bennigan's" with "run-of-the-mill" Eclectic food and "harmless" service that ranges from "pleasant" to "dazed and confused"; while most would give it a go "in a pinch", others insist it "needs to be reinvented"; N.B. there's been a post-*Survey* renovation.

Gypsy Rose 🕃 19 19 19 $26
Rte. 113, 505 Bridge Rd. (bet. Rtes. 29 & 73), Collegeville, 610-489-1600
☑ In a "beautiful setting" above a creek by the Perkimen in Collegeville, this "romantic" Eclectic has a lot of "warmth" along with a "nice view from an enclosed porch dining area"; while "the crabs star, the rest of the menu is good", and so is brunch.

Hadley's Bistro-American 🕃 19 19 19 $31
Sheraton Society Hill, 1 Dock St. (Walnut St., bet. Front & 2nd Sts.), 215-238-6656
☑ A newly redecorated New American in the Society Hill Sheraton that's a "comfortable", "lovely setting for better than average hotel food"; try it "after the theater."

Hamilton's Grill Room 🕃 23 18 19 $38
The Porkyard, 8 Coryell St. (N. Union St.), Lambertville, NJ, 609-397-4343
■ This "charmer" in Lambertville is "worth the schlep" for "cocktails in the boat house" bar or "thoughtfully prepared" Mediterranean dishes ("excellent" grilled seafood) outside in the "pretty courtyard" where it's BYO; big eaters find "portions small for the price."

Hank's Place 🕃⍢ 19 10 17 $12
Rtes. 1 & 100, Chadds Ford, 610-388-7061
☑ "Watch for Wyeths" at this "comfortable" Chadds Ford Greco-American "greasy spoon" that's a "hangout" for Brandywine Valleyans who "love breakfast"; most brave "mob" conditions for "honest food at old-fashioned prices", but a few find the eats "plain."

Happy Rooster 19 16 16 $38
118 S. 16th St. (Sansom St.), 215-563-1481
☑ A "unassuming", "classy" Center City Continental "institution" with a "great bar" ("the perfect martini") that's "still the best place to get a drink with the old boys club set"; most find the food "good" if "overpriced", but nonregulars complain that the staff "caters only to frequent patrons" and think the interior "needs refurnishing and fresh air."

Hard Rock Cafe ◐ [S] — | — | — | M
Reading Terminal Mkt., 12th & Market Sts., 215-238-1000
Philadelphia, one of the world's great rock 'n' roll towns, has finally been put on the map by this guitar-fueled chain; this outpost is a block from the Convention Center in the former Reading Terminal; the food is, well, casual, but the atmospherics (memorabilia, music) are the real draw.

Hardshell Cafe [S] 15 | 12 | 14 | $22
901 Market St. (9th St.), 215-592-9110
150 Rte. 73 N. (Rte. 70), Marlton, NJ, 856-983-3180
355 York Rd. (bet. County Line & Street Rds.), Warminster, 215-674-0600
◪ Diners say "stick to crabs" (especially the "delicious" garlic ones) when dining at this "family seafood" chain; despite gripes that it's "too commercial", there are "long waits", so they must be doing something right.

Harmony Vegetarian Restaurant [S] 20 | 14 | 18 | $18
135 N. Ninth St. (bet. Cherry & Race Sts.), 215-627-4520
◪ Many "can't believe" that dishes such as steamed 'beef' buns are made with faux meat at this Chinese "vegetarian heaven" in Chinatown that "gets better with time"; on the downside, the decor's "unmemorable" and a minority thinks the "phony meat doesn't cut it" ("stick to veggies").

Harry's Bar & Grill (CLOSED) 23 | 19 | 21 | $39
22 S. 18th St. (bet. Chestnut & Market Sts.), 215-561-5757
◪ A weekday-only, "somber" Center City Continental that's "solid in every respect"; "it can be a little intimidating for the solo diner", especially women, since "everything about this place is masculine"; still, some think "it wouldn't hurt" to open on Saturdays.

Hartefeld National [S] ▽ 21 | 23 | 20 | $30
1 Hartefeld Dr. (bet. Rtes. 7 & 141), Avondale, 610-268-8800
■ "There's no better way to end a round of golf" than to drop in at this bucolic Chester County American for "excellent food" with a "gorgeous" view ("if you like golfing scenery, this is the place"); "too bad it's not closer to civilization."

Haute To Trot [S] — | — | — | I
930 Locust St. (10th St.), 215-440-0930
This "excellent" Eclectic bistro "hidden" near Washington Square may have a silly pun for a name, but it also has "imaginative fare" (lunch and Sunday brunch only) and surprisingly friendly Franco-style service.

Havana [S] 16 | 14 | 16 | $21
105 S. Main St. (bet. Mechanic & New Sts.), New Hope, 215-862-9897
■ This "fun", "loud and youthful" New Hope Eclectic "hot spot" is "great for people-watching" from the "huge", "warm weather" "outdoor patio"; the "trendy menu" "usually delivers" and is priced "reasonably."

Herb Garden Café 22 | 17 | 20 | $29

19 S. Whitehorse Rd. (Rte. 23), Phoenixville, 610-935-5988

■ The many fans of this "charming" New American BYO say it just might be "the best-kept secret in Phoenixville"; "stylishly presented", "quality" dishes, "personal service" and a "homey" setting in a "pretty, old house" ("floor creaks") make it a "pleasant" place to "settle in for a long, romantic" meal; "take the drive once and you'll be going there again."

Hikaru 20 | 16 | 18 | $26

4348 Main St. (Grape St.), 215-487-3500 [S]
607 S. Second St. (bet. Bainbridge & South Sts.), 215-627-7110 [S]
108 S. 18th St. (bet. Chestnut & Sansom Sts.), 215-496-9950

◪ Japanese triplets with outposts in Center City, Manayunk and near South Street (Manayunk has "the best decor") providing "friendly" service and sushi that most consider "solid" and "reliable"; some counter "nothing exceptional, but nothing negative."

H.K. Golden Phoenix ◐[S] 22 | 15 | 19 | $18

911 Race St. (bet. 9th & 10th Sts.), 215-629-4988

■ "If you like seafood", this new, huge, "informal" Chinatown newcomer "can do no wrong", especially at the "great" Hong Kong–style dim sum brunch, already being called one of "the best in the city."

Homestead Restaurant 15 | 16 | 16 | $30

3 Village Rd. (bet. Dresher & Welsh Rds.), Horsham, 215-657-8840

■ A lakeside view and outdoor deck ("lovely setting") don't prevent critics from saying that this Horsham Eclectic that "used to be a favorite" is now too "inconsistent" in the food and service areas; perhaps management changes over the last year will help.

Hotel du Village [S] 23 | 23 | 22 | $44

2535 N. River Rd. (bet. Phillips Mill Rd. & Rte. 32), New Hope, 215-862-9911

■ An "elegant" Classic French in a "romantic" château on River Road, complete with "dark wood ceiling beams" and "two large fireplaces for cozy winter dining"; the staff is "very serious" and the food is "delectable."

Hot Tamales Cafe ⊄ 16 | 10 | 14 | $8

703 Walnut St. (7th St. at Washington Park), 215-574-8322
114 S. 20th St. (Sansom St.), 215-569-8511
524 S. Fourth St. (South St.), 215-922-3411 [S]

◪ There's "no better bargain" than these "cheap" ("and I mean cheap!"), "tasty", "fast-food–style" Mexican *hijos* near South Street and in Center City; some find the offerings "bland", but those on the run assert "both your tummy and pocket feel full when you leave."

House of Chen ●S   ▽ 17 | 13 | 16 | $17
932 Race St. (bet. 9th & 10th Sts.), 215-925-4248
■ There's "not much atmosphere" at this "traditional" Chinese in Chinatown but the "owner shakes your hand" and the chow's generally "reliable"; it's a "good bet" for a "late-night snack" (open until 5 AM).

Hunan Restaurant S   17 | 12 | 18 | $20
47 E. Lancaster Ave. (Rittenhouse Pl.), Ardmore, 610-642-3050
☑ Though many call this Main Line BYO Chinese an "old standard" that's still "dependable", others counter that it's "not as good as it used to be" and has an interior that "needs a face-lift."

Hunt Room S   ▽ 15 | 17 | 15 | $28
Desmond Great Valley Hotel, 1 Liberty Blvd. (Rte. 29), Malvern, 610-296-7300
☑ It seems many surveyors haven't been out to this American seafooder in "the middle of a god-awful corporate center" in Malvern since its remodeling and change of focus, but those who have claim it's "more open and bright" with food that's "improving"; consensus holds that it's "better at lunch."

Hymie's Merion Deli S   16 | 8 | 13 | $14
342 Montgomery Ave. (Levering Mill Rd.), Merion Station, 610-668-3354
☑ While surveyors "could live without the attitude" from the "crusty waitresses", and many call for better housekeeping, this Main Line Jewish-style deli "hangout" is still a "place to be seen on Sunday mornings"; sure, the fare is "typical", but for "grease and good times" this "institution" still has allure.

Il Giardino S   15 | 15 | 15 | $29
202 E. Lancaster Ave. (Church Rd.), Ardmore, 610-896-0705
☑ There's "good potential" at this Main Line "neighborhood" Italian, but right now most agree the food and service are too "inconsistent" to justify the "pricey" tab.

Il Portico S   22 | 23 | 21 | $46
1519 Walnut St. (bet. 15th & 16th Sts.), 215-587-7000
■ Yes, this "elegant" "beautiful" Restaurant Row Italian has "tuxedoed waiters" who are "serious about their food" and it delivers "superior", "melt-in-your-mouth" dishes; however, many find it "pretentious" and so "expensive" it's "made 'chutzpah' an Italian word."

Il Sol D'Italia   19 | 16 | 18 | $29
255 N. Sycamore St. (Rte. 431), Newtown, 215-968-5880
■ Newtowners enjoy this "casually elegant" Southern Italian for its "good food", "friendly" staff , "funky", "imaginative artwork" and jazz on Fridays and Saturdays, when there's a "bar scene."

Il Tartufo 🅂⊘   21   14   19 $30
4341 Main St. (Grape St.), 215-482-1999
■ Here's a "jewelbox hidden" among the power rooms in
Manayunk: an "outstanding", if "cramped", Northern
Italian BYO from the owner of Tira Misu and Il Portico;
admirers rave over the "hospitable staff" and "superb"
food ("try the artichokes") but warn that it's cash only.

Imperial Inn ◗🅂   20   13   17 $17
146 N. 10th St. (bet. Cherry & Race Sts.), 215-627-5588
■ "Order lots and share" at this "homey" Chinatown
Chinese "favorite" that "has looked the same for 15
years"; since other items can be "standard", many prefer
to go just for the "reliable" Sunday dim sum brunch ("get
there early"), perfect "when you don't want waffles."

Ingleneuk Tea House 🅂   15   15   18 $20
120 Park Ave. (Rte. 320), Swarthmore, 610-543-4569
▨ "Take a trip into yesteryear" at this "picturesque",
"homey" "institution" in Swarthmore known for its
"welcoming staff", "silver-haired" clientele, "nice family
atmosphere" and "delicious" sticky buns; some find other
items on the "old American menu" "ordinary."

INN AT PHILLIPS MILL 🅂⊘   25   26   23 $39
2590 N. River Rd. (Rte. 32), New Hope, 215-862-9919
■ "Simply the most romantic place I've ever dined" is the
sentiment on this "charming" BYO New Hope inn where the
French bistro dishes are "superbly prepared", service is
"impeccable" and the whole experience is "the perfect end
to a day in Bucks County" – "I'd move in if I could afford it."

Inn of the Hawke ◗🅂   ▽ 18   20   20 $24
*Inn of the Hawke, 74 S. Union St. (Mt. Hope St.),
Lambertville, NJ, 609-397-9555*
▨ The selling point of this Lambertville American is the
"lovely" patio, though the food is "good" and "getting better
each time" and there's "great conversation" at the bar.

Inn on Blueberry Hill ◗🅂   22   23   21 $40
*Almshouse Rd. & Rte. 611 (north of PA Tpke., exit 27),
Doylestown, 215-491-1777*
▨ Set in a "beautifully restored Victorian manor" with "very
comfortable dining chairs", this American comes through
with "delicious" food and a "pleasant" staff that's always
"trying"; a few dis the "view of Route 611 and the strip mall."

Inn Philadelphia 🅂   22   23   21 $38
251 S. Camac St. (bet. 12th & 13th Sts.), 215-732-2339
■ "Try a single malt by the fireplace" or an "elegant" dinner
in the "secret garden" at this "romantic" American-
Continental in a "handsome" townhouse tucked away in
Center City; the new chef is more than holding his own, as
is the usually "professional" service; P.S. tune in to the piano
player on Thursday–Saturday nights.

Io E Tu Ristorante S | 21 | 15 | 21 | $28 |
1514-20 S. Ninth St. (bet. Dickinson & Tasker Sts.), 215-271-3906
■ There's an "old-world attention to detail" at this family-run Italian, a "wonderful change from the other red gravy joints in South Philadelphia; "terrific", "belt-expanding" food is matched by a "really personal staff" with lots of "warmth and passion", though the room is "too gaudy" for some.

Isaac Newton's S | 15 | 14 | 16 | $18 |
18 S. State St. (Newtown-Yardley Rd.), Newtown, 215-860-5100
☑ Relativity speaking, there's a "younger crowd" (including "screaming babies") at this "noisy" Newtown stop that whips up "fun", "munchie" American food ("a Friday's with a little more class"); though ratings aren't stellar, most think it's "good for the beers [17 microbrews] and burgers."

ISABELLA'S S | 27 | 19 | 23 | $35 |
6516 Castor Ave. (bet. Hellerman & Magee Sts.), 215-533-0356
■ A French-Italian "find", "hidden" on a "dull, commercial" Northeast strip ("foie gras on Castor Avenue – wow"); "excellent", "imaginative" food from "super chef" Ben McNamara is presented "beautifully", the service is "friendly" and while the interior is "very cramped", that's a small price to pay since "if it were in Center City we would never get a reservation"; N.B. the food rating has rocketed three points since our last *Survey*.

Italian Bistro S | 16 | 16 | 17 | $21 |
211 S. Broad St. (bet. Locust & Walnut Sts.), 215-731-0700 ◗
1509 Hwy. 38 (Chapel Ave.), Cherry Hill, NJ, 609-665-6900
■ A chain Italian where the "food quality varies from location to location", therefore, it's not surprising that some label it a "good value" and "better than average", while others scoff "an Italian version of Bennigan's."

Jack's Firehouse ◗S | 18 | 20 | 18 | $35 |
2130 Fairmount Ave. (bet. 21st & 22nd Sts.), 215-232-9000
☑ "Be ready for the unusual" (meaning "lots of game dishes") when dining at Jack McDavid's "inventive" (some think "too far out") "upscale-casual" American in a Fairmount firehouse; while it's "fun" and Jack sure is "an original", the whole shebang strikes quite a few as "overpriced and overhyped."

Jake & Oliver's House of Brews S | – | – | – | M |
(nka Wichita Steaks and Brews)
22 S. Third St. (bet. Chestnut & Market Sts.), 215-627-4825
261 Montgomery Ave., Bala Cynwyd, 610-664-3000 **(CLOSED)**
The owner of these former sibling micro breweries has remodeled and renamed the South Third Street location as a tongue-in-cheek Western-style steakhouse serving moderately priced steaks and fixins (from Tex Mex chili to calamari to "Snazzy Chicken"), fit for the entire family, as well as for large groups.

JAKE'S ⬛　　　　　　　27 | 22 | 24 | $42
4365 Main St. (bet. Grape & Levering Sts.), 215-483-0444
■ Bruce Cooper's "first-class" New American is easily
"Manayunk's bright star", an "understated" "wonder" with
"knowledgeable" servers, an "outstanding" wine list and the
"best nouvelle cuisine around", though when it's crowded
you can "feel like a sardine"; don't leave without trying the
crab cakes or salmon.

Jamaican Jerk Hut ⬛⊘　　　21 | 10 | 17 | $15
1436 South St. (15th St.), 215-545-8644
■ An "interesting" Jamaican "dive" off Broad Street where
"jerk-food junkies" bliss out to "fantastic" "jerk pork to die
for" and listen to hot "steel drum" music on a seasonal
patio that "transports you to the Caribbean."

Jannie ⬛　　　　　　　▽ 21 | 21 | 22 | $21
Cottman Bustleton Shop Ctr., 2117 Cottman Ave.
(Bustleton Ave.), 215-722-6278
■ This "shiny clean" Chinese-Japanese "surprise" is one of
the "classiest" acts in Northeast Philadelphia; there's "light",
"superbly fresh", "ridiculously low-priced food", "very
attentive service" and a "big, open", "beautiful room"; truth
be told, "it doesn't belong in a shopping center."

JEAN PIERRE'S ⬛　　　　25 | 23 | 24 | $52
101 S. State St. (Centre Ave.), Newtown, 215-968-6201
■ Diners find a "touch of Le Bec-Fin in Newtown" at this
"memorable" Classic French that "feels like a country inn in
Provence"; its many fans enjoy being "pampered" during
the "exquisite", "absolute steal" three-course lunches.

Jefferson House ⬛　　　19 | 22 | 20 | $32
2519 DeKalb Pike (Germantown Pike), East Norriton,
610-275-3407
☑ The "beautiful setting" (a "grand old" mansion with
"white linen and crystal") is the star of this "dependable"
Montco International, a "safe place to take your parents" or
hold a wedding; there's "romantic seating on the veranda" if
you're just getting engaged.

Jim's Steaks ◐⬛⊘　　　20 | 9 | 14 | $8
400 South St. (4th St.), 215-928-1911
431 N. 62nd St. (bet. Callowhill St. & Girard Ave.),
215-747-6615
Roosevelt Mall, 2311 Cottman Ave. (Bustleton Ave.),
215-333-5467
☑ "Sloppy, greasy and damn good" is the consensus on
these cheese steak "landmarks" (the "crowded" flagship on
South Street is for "people-watchers"; other outposts are
in West and Northeast Philly) that are a "tradition" among
locals and tourists; while a few note "surly" service, most
agree it's "the fastest way to a heart attack" but "worth it."

J.J.'s Grotto   16 | 11 | 15 | $17

27 S. 21st St. (bet. Chestnut & Market Sts.), 215-988-9255

■ An Italian jazzery in a Center City cellar with hot tunes and "delicious pizza" (though other items are only "so-so"); foes sound a blue note for the "dingy", "rec-room" setting, but overall this place is an "upbeat", "after-hours hangout", so "put on your shades, grab a pie and stay a while."

Joe's Peking Duck House S   20 | 7 | 16 | $17

925 Race St. (bet. 9th & 10th Sts.), 215-922-3277
Marlton Crossing Shopping Ctr., 145 Rte. 73 S. (Rte. 70 E.), Marlton, NJ, 856-985-1551 ⊅

■ The decor's "uninspiring" at these Chinese siblings (the Chinatown original's downright "scruffy"), but the food's "reliable" and you can still get some of the "best Peking duck" around, even though "Joe's gone" away to Joseph Poon; service is "eat-and-run" "fast."

Joe's Tomato Pies S   ▽ 22 | 10 | 17 | $11

552 S. Clinton Ave. (bet. Bayard & Butler Sts.), Trenton, NJ, 609-393-3945

■ A "favorite" in Trenton for "inexpensive", "exceptional" pies ("wonderful thin white pizza") and Italian food ("ask to have your antipasti mixed"); fans note "it looks so awful on the outside, when you walk in you will be surprised."

John Harvard's S   16 | 17 | 17 | $20

1001 Springfield Sq. S. (Baltimore Pike), Springfield, 610-544-4440
629 W. Lancaster Ave. (Old Eagle School Rd.), Wayne, 610-687-6565 ◗

■ There's "stick-to-your-ribs", "surprisingly good" "pub grub with a twist" at these "noisy", "always jammed" yuppie and "kid-friendly" brew pubs ; service is "better than expected" and "with beer this good, bring a designated driver"; to detractors, "sounds great, comes up short."

Johnny Mott's S   19 | 13 | 19 | $27

Cedarbrook Hill Apts., 8460 Limekiln Pike (bet. Greenwood Ave. & Rte. 309 S.), Wyncote, 215-887-1263

■ An "old reliable" Italian seafooder in Wyncote featuring "huge portions" of "very good" food and a popular "bargain" early bird; to most people under 60, it's "ok" but "boring – like kissing your grandmother (who probably eats here three times a week)."

Joseph Ambler Inn S   22 | 23 | 21 | $36

1005 Horsham Rd. (bet. Stump & Upper State Rds.), North Wales, 215-362-7500

■ You'll find "lots of polished wood and glazed meat" at this North Wales country inn offering "wonderful" Traditional American food ("best rack of lamb this side of New Zealand"), "attentive" service and "cozy" rooms to stay the night; "eat on the terrace" when weather permits; if you're game the menu is too.

Joseph Poon [S] 22 18 22 $25
1002 Arch St. (10th St.), 215-928-9333
◪ "We're glad Joe's back" (his "enthusiasm is contagious") is the consensus on chef Poon's new Asian fusion BYO in Chinatown, where a "sweet staff" serves "large portions" of "weird combos that work" – most of the time, anyway, though a few judge the results "mixed"; P.S. free cooking lessons on Saturday are "a kick."

Joseph's Italian Cuisine [S] 23 16 21 $31
1915 E. Passyunk Ave. (bet. McKean & Mifflin Sts.), 215-755-2770
■ South Philadelphia Italian where "hunky guys from the neighborhood" deliver "elegantly prepared", "delicious" food ("exceptional sauces") amidst "pleasant" surroundings.

Jow's Garden [S] ▽ 21 17 21 $19
349 S. 47th St. (bet. Pine & Spruce Sts.), 215-471-3663
◪ Located in a tough part of West Philadelphia, this Italian-Thai is a "spicy little gem" that some say "deserves more attention" ("never crowded"), even if a few complain that the food combo is a "mismatch"; "unless you're a fire-eater", the flying tiger dish may be too hot.

Joy Tsin Lau ◐ [S] 18 12 15 $18
1026 Race St. (bet. 10th & 11th Sts.), 215-592-7226
■ The "tacky", slightly "shabby" interior at this Chinatown "standby" can't keep the crowds away from the "unusually tasty" dim sum at lunch (though other items are "average"); of course, "it would be nice if servers spoke English" (or "if I spoke Chinese").

Judy's Cafe [S] 21 13 18 $24
627 S. Third St. (Bainbridge St.), 215-928-1968
■ There's a "*Cheers*-like atmosphere" at this "quirky" Queen Village Eclectic known for "big portions" of "excellent" "comfort food with an edge" ("don't pass up the meat loaf and mashed potatoes"); the staff is "colorful enough to shame Crayola" and the "hip" clientele (a mix of "gays and straights") only a shade less "interesting."

JW's Steakhouse [S] ▽ 20 19 21 $43
Convention Ctr. Marriott, 1201 Market St. (12th St.), 215-625-6074
■ "Good for a hotel" is the reaction to this Convention Center Marriott steakhouse, where the room is "beautiful", the staff "attentive" and the presentations "very nice."

Kabul [S] 21 16 19 $21
106 Chestnut St. (bet. Front & 2nd Sts.), 215-922-3676
■ "The pumpkin entree is a wonderful surprise" at Philadelphia's only Afghan restaurant, a "low-key", "reasonably priced" Old City BYO with "intriguing flavors for both the demure and the daring" – "exotic, but easy to like."

Kaminski's ◐ [S] 13 | 10 | 14 | $17
1424 Brace Rd. (Rte. 561), Cherry Hill, NJ, 856-428-2555
■ "If you can tolerate the sports goons yelling over the TV", this "smoky" Cherry Hill "hangout" has an "extensive", "bar-style" menu of "cheap eats"; reviewers single out the "good roast beef sandwiches" and burgers, but add that the decor is in "need of sprucing up."

Kansas City Prime [S] 24 | 21 | 21 | $49
4417 Main St. (bet. Carson & Gay Sts.), 215-482-3700
◪ "Oversized portions" of beef that "melt in your mouth" are the hallmark of this "striking" Manayunk steakhouse, "worth a pilgrimage every year or so" for a cholesterol binge; while most agree you'll get "a good cut of meat", critics complain it's "seriously overpriced" and bemoan "tables too close together"; don't miss the "great bread pudding."

Katmandu [S] 15 | 19 | 14 | $22
415 N. Delaware Ave. (bet. Callowhill & Spring Garden Sts.), 215-629-7400
Waterfront Park, Rte. 29 (Trenton Thunder Stadium), Trenton, NJ, 609-393-7300
■ For "hot fun in the summertime", these island bistros (one in Trenton, the original near Penn's Landing) are "like a quick trip to the Caribbean" with reggae music and a "view of the water"; although ratings are average and "cover charges" (on weekends) are a turnoff, many say the "food is surprisingly good for a watering hole" "meat market."

Kaufman House [S] 20 | 18 | 20 | $33
Main St./Rte. 63 (1 mi. east of Rte. 29), Sumneytown, 215-234-4181
■ This "reliable" Traditional American near Lansdale is an "old favorite" for "delicious food" from an "artful menu"; the "1850s setting" is "relaxing" and if it gets too late you can always stay the night; dinner reservations are recommended on weekends.

Kawabata [S] 19 | 14 | 16 | $24
2455 Grant Ave. (Roosevelt Blvd.), 215-969-8225
■ A long-standing Northeast Japanese (the Chestnut Street location was sold) where the "dependable" sushi "rolls will rock you"; a post-*Survey* renovation and new menu should satisfy negativists.

KENNEDY-SUPPLEE MANSION 20 | 27 | 21 | $42
Valley Forge Nat'l Park, 1100 W. Valley Forge Rd. (Rte. 23), King of Prussia, 610-337-3777
■ It's sure "lovely to look at" say admirers of this "opulent", "old-fashioned" Continental in a "gorgeous mansion" at the edge of Valley Forge National Historical Park; but, as ratings suggest, the "inconsistent" food "doesn't always live up" to the "fabulously elegant" setting.

Khajuraho S   – | – | – | |
Ardmore Plaza, 12 Greenfield Ave. (Lancaster Ave.),
Ardmore, 610-896-7200
Erotic sculpture is only one of the surprises at this
"fabulous" and "desperately needed" Main Line BYO Indian
(pronounced ka-ju-RA-ho) in an Ardmore storefront; locals
savor the balance of spicy and subtle and seem almost
embarrassed at the budget prices.

Kimberton Inn S   22 | 24 | 23 | $34
Kimberton Rd. (Hares Hill Rd.), Kimberton, 610-933-8148
■ The owner "runs a tight ship" at this Chester County
"perfect country inn", a "romantic" gem that's a "nice
place to spend a Sunday" or a "special occasion"; the
Regional American food is "solid" and the staff "pleasant."

Kimono Sushi Bar S   ▽ 19 | 11 | 17 | $20
Lafayette Hills Shopping World, 519 Germantown Pike
(Church Rd.), Lafayette Hill, 610-828-6265
■ It might be "scruffy looking", but this Chinese-Japanese
mix in Lafayette Hill turns out "flavorful" rolls and other
"excellent" dishes; to some the "menu is difficult to
understand", but the "friendly" help will translate.

Kim's S   ▽ 22 | 7 | 17 | $18
5955 N. Fifth St. (Champlost Ave.), 215-927-4550
■ "A pile of beef, a hibachi and beer – what's not to like?"
about this nothing-fancy Korean BBQ joint in Olney; although
English is a second language, the experience is "great fun"
and a "value" to boot.

Kingdom of Vegetarians S   ▽ 19 | 13 | 20 | $15
129 N. 11th St. (bet. Arch & Race Sts.), 215-413-2290
■ The "creative", "all-you-can-eat dim sum" is the
attraction at this Vegetarian-Chinese in Chinatown; "sweet"
service is "quick" and "efficient."

King George II Inn S   21 | 20 | 20 | $33
102 Radcliffe St. (Mill St.), Bristol, 215-788-5536
■ This "lovely", "intimate" Bucks inn with "colonial
decor" and a "river view" ("watch boats sailing") is a
"civilized" "place to take your grandparents" for
"well-done" American-Continental food and also for
"caring", "unsnobby" service.

Knave of Hearts S   21 | 19 | 18 | $29
230 South St. (bet. 2nd & 3rd Sts.), 215-922-3956
■ "An oldie but goodie" sums up the sentiment on
this "quirky and quaint" International stop, where "we
remember why we love the '70s" (and forget we're on
South Street); the majority insists the "romance" is still
there and the "above-average" food (including the "best
brunch") is "consistently consistent."

Kobe Japanese Steakhouse 🅢   ▽ 22 | 21 | 21 | $27
Valley Forge Hilton, 251 W. DeKalb Pike, King of Prussia, 610-337-1200
■ "Go for the show" at this "fun", "unpretentious" King of Prussia Japanese steakhouse, where the "solid" food measures up to the chop-chop presentation.

Korea House 🅢   ▽ 17 | 7 | 16 | $16
117 S. 18th St. (bet. Chestnut & Sansom Sts.), 215-567-3739
■ "Why is it never crowded?" wonder admirers of this "old-fashioned" Korean BYO in Center City; though surroundings are "dreary" ("kimchi and short ribs on Formica"), most think the "good" barbecue and "great little side dishes" make up for it.

LA BONNE AUBERGE 🅢   24 | 26 | 23 | $58
Village 2 Apt. Complex (Mechanic St.), New Hope, 215-862-2462
■ "Take your checkbook and your appetite" to this "opulent country farmhouse" in a New Hope "condo complex" for "gourmet courses" of Classic French food from a caring "husband-and-wife team" and their "friendly" staff.

La Campagna 🅢   ▽ 23 | 17 | 21 | $30
60 E. Baltimore Pike (Diamond St.), Clifton Heights, 610-626-6036
■ A "neighborhood" Italian "find" in blue-collar Delco with "outstanding" food, a "friendly" staff and "modest prices"; it's a "real pleasure."

LA CAMPAGNE 🅢   26 | 24 | 23 | $46
312 Kresson Ave. (bet. Brace & Marlkress Rds.), Cherry Hill, NJ, 856-429-7647
■ Everything's "still in top form" at this "classic yet unpretentious" country French bistro in a "romantic" Cherry Hill Victorian home; while fans rhapsodize over "terrific", "unusual dishes" and "warm" service, a few critics carp that it's "overpriced" for a BYO.

La Cipolla Torta 🅢⊘   19 | 8 | 16 | $11
132 Market St. (bet. Front & 2nd Sts.), 215-629-5552
■ For "creative" pizzas in Old City, this "feisty" joint with "cute paintings" in a newly renovated dining room is "worth a drive across town"; the "funny guys behind the counter" turn out a mean onion pie, and sandwiches aren't bad either.

La Cocotte 🅢 (CLOSED)   22 | 19 | 21 | $39
124 W. Gay St. (bet. Church & Darlington Sts.), West Chester, 610-436-6722
■ Many think this "lovely" West Chester BYO is "as close to a small restaurant in France" as you can get; classic bistro food is "delightful" and the "dark", "low-key" atmosphere is "cozy" and "quaint", but "terrible acoustics" and "too-close-together tables" can put the kibosh on "romantic dinners."

La Collina [S] 21 | 19 | 20 | $40
37-41 Ashland Ave. (Jefferson St.), Bala Cynwyd, 610-668-1780
◪ Insiders insist this Italian seafooder in Bala Cynwyd offers the "best Dover sole" and "excellent appetizers" (especially for a "business lunch") served by "busybody waiters who make meals fun"; but critics counter it's "noisy", "old-fashioned and overpriced."

LA FAMIGLIA [S] 26 | 23 | 23 | $51
8 S. Front St. (bet. Chestnut & Market Sts.), 215-922-2803
■ An "amazing wine list", "fabulous" food, "wonderful old-world charm" and "professional service" make this "authentic" Old City Italian one of the best "special occasion" spots in town; while a few find the atmosphere "stuffy" and "pretentious", the majority maintains it's "still great after all these years."

La Familia Sonsini [S] ▽ 18 | 21 | 18 | $35
202 Old Marlton Pike (bet. Hartford Rd. & Rte. 70), Medford, NJ, 609-654-5217
◪ Supporters say this "beautiful", family-run Eclectic (French/Italian/Cajun/Creole) BYO "hidden" in Burlco boasts "imaginative" food and a "pleasant" staff; but while foes concede the "decor is interesting", they snipe "service is slow" and they're "not quite sure what the food style is."

La Forno [S] ▽ 17 | 11 | 18 | $16
831 N. Providence Rd. (Monroe St.), Media, 610-891-9950
■ This "friendly", "accomodating" Delco Italian BYO is "always busy" and the reason is the "fine" brick-oven pizza; the only "ok decor" is offset by the "excellent amount of food for the money."

LA FOURCHETTE [S] 25 | 23 | 24 | $48
(nka Fourchette 110)
110 N. Wayne Ave. (Rte. 30), Wayne, 610-687-8333
■ New owners took over this Main Line spot post-*Survey* and installed a lower-priced American grill–French bistro menu (thus outdating our ratings); only time will tell if it can maintain its reputation for "excellent food", "wonderful service" and "lovely" atmosphere.

La Grolla 22 | 18 | 21 | $30
782 S. Second St. (bet. Catharine & Fitzwater Sts.), 215-627-7701
■ The "claim to fame is game" at this "unpretentious", "homey" Northern Italian South Street "find"; sometimes "your long lost Italian grandma's in the kitchen" and "personal service" always adds to the "pleasant" ambiance.

Lai Lai ▽ 16 | 15 | 19 | $17
1119 Walnut St. (11th St.), 215-440-7866
■ If you're "outside Chinatown", this "standard" Center City Chinese is ok for "walk-ins" or "takeout after work"; "service is good" and there's a "reasonable lunch menu."

La Locanda del Ghiottone 🅂⌐   24 | 16 | 18 | $23
130 N. Third St. (Arch St.), no phone

■ Like a "phoenix from the ashes", this popular Old City Italian BYO has arisen newly renovated after a fire and is serving "huge portions" of "authentic", "delicious", "fresh" food that's "great for the price"; however, "it's crowded", there's a "no reservations" policy and you may "have to wait half your life for a table."

Lamberti's Cucina 🅂   16 | 14 | 16 | $20
(fka Pasta Blitz)
212 Walnut St. (bet. 2nd & 3rd Sts.), 215-238-0499
Krewstown Rd. Shopping Ctr., 9321-23 Krewstown Rd. (Grant Ave.), 215-671-9919
Feasterville Plaza, Bustleton Pike (Street Rd.), Feasterville, 215-355-6266
1491 Brace Rd. (Rte. 561), Cherry Hill, NJ, 856-354-1157
(fka Ristorante Lamberti's)

■ "When time's more important than taste", these "convenient", "fun, upbeat", "big-portioned" Italians are "perfectly adequate"; the Cherry Hill branch seems to be a cut above the rest.

Lambertville Station 🅂   18 | 19 | 18 | $28
11 Bridge St. (at foot of bridge), Lambertville, NJ, 609-397-8300

☑ Surveyors are on two different tracks about this Lambertville New American in a "picturesque" "old converted train station": fans feel it's a "must for unusual fare", "friendly service", a "relaxing" atmosphere and "inexpensive" prices, while a handful of critics call it a "tourist trap"; but most maintain "it's a good place to stop after a day of antiquing."

Lamb Tavern 🅂   18 | 18 | 19 | $30
865 W. Springfield Rd. (Rte. 320), Media, 610-544-3300

■ "Solid if unadventurous" Traditional American in Media where "homey" fare is served by "caring" folks in "historic" 1739 digs; it's a "dependable" "reminder of genteel times" for the "blue-haired" set.

Landing, The 🅂   20 | 22 | 17 | $32
22 N. Main St. (Bridge St.), New Hope, 215-862-5711

■ "Well worth finding", this "warm and cozy" Regional American has a "terrific setting on the Delaware" in New Hope; though the food is "creative" and "well-prepared" ("good crab cakes") the "lovely views" are the star.

La Padella 🅂   18 | 17 | 18 | $27
Grant Plaza II, 1619 Grant Ave. (bet. Bustleton Ave. & Krewstown Rd.), 215-677-7723

■ This "surprisingly good" Northern Italian in a Northeast shopping center "exceeds expectations"; "prices are reasonable for the quality", and the "delicious lunch buffet" is "a steal."

La Paella Tio Pepe　　　　19 | 18 | 19 | $27
12012 Bustleton Ave. (bet. Byberry Rd. & Hendrix St.),
215-677-8016
■ "Delightful" Northeast Spanish dishing out "classic
multiple courses" of "earthy", "authentic" food like "well-
prepared paella"; for most it's a "why-don't-we-come-here-
more-often kind of place" because it's downright "pleasant."

La Pergola S　　　　18 | 12 | 18 | $19
42 Shewell Ave. (Main St.), Doylestown, 215-230-9936
726 West Ave. (Rte. 611), Jenkintown, 215-884-7204
■ These Jewish-Mediterranean twins in Jenkintown and
Doylestown may be "decorated like dime stores", but
the "tasty", "freshly made" food makes it "great for
vegetarians"; while most "wouldn't drive too far for them",
they're "happy they're in the neighborhood."

La Terrasse S　　　　22 | 22 | 20 | $36
3432 Sansom St. (bet. Chestnut & Walnut Sts.), 215-386-5000
■ "Back from the dead and better than before" is what fans
are saying about the "rebirth" of this long-closed "classic"
French bistro on the Penn campus; lovingly redone in
"beautiful light woods", it's "stunning and elegant", with
"excellent food" and "pleasant service"; the "tinkling piano"
and "wonderful outdoor dining area" are other assets; a few
foes sniff it's just a "shadow of its former self", but the vast
majority exclaims "welcome back, old friend!"

Latest Dish, The ◗S　　　22 | 18 | 18 | $21
613 S. Fourth St. (bet. Bainbridge & South Sts.), 215-629-0565
■ This "strong newcomer" off South Street has "delicious",
"eclectic" New American food and a "hip", "intimate" feel;
some of the staff may "fulfill the dumb model stereotype",
but "amazing prices" may make it the "best deal in town."

Lauren's S (CLOSED)　　　– | – | – | M
(fka American Bistro)
Village Mall, 1 Morton Ave. (Rte. 420), Morton, 610-543-3033
While they're "working hard to recapture the former magic"
of this Delco Eclectic bistro, respondents are split on the
food, with a few saying "still great" but others noticing a
"drop in quality" and dishes with "too many ingredients";
N.B. recent menu changes mean lower prices, fewer game
dishes and more French and Asian fusions.

La Veranda S　　　　23 | 21 | 19 | $41
Penn's Landing, Pier 3, Columbus Blvd. (bet. Arch &
Market Sts.), 215-351-1898
■ A "hangout" for "politicos" and other "well-connected"
types, this Penn's Landing Italian seafooder serves "superb"
food in "generous portions" and offers "great waterfront
views"; however, even admirers admit "unless you're
somebody, service is slow" and "snooty", and the "wait is
bad even with reservations."

La Vigna S   20 | 17 | 20 | $30 |
1100 S. Front St. (Federal St.), 215-336-1100
■ An "upscale" South Philly Northern Italian that's a "best buy" for "consistently good", "down-to-earth" food and "unobtrusive" service; it's a "tight, crowded place", so you may be more comfortable out on the patio.

LE BAR LYONNAIS   29 | 24 | 25 | $42 |
1523 Walnut St. (15th St.), 215-567-1000
■ "Why pay Le Bec-Fin prices when you have Le Bar downstairs?"; this "cozy" "gathering place" beneath Georges Perrier's older, "pomp and circumstance" shrine features a "sophisticated" French bistro menu and is a "romantic spot for drinks and dessert"; it may be "cramped" and "smoky", but "it's where those who really know great food at great prices go."

LE BEC-FIN   29 | 29 | 29 | VE |
1523 Walnut St. (bet. 15th & 16th Sts.), 215-567-1000
■ It's No. 1 across-the-board for food, decor and service in Philadelphia and "everything they say about" Georges Perrier's "world-class" Classic French on Restaurant Row "is true": "exquisite and perfect" cuisine, "gorgeous" decor and "impeccable" yet "unintimidating" service; while wallet-watchers warn it's "expensive" (the prix fixe dinner is $118), devotees dub the $36 lunch a "bargain" because "if you die and go to 'food heaven', Le Bec-Fin will be the name over the door."

Le Bus S   19 | 14 | 15 | $18 |
3402 Sansom St. (34th St.), 215-387-3800 ⊟ (CLOSED)
135 S. 18th St. (Rittenhouse Sq.), 215-569-8299 ⊟
4266 Main St. (bet. Green & Shurs Lns.), 215-487-2663
◪ These "cheap" Eclectic "staples" sell "fabulous" bread, "good sandwiches, salads" and "healthy lunches on-the-run" (University City is a cafeteria, Center City is a takeout and Manayunk is a sit-down); though servers "couldn't care less" and "noise can be deafening", they're "heaven for yuppie parents with out-of-control kids" and still "reliable" "for good food or hanging out."

Le Champignon - Tokio ●S   ▽ 18 | 13 | 16 | $30 |
122 Lombard St. (Front St.), 215-922-2515
◪ While some are impressed with the "varied" mix of Japanese and Classic French food featured at this "funky" Society Hill mainstay, others call it a "surreal juxtaposition" and say "it should be one or the other"; for that, you could stroll over to its next door sibling, which is strictly a sushi bar and is unrated.

Le Colonial [S] — | — | — | M

1623 Walnut St. (bet. 16th & 17th Sts.), 215-851-1623

This new Restaurant Row outpost of NYC's posh and popular Vietnamese wows even the most jaded of trendies with its savory nibbles, sumptuous, turn-of-the-century Saigon decor and decent wine list; the upstairs lounge is a hot-spot if you're over 30.

Lee Ho Seafood Place ◐ [S] ▽ 20 | 10 | 15 | $17

941 Race St. (bet. 9th & 10th Sts.), 215-922-6336

■ "Accommodating" Chinatown Chinese cooks up "unusual seafood" at "good value" prices; it's an outlet for the adventurous, but timid palates can do ok as well.

Lee How Fook [S] ≠ 23 | 8 | 18 | $17

219 N. 11th St. (bet. Race & Vine Sts.), 215-925-7266

■ A "pool hall is more attractive" than this "authentic" Chinatown BYO, but "superb" Chinese "home cooking" at "dirt-cheap" prices more than makes up for it; regulars recommend the salt-baked shrimp and the "best hot and sour soup" around.

Lemon Grass Thai [S] 21 | 16 | 19 | $22

3626-30 Lancaster Ave. (north of 36th & Market Sts.), 215-222-8042

■ "Little-known", "terrific" Thai "gem" in West Philly that dishes up "sublime classics", including "lots of vegetarian choices"; while the atmosphere is "pretty" and "calm", the neighborhood can be "creepy" after-hours; the Lancaster County branch is larger but has a similar menu.

Lenape Inn [S] 20 | 22 | 19 | $34

1333 Lenape Rd. (bet. Rtes. 52 & 100), West Chester, 610-793-2005

■ "Be sure to sit by the windows" because the "main draw" at this Chester County Continental is the "beautiful view" of the Brandywine Creek; the "good food" is "pleasantly surprising" and the "serene setting is nice for special occasions."

Le Petit Cafe [S] 23 | 18 | 22 | $32

7026 Terminal Sq. (Market & 69th Sts.), Upper Darby, 610-352-8040

■ The "delicious" French cuisine at this "intimate" Upper Darby BYO, run by a "wonderful" husband-and-wife team, is "as well thought out as the lovely atmosphere" that's straight out of "the Left Bank"; while "parking is a pain" and "tables are too small", it's "tiny but terrific."

Liberties ◐ [S] 17 | 16 | 17 | $26

705 N. Second St. (Fairmount Ave.), 215-238-0660

◪ The verdict is mixed on this Northern Liberties American-International: loyalists find the "cozy bar atmosphere" "fun for a group" and the food "good and reliable"; but foes say it's "lost its innovativeness and upscale crowd."

LionFish [S]🚫 ▽ 17 | 17 | 21 | $11

614 N. Second St. (bet. Fairmount Ave. & Spring Garden St.), 215-829-9103

■ There are "superfriendly owners" at this Northern Liberties Eclectic "hangout" that's about "as good as a coffeehouse gets"; "it can be smoky", but what do you expect from a "cool beatnik" atmosphere?

Little Fish [S]🚫 22 | 14 | 20 | $22

600 Catharine St. (6th St.), 215-413-3464

■ For "fresh fish" and "no-frills", it's tough to beat this "tiny" New American BYO with "big flavors" in a "scruffy" South Philly storefront; the chef in the open kitchen "talks to you" while whipping up "imaginative" seafood dishes and service is "wonderful" and "friendly."

Little Pete's ◐[S]🚫 13 | 8 | 14 | $12

219 S. 17th St. (Chancellor St.), 215-545-5508

■ "Typical diner food" and "waitresses from another era" characterize this "consistent" 24-hour "hash house" off Rittenhouse Square that acts as "the de facto commissary for the old folks in the William Penn House"; it's "literally a 'greasy spoon'", but with "large portions" and "bargain" prices, it's also a "doggy-bagger's heaven."

London Grill [S] 20 | 18 | 19 | $30

2301 Fairmount Ave. (23rd St.), 215-978-4545

■ For many, this "consistently imaginative" Fairmount New American is their "favorite neighborhood restaurant" and it's particularly "good after the Art Museum"; a "cool bar" explains why fans "always leave in a positive mood."

Lone Star Steakhouse [S] 14 | 14 | 16 | $21

11295 Roosevelt Blvd. (Red Lion Rd.), 215-969-7800

2452 Rte. 38 (near Cherry Hill Mall), Cherry Hill, NJ, 856-482-7727

505 W. Ridge Pike (Chemical Rd.), Conshohocken, 610-834-9394

500 Rte. 73 S. (¼ mi. north of Rte. 70), Marlton, NJ, 856-988-6737

1521 Blackhorse Pike (Rte. 42 S.), Turnersville, NJ, 856-262-1737

101 Laurel Oak Rd. (White Horse Rd.), Voorhees, NJ, 856-309-2121

◪ If your idea of "fun" is "throwing peanut shells on the floor" and watching waiters perform "tacky line dances", then this "hokey" steakhouse chain with Cajun-Creole accents fills the bill; however, while a minority claims it's "family-friendly" and "decent for the money", most suggest it's a "nightmare version of the Outback" and that if it's prime meat you seek, saddle up and skedaddle.

Long's Gourmet Chinese 🅂
18 | 14 | 18 | $19

*2018 Hamilton St. (bet. Callowhill & Spring Garden Sts.),
215-496-9928*

☑ The long and short of it is that reaction to this "low-key"
Chinese near the Art Museum is mixed; insiders insist it's
"regaining its quality" with new owners serving "healthful"
dishes ("love the pepper pot soup"); dissenters insist
"quality has slipped" and call it "a ghost of its former self."

Loose Ends (CLOSED)
21 | 14 | 19 | $25

517 Station Ave. (Rte. 30), Haddon Heights, NJ, 609-546-9777

■ They have the "well-prepared" food part all tied up at
this "imaginative" International BYO in Camden County
where "good prices" and a "supernice" attitude also help
offset the fact that the room is "not much to look at."

Los Amigos'
New Mexico Grille 🅂 (CLOSED)
18 | 15 | 16 | $21

50 S. Second St. (bet. Chestnut & Market Sts.), 215-922-7061

☑ Reviewers have mixed feelings about this Old City
Southwestern stalwart; supporters say it offers "creative"
fare that's "great value for the money", but phobes find
it's "looking tired" and say the food is only "average."

Lucy's Hat Shop 🅂⊘
– | – | – | M

247 Market St. (bet. 2nd & 3rd Sts.), 215-413-1433

Only time will tell whether diners will take their hats off to
this attractive Old City American-Continental newcomer,
set in a former millinery shop; its prospects look good
since a lively, younger crowd is currently flocking to the
imaginative weekend brunches and nighttime bar action.

Luigi's at the Canal House 🅂
18 | 18 | 17 | $28

*28 W. Mechanic St. (bet. Main & New Sts.), New Hope,
215-862-2069*

■ "The food is good" at this "peaceful" Italian on the Canal
in New Hope, but the "tasteful decor" and "intimate and
charming" "ambiance carry" the place; consider a visit
"after recitals" at the Bucks County Playhouse.

Ly Michael's 🅂
21 | 17 | 20 | $26

7552-54 Haverford Ave. (City Ave.), 215-879-8868

☑ "They're really trying" at this "elegant" Asian-French in
"blue-collar" Overbrook Park (but "near the Main Line");
pros offer high praise, calling it a "poor man's Susanna Foo",
with "excellent" "modern" food and "attentive help"; a
few quibble it's only "average", but the majority maintains
it's a "promising" "diamond in the rough."

Maccabeam 🅂
19 | 7 | 14 | $12

128 S. 12th St. (bet. Sansom & Walnut Sts.), 215-922-5922

■ At this "authentic" glatt kosher Middle Eastern in Center
City, the "fresh", "no-nonsense" fare includes a "fabulous
salad sampler"; despite "no atmosphere" and "grumpy
waitresses", it's still "the closest thing to being in Tel Aviv."

Mace's Crossing S 13 13 14 $18
1714 Cherry St. (17th St.), 215-564-5203
■ "Don't expect too much" at this "rustic" "neighborhood tavern" off the Parkway; regulars say forget the American grub "prepared without caring" and stick to a "beer with friends after work" – you won't get crossed up.

MADEMOISELLE DE PARIS (CLOSED) 27 20 19 $12
122 S. 18th St. (Sansom St.), 215-751-0670
■ "Let *me* eat cake" swoon fans of this "civilized", "exquisite pâtisserie" off Rittenhouse Square where "beautiful" creations are "so good you need a cigaret afterward"; decor is "a little ooh-la-la over the top" and "snotty service" is "right from Paris."

Mad 4 Mex ◗S – – – I
Shops at Penn, 3401 Walnut St. (Moravian Ct.), 215-382-2221
Budget-conscious University City dwellers flock to this "solid" Mexican for the "best burritos under $10", plus "hearty" lunch specials and a decent beer list; it's an offshoot of a chain.

MAINLAND INN S 27 25 26 $42
17 Main St. (Sumneytown Pike), Mainland, 215-256-8500
■ This "hard to beat" New American in an "idyllic pastoral setting" near Lansdale might be the "best-kept secret" in rural Montco; the "sophisticated menu", "excellent food" and "lap of luxury" atmosphere are lovingly maintained by "owners and a staff with a passion that makes for a great restaurant"; acolytes urge "if you haven't been there yet, go."

Main-ly Desserts S 21 16 17 $15
4247 Main St. (Rector St.), 215-487-1325
■ "Wherever you eat in Manayunk, don't get dessert" because this "cute" coffeehouse-cum-American is "always delicious", satisfying sweet tooths with "fattening delights" and others with "creative food" (including a "great" Sunday brunch); outstanding "people-watching" compensates for "cramped" space – all in all, it's "Main-ly heaven."

Malvern Meeting House S 14 12 17 $19
536 Lancaster Ave. (bet. Rtes. 202 & 352), Malvern, 610-644-0220
☑ There's no meeting of the minds on this Malvern Southern Italian: while loyalists like the homemade specialties and "reasonable" prices at this "informal", family-oriented "neighborhood place", foes frown about "mediocre" food and say the "old decor needs updating."

Mama Palma's S⊄ – – – M
2229 Spruce St. (23rd St.), 215-735-7357
This "adorable" Fitler Square spot is "what a brick-oven pizzeria should be", with "fresh ingredients" and "inventive", International-themed low-fat toppings at "a good price"; it's an excellent "date place" and "kid-friendly" as well.

Mama Rosa (CLOSED) ▽ 22 | 8 | 13 | $16
3838 N. Broad St. (Pike St.), 215-225-2177
■ The few surveyors who know this Broad Street BBQ joint say it serves "down-home Soul food at its best"; "excellent portions" and "friendly service" help make up for the lack of decor.

Ma Ma Yolanda's [S] 17 | 15 | 17 | $25
746 S. Eighth St. (bet. Catharine & Fitzwater Sts.), 215-592-0195
◪ Surveyors are on the fence when it comes to this long-standing South Philly Northern Italian: while many enjoy "simple", "quintessential" dishes like the "best homemade pasta in town" and the "cute interior", dissenters insist the "food is nothing to make you wish you were Italian" and gripe they "can't get past the decor."

Mamma Maria ◐ [S] 20 | 13 | 19 | $33
1637 E. Passyunk Ave. (bet. 11th & 12th Sts.), 215-463-6884
■ "What a blast!" is the consensus on this family-run ("like being at my in-laws for Christmas") South Philadelphia BYO Italian that reopened mid-*Survey* after a 1997 fire; while à la carte dishes will soon be available, the fixed price menu is a must-try "multiple-course feast" of "honest, down-to-earth" food made by Mamma herself; "come hungry and be prepared to eat."

Manayunk Brewing Co. [S] 15 | 17 | 16 | $21
4120 Main St. (Farmer's Market), 215-483-8220
◪ "Cavernous" brewpub under the Manayunk Farmer's Market with "decent" to "mediocre" pub grub and "nice" jazz and blues; try it "if you're single", since the only thing that "exceeds the flow of beer is the flow of hormones."

Manayunk Farmer's Market [S] ≠ 19 | 12 | 14 | $11
4120 Main St. (Shurs Ln.), 215-483-0100
■ There's "something for everyone" (though it's "no Reading Terminal") at this "fun", "lively" Manayunk landmark where a "variety" of people and edibles meet; though the "noise level is like being on a runway", you can "sit out on the deck" between purchases.

Mandarin Garden [S] 20 | 15 | 19 | $19
91 N. York Rd. (Davisville Rd.), Willow Grove, 215-657-3993
■ "Above-average" Chinese near the train station in Willow Grove that's one of the "best for the money"; "imaginative" food – like "great shrimp with toffee walnuts" – is "consistent" and the staff is "warm and friendly."

Manila Bay Bar & Grill [S] ▽ 19 | 11 | 19 | $19
6724 Castor Ave. (bet. Kerper & Knorr Sts.), 215-722-7877
■ "It's not fancy, but the food is like home even if you're not Filipino" say fans of this Southeast Asian in the Northeast; while the "dive" atmosphere is "depressing", "earthy", "authentic" cooking and a "nice" staff help offset it.

Marabella's [S] 15 | 15 | 15 | $22
401 E. City Ave. (Monument Rd.), Bala Cynwyd, 610-668-5353
602 Skippack Pike (Penllyn-Blue Bell Pike), Blue Bell, 215-641-9100
◪ An Italian minichain that's a "steady", "good family spot" for "decent food" at "economic" prices; dissenters say they "used to be better" and now serve "undistinguished", fare in a "sterile atmosphere"; bonus for parents: it's so "noisy you can't hear your kids scream."

Marathon Grill 18 | 11 | 14 | $12
1339 Chestnut St. (13th St.), 215-561-4660
Suburban Station, 1617 John F. Kennedy Blvd. (16th St.), 215-564-4745
1818 Market St. (18th St.), 215-561-1818
121 S. 16th St. (Sansom St.), 215-569-3278 [S]
◪ Surveyors are divided on these "basic", "clean" American "lunch spots"; while many cheer the "fantastic and cheap" "power lunch" ("best" chicken Caesar salad), others find it "fast food" served with "attitude"; a sibling is due to open in the former Diner on the Square.

Marbles [S] 14 | 11 | 14 | $20
818 W. Lancaster Ave. (Bryn Mawr Ave.), Bryn Mawr, 610-520-9100
■ The "awful acoustics" at this Main Line Eclectic could make you lose your marbles; but that doesn't keep it from being a "favorite spot of the Bryn Mawr crowd" that goes for "huge portions" of "unspectacular" food at "reasonable" prices and to ogle the "beautiful bartenders."

Marco Polo [S] 18 | 14 | 17 | $23
Elkins Park Sq., 8080 Old York Rd. (Church Rd.), Elkins Park, 215-782-1950
◪ "Friendly" "chef Lo gets high grades" at this Montco Italian; the decor's "not beautiful, but clean and functional" and the service is "accommodating"; even the less-enthused say it's a "decent" "neighborhood place."

Marco's ⊄ 24 | 15 | 23 | $22
232 Arch St. (bet. 2nd & 3rd Sts.), 215-592-8887
■ "What a delightful find" is the response to this "energetic" newcomer to Old City with a "friendly" staff and "creative" Eclectic cooking from the former chef at Cafe Nola; as for "cozy", well, "you sit closer to your neighbor than your date"; BYO helps keep it "reasonably priced."

Marco's Cafe [S] ▽ 24 | 20 | 23 | $34
403 N. Haddon Ave. (bet. Hawthorne & Rhoades Aves.), Haddonfield, NJ, 856-428-9839
■ "Charming" International BYO "find" in the former Food for Thought space in Haddonfield; "creative", "beautifully plated" fare served in an "intimate" setting makes the experience "a real pleasure."

Margaret Kuo's Mandarin [S] | 20 | 15 | 19 | $22
190 Lancaster Ave. (Rte. 30), Frazer, 610-647-5488
◪ "Not your typical Chinese", this BYO Asian in Chester County offers "careful presentation", "top-of-the-line" food, a "kind, knowledgeable" staff, and "good lunch specials."

Marker, The [S] | 23 | 23 | 22 | $42
Adam's Mark Hotel, City Ave. & Monument Rd., 215-581-5010
■ This "civilized" Eclectic in the Adam's Mark offers "delicious" food served in "elegant" surroundings by an "accommodating" staff; a "fantastic Sunday brunch" and a "first-rate piano player" also hit the mark.

Marrakesh [S]💳 | 19 | 22 | 19 | $29
517 S. Leithgow St. (bet. 4th & 5th Sts.), 215-925-5929
■ It's "a little over-the-top with the *Arabian Nights* shtick", but sybarites are here for the show rather than the "average" Moroccan food that's "eaten with your hands"; as "exotic" experiences go, this one's "fun", "at least once."

Marra's [S]💳 | 18 | 10 | 14 | $17
1734 E. Passyunk Ave. (bet. Moore & Morris Sts.), 215-463-9249
■ "Stick to the pizza" ("great", "cheap" "thin-crust" pies) at this South Philly Italian with "zero atmosphere"; while most think service from "waitresses who talk like Rocky" is "rude", others insist it's "less surly than before."

Marshalton Inn [S] | 22 | 24 | 21 | $36
1300 W. Strasburg Rd./Rte. 162 (Sugar Bridge Rd.), Marshallton, 610-692-4367
■ "Bring your appetite" to this "quaint" Traditional American that's just west of West Chester; "creative", "first-class" colonial fare, served "by the fire" in a "romantic" 1814 inn, is a "postcard experience" "worth the drive."

Marsilio's | ▽ 21 | 16 | 19 | $29
541 Roebling Ave. (Chestnut St.), Trenton, NJ, 609-695-1916
◪ Loyalists like the "bargain lunches" at this long-standing Italian in Trenton's Chambersburg section; but cynics counter it's merely "run of the mill."

Martine's Fine Food [S] | ▽ 21 | 23 | 18 | $24
7 E. Ferry St. (Main St.), New Hope, 215-862-2966
■ The few surveyors who know this "tiny but tasty" New Hope Eclectic say its name is right on the money; the "relaxing" atmosphere also makes it a "nice place to go just for a drink" and people-watching out on the patio.

Martini Café ◐ | 12 | 14 | 17 | $25
622 S. Sixth St. (Bainbridge St.), 215-629-0661
◪ "No need to wear black" at this "relaxed" Eclectic-Italian off South Street, a "trendy" spot with a "great-looking staff and crowd"; though appetizers are "ok", many skip the food ("leaves much to be desired") and proceed with the "cigar-smoking suits" right to the long martini list.

Martini's Lounge & Restaurant S | 18 | 19 | 17 | $25
1836 Callowhill St. (19th St.), 215-557-9533
■ The "food's surprisingly good" at this "hip" Eclectic near the Free Library; though it's hard to see ("they should spend more on light bulbs"), "show up a few times" and you're "treated like family."

Mayfair Diner ◐S | 16 | 12 | 17 | $13
7373 Frankford Ave. (Bleigh St.), 215-624-8886
■ This "busy, busy" Lower Northeast diner "institution" with a "drop-in-anytime" atmosphere "brings back childhood memories" to those who love "the dazzle of its old chrome" and "hearty, old-fashioned" food "like Mama used to cook"; a few contrarians counter it's "pedestrian."

McGillin's Olde Ale House ◐ | 14 | 17 | 16 | $14
1310 Drury St. (bet. Chestnut & Sansom Sts.), 215-735-5562
■ It's "worth the search" for this Center City "institution" where "hearty" "Irish bar basics" come with "lots of history" (it's the city's oldest operating pub); though "most people come for the drinking", lunch is "a value."

Meiji-En S | 20 | 22 | 19 | $30
Pier 19, Columbus Blvd. (bet. Callowhill & Spring Garden Sts.), 215-592-7100
■ "Serene, gorgeous" Japanese next to Dave & Buster's on Columbus Boulevard offering an "entertaining" hibachi "culinary show" and "romantic" river views, as well as a "fantastic" jazz brunch; N.B. they've added an AYCE sushi buffet for happy hour Monday–Friday.

Meil's S⌿ | 23 | 14 | 20 | $24
Bridge & Main Sts., Stockton, NJ, 609-397-8033
■ "Huge portions" of American "comfort food" are the specialty at this "fun" Stockton BYO; "wonderful breakfasts" and "stick-to-your-ribs" lunches and dinners ("forget about low-fat") are served up in a "relaxed" atmosphere.

Melrose Diner ◐S⌿ | 16 | 12 | 17 | $13
1501 Snyder Ave. (bet. 15th St. & Passyunk Ave.), 215-467-6644
☑ "You don't mind being called hon" at this "quintessential" South Philly diner that serves unparalleled pancakes and pies round the clock; its few critics scoff it's "living on its reputation" and dislike "sitting with strangers", but others go for the "cheap" "classic" eats and "salty" staff ("some of the waitresses voted for Ike.")

Mel's Italian S | 15 | 10 | 14 | $31
201 Jefferson St. (76 W., Belmont exit), Bala Cynwyd, 610-668-1712
☑ Supporters say there's "solid" cooking and tout the "all you can eat mussels on Monday" at this Northern Italian in a "weird location" across from Manayunk; however, many who find the food is "fair at best" and the "decor needs sprucing up" claim they won't be playing the "waiting game."

Melting Pot [S] 15 | 15 | 17 | $25
8229 Germantown Ave. (Southampton St.), 215-242-3003
◩ "Fun and games for the whole family" is the idea behind this "unusual", "do-it-yourself fondue" joint in Chestnut Hill that serves "huge portions"; but phobes say it's "way too time consuming" and "the novelty of cooking your own dinner wears off pretty quickly."

Mendenhall Inn [S] 23 | 23 | 23 | $39
Mendenhall Hotel, Rte. 52 (1 mi. from Rte. 1 S.), Mendenhall, 610-388-1181
■ "A worthy destination" in southern Chester County, this New American offers "delicious" food, a "glorious" setting with "great gardens" and "attentive service"; it's "always enjoyable", particularly for special "romantic" occasions.

Mexican Food Factory [S] 19 | 16 | 17 | $21
601 W. Rte. 70 (Rte. 73), Marlton, NJ, 856-983-9222
■ "Authentic", "always fun" Marlton Mexican that's "worth the wait" (they work at a "siesta's pace") for "gigantic" portions of "innovative" food; it's "reasonably priced" and there are "excellent specials."

Mexican Post ◐[S] 16 | 12 | 15 | $16
104 Chestnut St. (Front St.), 215-923-5233
■ "When you're hungry but not too picky", this Old City Mexican "hole-in-the-wall" can fill the bill with "average" fare; it's "cheap and quick", but "don't go out of your way."

Mia's [S] (CLOSED) 19 | 20 | 19 | $28
Warwick Hotel, 1701 Locust St. (17th St.), 215-545-4655
■ This "better than expected" Mediterranean in the Warwick serves "superb" meals in a "lovely", "elegant" room off the lobby; a "great piano player" and "wonderful" list of wines by the glass are other pluses.

Michael's Family Restaurant ◐[S] 13 | 11 | 14 | $16
3340 Street Rd. (Richlieu St.), Bensalem, 215-638-2283
■ There's "affordable" but "not inspiring" fare at this "typical" Bensalem diner; while "you can make a meal out of the salad bar", most moan "you get a lot but nothing hits the spot."

Michael's Ristorante [S] 19 | 17 | 18 | $27
824 S. Eighth St. (Christian St.), 215-922-3986
■ "They make you feel at home" at this "intimate", "better than average" South Philly Italian; the "staff is friendly", the atmosphere is "relaxed" and it's "fairly priced."

Minar Palace 20 | 5 | 14 | $12
1605 Sansom St. (bet. 16th & 17th Sts.), 215-564-9443
■ "More a hut than a palace", this Center City Indian BYO turns out "huge portions" of "consistently delicious", "masterfully spiced" food at "cheap" prices; but considering the decor rating, some say "takeout is the best plan."

Mirna's Cafe [S] ≠ — 22 | 12 | 18 | $28
417 Old York Rd. (West Ave.), Jenkintown, 215-885-2046
■ "Outstanding", "creative" Eclectic-Mediterranean BYO in a "cramped" Jenkintown storefront that's "always too congested and noisy" on weekends; while some say service can come with "attitude", this "hot spot" remains a "local favorite."

Monk's Café ◐ [S] — 20 | 17 | 17 | $21
264 S. 16th St. (Spruce St.), 215-545-7005
■ This "cozy" Center City Belgian bistro boasts "fine pommes frites", mussels and an "outstanding beer selection"; "reasonable" prices also make it an appealing "place to hang out."

MONTE CARLO LIVING ROOM [S] — 26 | 24 | 24 | $51
150 South St. (2nd St.), 215-925-2220
■ An "elegant" Italian with "warm, attentive" service that's a "romantic" retreat from the hustle of South Street; chef Nunzio Patruno "has hands of gold", and the "decadent" disco upstairs is the place to work off the calories; it's "expensive", but a "wonderful special event experience."

Montserrat ◐ [S] — 14 | 13 | 15 | $19
623 South St. (bet. 6th & 7th Sts.), 215-627-4224
◩ This South Street New American with "fun outdoor tables" in the thick of "people-watching" action reminds some of a "Greenwich Village cafe"; but while some laud the veggie choices on the menu, critics counter the "food is so-so" and the place "needs a face-lift."

Moonstruck [S] — 20 | 21 | 20 | $31
7955 Oxford Ave. (Rhawn St.), 215-725-6000
■ A Northeast Italian that's called a "remarkably good neighborhood restaurant" with "consistently fresh" food, "beautiful", "romantic" decor, "excellent service" and "fair prices"; in short, "this place is a joy."

More Than Just Ice Cream ◐ [S] ≠ — 20 | 14 | 16 | $12
1119 Locust St. (11th St.), 215-574-0586
■ "Much more" proclaim fans of this Center City American "dessert lover's paradise" that moved post-*Survey* to new digs two blocks away from the original; the devoted say "starve yourself all day, then indulge" in the "mile-high" apple pie ("one slice will feed a football team"), the "best" carrot cake and "great" Sunday brunch (oh yeah, they have ice cream too).

Moriarty's ◐ [S] — 14 | 13 | 15 | $16
1116 Walnut St. (11th St.), 215-627-7676
■ "For a bite" "before or after the theater", this "average", "inexpensive" Center City pub "convenient" to the Forrest ("location, location") is "comfortable" enough; fortunately, it "doesn't pretend to be more than it is."

Morning Glory Diner S⊘   ▽ 23 | 18 | 23 | $14
735 S. 10th St. (Fitzwater St.), 215-413-3999
■ "You go, girl!" is the reaction to Samantha Mickey's "bustling little corner diner" in the heart of South Philly, where "good home cooking", "friendly service" and "cool" coffee mugs rule from morning through dinnertime.

MORTON'S OF CHICAGO S   26 | 21 | 23 | $49
1 Logan Sq. (19th St., bet. Benjamin Franklin Pkwy. & Cherry St.), 215-557-0724
■ The Logan Square location of this "decadent" chain is "always reliable" for "huge portions" of "top-quality" steaks, with a side of cigars; it's "especially good for expense accounts", pulling in "power people" who are there to "chew the fat"; a move to Walnut Street is planned for late 1999.

Moshulu S   17 | 25 | 18 | $38
735 S. Columbus Blvd. (South St.), 215-923-2500
☑ "Sailors never had it like this" on a "beautifully appointed" ship berthed on the southern edge of Penn's Landing; while some call it a "pleasant" place to "entertain out-of-towners" because it "harbors tasty" International fare, others pan "ho-hum food" and "steerage-class" "attitude."

Mother's S   16 | 14 | 15 | $23
34 N. Main St. (bet. Bridge & Randolph Sts.), New Hope, 215-862-9354
☑ Some of the tourists flocking to New Hope head for this "fun" American on Main Street for "ok" "comfort food"; but a number of detractors insist that "it's nothing like it used to be" and "if Mother cooks like this, I'll go live with Dad."

Mr. Martino's Trattoria S⊘   21 | 20 | 21 | $22
1646 E. Passyunk Ave. (12th St.), 215-755-0663
■ "Small, friendly trattoria serving wonderful food" is the consensus on this South Philly storefront Italian BYO that "looks like a movie set" "out of the '40s"; one complaint – the "menu is limited" and "they need to change it."

Mrs. London's Cafe (CLOSED)   22 | 20 | 19 | $32
Meadows Edge Mktpl., 515 Rte. 73 S. (bet. Brick & Evesham Rds.), Marlton, NJ, 609-983-7744
☑ "Innovative" International seafooder in an "unexpected" "Victorian setting" in Marlton with "excellent" cuisine, "cozy", "charming" ambiance and "helpful" service; however, dissenters who find it "overrated" with "poor" service caution "you wait even with reservations."

Murray's Deli S⊘   17 | 7 | 13 | $14
285 Montgomery Ave. (Old Lancaster Rd.), Bala Cynwyd, 610-664-6995
☑ A "classic" Main Line deli with "huge portions" of "fresh, simple food" ("stock up on cholesterol"); foes find the fare "ordinary" and say the place could use some spiffing-up; all advise "try not to take the rude service personally."

Museum Restaurant S   19 | 20 | 19 | $24

*Philadelphia Museum of Art, Benjamin Franklin Pkwy. &
26th St., 215-684-7990*

■ 'Tis the Cezanne to have a look at this "civilized respite"
inside the Art Museum; the "excellent" Continental food
is a "surprise" (try the "varied buffet for a light meal") and
the "tablecloths are a work of art"; it's not too much Monet,
so even the "ladies who lunch" might want to get in
the van and go.

Mustard Greens S   23 | 18 | 20 | $23

622 S. Second St. (bet. Bainbridge & South Sts.), 215-627-0833

■ "Gourmet Chinese" off South Street "outclasses
Chinatown" with "refined", "died-and-gone-to-heaven"
food that's "light", "healthy and fresh" ("green beans like
candy"); the setting is "attractive" and staff is "attentive."

My Thai S   21 | 17 | 20 | $21

2200 South St. (22nd St.), 215-985-1878

■ "A hidden treasure" in the South Street neighborhood
that "surprises outsiders" with "delightful, delicately
seasoned" Thai cooking; the decor is "attractive", service
is "thoughtful" and the "price is reasonable."

Nais Cuisine S   24 | 14 | 21 | $31

13 W. Benedict Ave. (Darby Rd.), Havertown, 610-789-5983

■ "Top-drawer" French-Thai BYO "gem" in a "plain"
"old house" in Havertown with "memorable meals" and
"moderate prices"; while the "menu hasn't changed much"
and some think the "rich" food needs some "updating",
devotees declare it's "always enjoyable" and more than
just a "Nais try."

Nan   – | – | – | M

4000 Chestnut St. (40th St.), 215-382-0818

A French-Thai BYO in University City with sublime food from
the chef of the late, great Alouette, and a restful, inviting
atmosphere; it's certainly one of the better newcomers.

New Corned Beef Academy   17 | 10 | 15 | $11

1605 Walnut St. (16th St.), 215-561-6222

◪ Familes and businessman alike scarf down "filling"
sandwiches at this "clean" Center City Jewish deli with
"top quality corned beef and turkey" and "quick" service;
the few naysayers say it's "nothing like the original" and
"average at best", but most deem it a "winner", especially
for takeout and lunch.

New Delhi S   19 | 11 | 16 | $15

4004 Chestnut St. (bet. 40th & 41st Sts.), 215-386-1941

◪ "The buffet rules" at this University City Indian whose
"bargain" "meal deals" are a "favorite" of students; but
foes feel the food is "indistinguishable" from others of its
ilk, adding the setting may be "spacious", but it could
use some spiffing-up.

New Orleans Cafe 🆂　　　▽ 23 | 15 | 17 | $27 |
1423 Chester Pike (Simpson Ave.), Eddystone, 610-872-5445
New Orleans Cafe II 🆂
9 Kline's Ct. (Bridge St.), Lambertville, NJ, 609-397-2322
☑ For many, these "authentic" Cajun-Creole twins – in blue-collar Eddystone and trendy Lambertville – serve up "heaven on a plate", with "generous portions" of "spicy treats"; however, as ratings suggest, critics think "service needs improvement."

New World Cafe (CLOSED)　　20 | 15 | 17 | $29 |
2114 Branch Pike (bet. Cinnaminson Ave. & Rte. 130), Cinnaminson, NJ, 609-786-7022
■ It's "quite a surprise for a neighborhood joint" say some about this "interesting", "imaginative" International BYO "hidden" off the highway in Cinnaminson; the service is "disorganized", but the "art-filled" atmosphere is "relaxing."

Nicholas Nickolas　　　　　22 | 25 | 23 | $50 |
(nka Nick's Fishmarket & Grill)
Rittenhouse Hotel, 210 W. Rittenhouse Sq. (bet. 19th & 20th Sts.), 215-546-8440
☑ This "fancy in a flashy way" seafooder has a "beautiful, breathtaking view" of Rittenhouse Square; the food can be "delicious", but it's "priced for millionaires", and what is "superb service" to some is "pretentious" to others.

Nick's Bar & Grill ◐🆂　　　20 | 21 | 21 | $27 |
Rittenhouse Hotel, 210 W. Rittenhouse Sq. (bet. 19th & 20th Sts.), 215-546-8440
■ "Try to get a window seat" at this American "oasis of sophistication" downstairs from Nicholas Nickolas in the Rittenhouse; "upscale hamburgers", "beautiful decor", a "great piano bar" and the fact that "cigar smokers are welcome" also mean it's a "high-class singles bar scene."

Nifty Fifty's 🆂⊘　　　　　16 | 17 | 16 | $10 |
2491 Grant Ave. (Roosevelt Blvd.), 215-676-1950
1356 E. Passyunk Ave. (10th & Reed Sts.), 215-468-1950
1900 MacDade Blvd. (Rte. 420), Folsom, 610-583-1950
■ "You get a sunburn from all the neon" at these "fun", "affordable", faux-'50s "retro" eateries that are best for "juicy burgers" and "old-time" shakes; the astute ask "why bother to eat at a fake diner in a city full of authentic ones?" but "kids love it."

Nonna's 🆂　　　　　　　　21 | 21 | 18 | $36 |
211 Haddonfield-Berlin Rd. (Brace Rd.), Cherry Hill, NJ, 856-795-1778
☑ Loyalists like the "creative" cuisine and "lovely setting" at this Cherry Hill New French–Northern Italian BYO; but detractors deem it "uneven" (it goes from being "delicious" to "disappointing"), adding the service "needs help."

Noodle Heaven S   15 | 12 | 15 | $17 |
224 S. Broad St. (Locust St.), 215-735-6191
☑ This "no-surprises" Chinese BYO on the Avenue of the
Arts is "ok" for a "quick meal" and a "good pre-theater
choice"; but foes maintain the food is "bland" and the
"service surly" ("it should be called Noodle Purgatory").

Norma's Middle Eastern   ▽ 20 | 11 | 18 | $17 |
Restaurant
*Barclay Shopping Ctr., Rte. 70 E. (Rtes. 41 & 295), Cherry
Hill, NJ, 856-795-1373*
■ Chef "Norma has a nice touch with traditional Middle
Eastern food" say supporters of this "solid", "inexpensive"
Cherry Hill BYO; the "Saturday night belly dancer" adds
an exotic element.

North Sea ◗S   – | – | – | M |
153 N. 10th St. (Race St.), 215-925-1906
The few surveyors who know this Cantonese in Chinatown
praise the "fine" seafood produced by a "chef who
entertains special requests"; the fact that it's "mostly
patronized by Chinese" testifies to its "authenticity."

North Star Bar S   17 | 16 | 17 | $20 |
2639 Poplar St. (27th St.), 215-235-7827
■ This Fairmount Eclectic "bargain" boasts "better than
average bar food" and "cool" live bands; as for the decor,
fans find it "funky" but the more fastidious grouse that it
"has the atmosphere of a garage."

Nul Bom S   19 | 15 | 18 | $25 |
*101 Washington Ln. (bet. Rtes. 73 & 611), Jenkintown,
215-884-5100*
■ "Unusual" Japanese-Korean "discovery" with "delicious
sushi" and "great barbecue" located on the ground floor
of a Jenkintown high-rise; "the only complaint is finding
someone who speaks English."

Odette's S   19 | 20 | 19 | $36 |
S. River Rd. (Rte. 232), New Hope, 215-862-2432
☑ Loyalists like the "relaxing dinners", "scrumptious Sunday
brunch", "romantic" atmosphere, "fantastic" river views
and "entertaining" piano bar at this American-Continental
just outside of New Hope; while a few cons charge the
food is "inconsistent" and "it was better years ago", most
"always have a good time" here.

Old City Coffee   21 | 17 | 18 | $8 |
221 Church St. (bet. 2nd & 3rd Sts.), 215-629-9292 S
Reading Terminal Mkt., 1136 Arch St. (12th St.), 215-592-1897
■ There's "very good coffee, muffins, scones" and an
"upbeat staff" at this American bakery in a "nice space"
that's like a "parlor in an old house" in Old City; N.B. the
Reading Terminal branch is a microroastery, not a restaurant.

OLD GUARD HOUSE INN   23 | 21 | 23 | $39
953 Youngsford Rd. (Righters Mill), Gladwyne, 610-649-9708
■ "An old favorite, especially in winter", this "cozy,
romantic" and "reliable" Main Liner offers "solid" Traditional
American fare like "wonderful rack of lamb"; it's a "blue-hair
heaven" where "they're always nice to Mother."

Old Mill Inn   18 | 19 | 18 | $24
Horsham & York Rds. (Rte. 263), Hatboro, 215-672-6593
☑ "They got the old part right" at this American-Continental
"standby" in a "rustic" 1798 inn in Hatboro; but while some
surveyors say it's a "nice place for an important dinner",
phobes find the menu "tired"; the philosophic shrug the
"food is mediocre, but there's plenty of it."

Old Original Bookbinders S   19 | 18 | 18 | $42
125 Walnut St. (2nd St.), 215-925-7027
☑ This "legendary" seafooder on Society Hill, serving
"fabulous crab cakes" and lobster, is a "great place for
anyone who loves tradition"; but while insiders insist
"choose plain seafood" and "you won't be disappointed",
a growing number of critics carp about "astronomical
prices" and say it "doesn't live up to its reputation."

Olga's Diner ◐S   12 | 10 | 14 | $15
Rtes. 70 & 73, Marlton, NJ, 856-596-1700
☑ A few fans praise "worthwhile desserts" at this 24-hour
"landmark" "Joisey" diner in Marlton and night owls love
the hours, but the majority maintains it's "seen better days" –
and a slip in ratings across the board supports them.

Opus 251 S   23 | 23 | 22 | $41
*Philadelphia Art Alliance, 251 S. 18th St. (Rittenhouse Sq.),
215-735-6787*
■ "An outstanding newcomer", this "innovative" country
American with Asian accents in the Art Alliance off
Rittenhouse Square serves "exquisitely prepared food"
in an "elegant" atmosphere with a "European feel" and
"attentive service"; "lunch on the patio is wonderful."

Orfèo   19 | 15 | 17 | $23
2029 Walnut St. (bet. 20th & 21st Sts.), 215-567-5000
☑ A "hidden, little treasure", this Asian-inspired Continental
in Center City "takes culinary risks" with "imaginative",
"subtly" flavored food and pros pronounce it "always a
pleasure"; but contrarians complain the fare is "variable" –
"from good to fair" – and the "setting is spartan."

Ortlieb's Jazzhaus ◐S   16 | 16 | 17 | $21
847 N. Third St. (Poplar St.), 215-922-1035
■ "Go for the music and drinks" at this "comfortable"
Northern Liberties jazz joint that jumps; the "decent" New
Orleans food is "fairly priced" and "will do in a pinch."

Otto's Brauhaus 🅂   18 | 16 | 19 | $21
233 Easton Rd. (Pine Ave.), Horsham, 215-675-1864
◼ It's "Oktoberfest anytime" at this "dependable", "honest" Montco German with "good", "reasonably priced" "stick-to-your-ribs home cooking"; "the Sunday buffet dinner is highly recommended."

Outback Steakhouse 🅂   18 | 15 | 17 | $23
3240 Tillman Dr. (Street Rd.), Bensalem, 215-633-8228
230 E. Lake Dr. (Rte. 38), Cherry Hill, NJ, 856-482-1350
Glen Eagle Shopping Ctr., 561 Glen Eagle Sq. (Rte. 202), Glen Mills, 610-558-0644
610 Old York Rd. (Fairway Rd.), Jenkintown, 215-886-5120
1162 Baltimore Pike (Sproule Rd.), Springfield, 610-544-9889
◪ "Big steaks", "big waits" and beepers are givens at these "noisy", "crowded" branches of the Down Under–themed steakhouse chain; supporters say the "belly filling" beef and the bloomin' onion are "good bangs for the buck", but cynics sneer the "salty", "run-of-the-mill" fare isn't for "this Yank."

OVERTURES 🅂   26 | 24 | 23 | $36
609-611 Passyunk Ave. (bet. Bainbridge & South Sts.), 215-627-3455
◼ Insiders insist this Mediterranean BYO "hideaway" off South Street is the "city's best value"; "astonishingly" "sophisticated" cuisine, "European service at its most professional" and a "romantic atmosphere" add up to a "great date" place for making overtures.

Ozzie's Trattoria 🅂   ∇ 20 | 14 | 20 | $30
1651 E. Passyunk Ave. (bet. Morris & 12th Sts.), 215-755-1981
◼ The few who know this "friendly," "neighborhood" Italian report it does "good basic" dishes like "melt-in-your-mouth veal" and some of "the best mussels in South Philly"; it's nothing fancy, but there's "super service."

Pace One 🅂   21 | 21 | 20 | $35
Glen Mills & Thornton Rds., Thornton, 610-459-3702
◼ "If you can find" this "lovely" country American tucked away in Thornton, you'll discover "well-prepared" food ("outstanding desserts") served in a "very pleasant setting" with "consistent service"; it's "expensive", but most maintain it's worth the "trek for a treat."

Pacific Grille 🅂   19 | 13 | 17 | $26
Village II Shoppes, 1200 S. Church St. (Academy Dr.), Mt. Laurel, NJ, 856-778-0909
◪ "Innovative" California-accented seafood dishes like "excellent crab cakes" are the draw at this "out of the way" BYO in Mount Laurel; even though some say the food can be "inconsistent" and the decor "depressing," overall it's a "great buy."

Paganini 🖪   18 | 17 | 15 | $28
81 W. State St. (bet. Clinton & Court Sts.), Doylestown,
215-348-5922
☑ Supporters of this Doylestown Northern Italian swear not
even "slow", "robotlike service" can spoil "consistently
good, moderately priced food", including "excellent
homemade pastas"; however, disgruntled critics say "it's
not as good since it moved to larger quarters" and a slip
in ratings across the board supports this stance.

Painted Parrot Cafe 🖪   19 | 14 | 15 | $18
211 Chestnut St. (bet. 2nd & 3rd Sts.), 215-922-5971
☑ An "amazing" all-you-can-eat "Wednesday night dessert
buffet" will "send anyone into sugar shock" at this Old City
New American BYO, although some squawk dishes "look
better than they taste"; all agree service can be "flaky."

Palace of Asia 🖪   23 | 19 | 20 | $25
Best Western Inn, 285 Commerce Dr. (bet. Bethlehem Pike
& Susquehanna Rd.), Fort Washington, 215-646-2133
■ "The reigning king of Indian food" is in a "setting fit for
a queen", "hidden" in a Fort Washington Best Western;
"aromatic", "top-of-the-line" cuisine is served by a "helpful"
staff; overall, it's an "excellent" choice.

Palladium   17 | 21 | 15 | $27
3601 Locust Walk (36th St.), 215-387-3463
☑ This "preppy" International on the Penn campus exudes
"Ivy League charm" – "you feel like you're on the set of *Love
Story*"; but the food is "inconsistent", and as for the student
service, "there's a difference between lazy and leisurely";
perhaps the safest bet is "drinks outside" on the terrace.

PALM 🖪   23 | 19 | 22 | $42
Park Hyatt at the Bellevue, 200 S. Broad St. (Walnut St.),
215-546-7256
☑ "Politicos" and "loud men with money" "chow down"
among the "noise", "crowds" and "cartoons" on the wall
at this "high testosterone level" Center City steakhouse;
though critics call it "pretentious", "overrated" and
"overpriced" – "the only thing they don't charge for is
oxygen" – most maintain it's "the place to see and be
seen" and the food is "terrific."

PAMPLONA 🖪   22 | 19 | 18 | $25
225 S. 12th St. (Locust St.), 215-627-9059
■ "Trendy, tasty tapas" "fun" for "sharing with friends"
are the focus at this "chic" Center City Spanish; even
though the "decibel level is ear splitting" ("if you're not
deaf by the end of the meal", you're on your way) and
servers can be "too cool for their customers", it makes for
a "great night out."

Paradigm 🅢   20 23 18 $33
239 Chestnut St. (bet. 2nd & 3rd Sts.), 215-238-6900
■ "Wear black and be beautiful" at this "loud", "au courant"
Old City newcomer with a staff that looks "like models" who
"almost scream 'we are so New York'"; comments on the
International cuisine range from "inventive" to "ok", but
the "cutting-edge decor", including "hilarious" "see-through
bathroom doors" that fog when locked, gets the attention.

Passage to India 🅢   20 16 19 $23
1320 Walnut St. (Juniper St.), 215-732-7300
☑ Loyalists particularly like the "good-deal lunch buffet"
at this "cut-above" Center City Indian; while service can
be "slow", it's "friendly", and the "lovely, romantic
atmosphere" includes "live piano music."

PASSERELLE   24 25 23 $46
175 King of Prussia Rd. (Lancaster Ave.), Radnor, 610-293-9411
■ "Words can hardly do justice" to the "impressive" food,
"gorgeous", "romantic setting" and "well-timed" service at
this Radnor New American that's a Main Line "special-
occasion" "favorite"; to the few who sniff "stuffy" and
"fancy-schmancy", hordes retort it's "first-class in every
way" and "makes you feel elegant."

Pastaria at Franco & Luigi's ⊉   ▽ 20 14 19 $23
1547-49 S. 13th St. (Tasker St.), 215-755-8903
■ "Superb" live opera singing and "good", inexpensive"
Italian fare hit high notes at this "fun", "friendly" South
Philly BYO; order simply and "you won't be disappointed."

Pastavino Trattoria 🅢   ▽ 19 17 15 $23
*Kings Hwy. Commerce Ctr., 124 E. Kings Hwy. (Lenola Rd.),
Maple Shade, NJ, 856-727-1001*
■ "Easy, reliable choice" for "family" Italian in Maple
Shade with "large portions" of pasta and "reasonable
prices"; there's also a "flavorful heart-healthy selection"
on the menu that includes grilled fish.

Pat's King of Steaks ◗🅢⊉   18 7 13 $8
1237 E. Passyunk Ave. (bet. 9th & Wharton Sts.), 215-468-1546
☑ This 24-hour "South Philly classic", across from archrival
Geno's, is a "must for out-of-towners" looking to absorb
"authentic" steaks and atmosphere (as well as "grease and
more grease"); the fit-for-a-king steaks may be "mouth-
watering", but servers "act like they're doing you a favor."

Pattaya Grill 🅢   22 18 19 $20
4006 Chestnut St. (40th St.), 215-387-8533
☑ While supporters say this "pleasant" University City
French-Thai offering "fine" food, including wild game
like ostrich and alligator, is "solid" and "reasonably
priced", critics call the menu "schizophrenic" and "too
variable"; for the "best seating", try the "beautiful sunroom."

Peacock on the Parkway   18 | 18 | 17 | $25 |
1700 Benjamin Franklin Pkwy. (17th St.), 215-569-8888
■ This Eclectic-Mediterranean peacock is "trying to fly" on the Parkway, and most times it does, dishing out "hearty", "delicious" "lunch bargains" and "great seafood"; the "small, pretty space" and "friendly proprietors" are pluses.

Peking Restaurant S   21 | 19 | 21 | $21 |
Granite Run Mall (Rtes. 1 & 352), Media, 610-566-4110
■ "Amazing" Chinese "winner" with "gracious service", that moved to a new "much prettier and lighter space" within Granite Run Mall, resulting in an improved decor rating; adherents say it's "considerably better" than most Asians outside of Chinatown, offering "impeccably" presented food "so good you can't believe you're in a mall."

Penang S⌀   – | – | – | M |
117 N. Tenth St., 215-413-2531
This boldly decorated Chinatown yearling features an open kitchen turning out the exotic tastes of Malaysia; there's hearty noodle dishes for the timid, fish-head casseroles for the adventurous and amazingly friendly service, especially given its New York minichain roots.

Pepper's Cafe ⌀   – | – | – | I |
2528 Haverford Rd. (Eagle Rd.), Ardmore, 610-896-0476
This tiny, casual American BYO is still not well known; the interior is dominated by a 10-seat counter next to a chef station whipping up salads, sandwiches and pasta dishes; a redo means dining on the outdoor deck is now a treat.

Persian Grill S   21 | 11 | 18 | $22 |
637 Germantown Pike (Joshua Rd.), Lafayette Hill, 610-825-2705
■ "Bring a hearty appetite" and ignore the "tacky decor" at this "secret" Montco Middle Eastern with "tasty", "authentic", "reasonably priced" food; still, one wag wonders "the ground lamb dishes are fit for a sultan, but what would he be doing at a Formica table?"

Philadelphia Fish & Co. S   20 | 15 | 17 | $28 |
207 Chestnut St. (2nd St.), 215-625-8605
■ "A terrific catch" is what you'll net at this "fresh", "dependable" Old City American seafooder with "the best true low-fat choices", "bargain lunches" and "beautiful presentations" from new chef Trish Morrissey; while aesthetes agree the atmosphere is "cafeteria-like", a post-*Survey* renovation may blunt that barb.

Philly Crab & Steak House S   ▽ 22 | 14 | 19 | $25 |
Grant & Academy Shopping Plaza, 3334 Grant Ave. (Academy Rd.), 215-856-9510
■ By Northeast "neighborhood" standards, this American-Eclectic is "a real gem" with "well-done" steaks and seafood, including crab cakes; however, critics snap the "tables are cramped" and the "noise" can be "horrendous."

Pho 75 [S]⇏ 21 | 8 | 16 | $9

1122 Washington Ave. (12th St.), 215-271-5866
823 Adams Ave. (Roosevelt Ave.), 215-743-8845

◪ A "basic Vietnamese soup kitchen" chain with links in South Philly and the Northeast, this duo offers "unique" "cheap" dishes to those in need of sustenance or who love the experience of group-slurping, despite the "bleak", "not-so-Pho-bulous" setting.

Pho Xe Lua [S] ▽ 20 | 9 | 17 | $15

907 Race St. (bet. 9th & 10th Sts.), 215-627-8883

■ The few surveyors who know this undiscovered Viet-Thai in the heart of Chinatown swear it's a "great value" for filling pho, succulent seafood and fresh mango milk shakes; it's closed Wednesdays.

Pietro's Coal Oven Pizzeria [S] 17 | 15 | 14 | $17

1714 Walnut St. (bet. 17th & 18th Sts.), 215-735-8090

■ "Classy" pizzeria just off Rittenhouse Square serving "thin, tasty" pies cooked in a coal-fired oven ; however, even fans feel the "slow", almost "nonexistent" service and "cash only" policy are problems; N.B. a new South Street location is scheduled to open in mid '98.

Pineville Tavern [S] 15 | 11 | 17 | $18

Rte. 413 (Township Line Rd.), Pineville, 215-598-7982

■ Despite tepid ratings, an "interesting combination" of "bikers" and "yuppies" congregate at this "friendly", "no-frills" Bucks County roadside bar with "basic", "filling" American food; the reason? it's "cheap, honey."

Pink Rose Pastry Shop [S]⇏ 24 | 19 | 16 | $10

630 S. Fourth St. (Bainbridge St.), 215-592-0565

■ "Save room" for a "sweet treat" at this "cute" "pink" dessertery off South Street that's like "an English country inn transplanted to an urban setting"; "drooling" addicts ask "did we die and go to heaven?" and hardly notice the "sleepwalking" staff.

Pippo's Fantastico [S] 16 | 16 | 17 | $25

765 Second St. Pike (Street Rd.), Southampton, 215-953-7775

◪ Fans of this "pleasant, attractive" Bucks County Italian that's "dressy for the neighborhood" say it serves "huge portions" of "well-prepared" food, including "good" pizza and pasta; however, cynics claim the cooking is only "so-so", adding "nothing is fantastico here except the prices."

Pizzicato [S] – | – | – | M

248 Market St. (3rd St.), 215-629-5527

This cool-looking, Old City yearling might come across as just another brick-oven pizzeria, but there's a sense of style in the contemporary takes on traditional Italian dishes and a warmth in the staff; yes, the pies are good, too.

Plough & the Stars ◗Ⓢ   21 | 23 | 20 | $24
123 Chestnut St. (2nd St.), 215-733-0300
■ "Outstanding newcomer" that's "trendy without being overwrought" is the verdict on this Old City "nouvelle Dubliner" with "interesting" contemporary Irish cuisine served in a "romantic" "Celtic rococo" room by a "friendly staff that evokes memories of the Emerald Isle"; it's "sometimes too noisy at night", so "try brunch."

Plumsteadville Inn Ⓢ   20 | 22 | 20 | $30
Rte. 611 & Stump Rd. (3 mi. north of Doylestown),
Plumsteadville, 215-766-7500
■ "Charming" and "rustic" Continental "sleeper" serving "wholesome", "tasty" cooking in an Upper Bucks County 1751 inn that looks "like a 3-D Christmas card in December"; "Sunday brunch is special."

Pollo Rosso Ⓢ   20 | 17 | 20 | $25
8229 Germantown Ave. (Southampton Ave.),
215-248-9338
■ "Popular", "friendly" and "family-oriented" Italian in Chestnut Hill known for "well-prepared pizzas and pastas" and the "world's best bread pudding"; while a few foes frown it's "crowded", "dark" and "noisy", most think it's a very "good value", "if you can get in."

Pompano Grille Ⓢ   – | – | – | M
(nka Bohemian Bistro)
Bainbridge & Fifth Sts. (1 block from South St.),
215-923-7676
After three years in this Queen Village location, chef-owner Bill Beck has turned off the neon and uprooted the palm trees to create a different style of warmth – a cozy Bohemian lounge; while there's now a new European bistro menu that's less expensive, patrons can continue to enjoy rooftop dining in the summer.

Ponzio's Kingsway ◗Ⓢ   17 | 12 | 17 | $18
7 W. Rte. 70 (Kings Hwy.), Cherry Hill, NJ, 856-428-4808
◪ A retail bakery on the premises ensures "there's nothing you can't get" at this " solid", "old-time" Cherry Hill diner "institution" that's "power-breakfast central"; but while some insist this is the place for an "inexpensive family feed", others argue "it's really gotten expensive."

Poor Henry's ◗Ⓢ   ▽ 18 | 18 | 20 | $18
829-51 N. American St. (bet. Brown & Poplar Sts.),
215-413-3500
■ This "quintessential brewpub" in Northern Liberties offers "fresh" beer and a "wide-range" of "good" American-Continental food in a "comfortable" "warehouse" space that reflects its past as the Ortlieb beer factory; the "location is so-so", but "parking is free."

Porcini 23 | 13 | 20 | $24
2048 Sansom St. (bet. 20th & 21st Sts.), 215-751-1175
■ Despite its mushrooming popularity, devotees gladly brave "long lines", "cramped", "crowded" quarters and "small portions" at this Center City Italian BYO for "wonderful", "fresh, light, delicious dishes" and "very friendly" service; in short – a "great neighborhood spot."

Portofino 18 | 14 | 17 | $27
1227 Walnut St. (bet. 12th & 13th Sts.), 215-923-8208
■ "Ordinary" but "reliable" "traditional" South Philly Italian smack in the Center City theater area with "agreeable service"; it's a decent bet "before a show", but "not as the focus of your evening."

Port Saloon (CLOSED) ▽ 16 | 18 | 17 | $29
735 S. Columbus Blvd. (Pier 34), 215-923-2500
☑ A Southern Italian on the dockside of the Moshulu at Penn's Landing; supporters like the "fun outdoor dining" with river views, but foes say the food is "inconsistent" ("they must throw their chefs overboard") and "overpriced."

Primavera Pizza Kitchen 🅂 18 | 22 | 17 | $24
7 E. Lancaster Ave. (Cricket Ave.), Ardmore, 610-642-8000
☑ Fans of this "primo" Main Line Italian, in a "former bank" that "looks like a museum" with "cool murals", praise the "reasonable prices" "excellent pizzas" and pastas; but a minority maintains the food is only "average" and the "hostesses act like they're from Pathmark."

Prime Rib 🅂 – | – | – | E
Warwick Hotel, 1701 Locust St. (17th St.), 215-772-1701
The showy D.C. and Baltimore steakhouse chain has swanked up a smashing space in the Warwick, with plush, leopard-print carpet, onyx walls and a baby grand, all to attract an older crowd hungering for the old days; huge portions of excellent, traditional food (the signature prime rib can feed an army) are served impeccably.

Provence 🅂 22 | 17 | 19 | $33
379 Lancaster Ave. (opp. Haverford College), Haverford, 610-896-0400
■ Chef-owner Francis Treciak is "always trying something new" and offers "imaginative food that generally works" at this "bit of France" in a "comfy" Haverford "barn"; it's "lovely for lunch and charming for dinner."

Pub Restaurant 🅂 19 | 14 | 18 | $23
Airport Circle & Rte. 130, Pennsauken, NJ, 856-665-6440
☑ "It's like eating at a football training camp" at this Pennsauken American serving "huge portions" of decent steak and "the Delaware Valley's best salad bar"; while the "'50s decor" means the atmosphere's "not that great", most insist this survivor is "one of the best bargains around"; so "keep those steakhouse chains, we'll take the Pub."

Purple Sage [S] (CLOSED) | 19 | 12 | 15 | $23 |
7540 Haverford Ave. (Sherwood Ave.), 215-879-3400
◪ Chef Ruth Breuninger's Overbrook Park International BYO offers "generous portions" and a "wide variety of excellent fresh food" at a "good price"; even though they need to "get their act together" when it comes to the "tasteless" decor and "slow service", boosters believe with tweaking it "could be a star."

Rachael's Nosheri | 18 | 9 | 16 | $12 |
120 S. 19th St. (Sansom St.), 215-568-9565
◪ A "typical yiddishe mama", Jewish-style deli in Center City that's "ok for lunch" when you need a cabbage borscht or "mile high" corned beef fix; there's "friendly service" and "no one leaves hungry."

Rajbhog Indian Vegetarian [S] | – | – | – | I |
738 Adams Ave. (Roosevelt Blvd.), 215-537-1937
The name of this kosher vegetarian Indian in a Northeast shopping center means "a feast for royalty" in Hindi, and diners certainly feel pampered after sampling the wide variety of authentic food and listening to the sitar music.

Ralph's [S]⊄ | 22 | 13 | 18 | $24 |
760 S. Ninth St. (bet. Catharine & Fitzwater Sts.), 215-627-6011
■ South Philadelphia red sauce "institution" for "plentiful" portions of "still great" "traditional" cooking, including "the best veal" and "wonderful mussels"; the staff is "macho" and "uppity" (but "charming"), it's "too loud" and "tables are too close together", but that's why it's "the real deal."

Rangoon [S] | 22 | 14 | 20 | $19 |
112 N. Ninth St. (bet. Arch & Cherry Sts.), 215-829-8939
■ There's "lots more space" in the new Chinatown digs of this Burmese stop ("the only one in town") known for a "gracious and knowledgeable" staff that guides patrons through the "spicy", "delicious" menu full of "singing flavors"; clearly, a "wonderful sleeper."

Ray's Cafe & Tea House [S] | 22 | 17 | 19 | $18 |
141 N. Ninth St. (bet. Cherry & Race Sts.), 215-922-5122
■ "Delicious dumplings and amazing coffee" (they "make brewing a cup into a show") are the hallmarks of this much-praised Chinese coffee shop; a few grumble over the cost ("the $8 cup of Blue Mountain is overpriced"), but most think the java is "worth every decadent drop."

READING TERMINAL MARKET ⊄ | 24 | 17 | 17 | $12 |
51 N. 12th St. (Arch St.), 215-922-2317
■ "Forget the Liberty Bell" and head to Philadelphia's "must-see", "no-pretensions" farmers market next to the Convention Center; it's an "Eclectic" "quick-meal central" that's "always an adventure" offering "food of every description" and a "funky" "people-watcher's" setting: "if you can't find something you like, you must be dead."

Red Hot & Blue S   17 13 15 $18
Holiday Inn, Rte. 70 & Sayer Ave. (opp. Garden State Park),
Cherry Hill, NJ, 856-665-7427
☑ A southern barbecue joint in Cherry Hill with "killer onion
loaf", a "first-rate pulled pork sandwich" and "good ribs";
a few snobs say "not North Carolina but not bad BBQ for
NJ"; P.S. there's also "great", if "loud", live blues music
on Friday and Saturday nights.

Regatta Bar & Grille S   ▽ 13 15 15 $24
Philadelphia Marriott West, 111 Crawford Ave. (bet. Rtes. 76
& 476), West Conshohocken, 610-260-9427
☑ "Lively" Traditional American in the West Conshy Marriott
with "acceptable" food and "cute" decor ("fun having an
eight man shell hanging over your head"); "brunch with
the grandkids is a bargain."

Rembrandt's S   19 18 19 $27
741 N. 23rd St. (Aspen St.), 215-763-2228
■ An "always pleasant" "popular Art Museum–area" stop
in Fairmount that "keeps going and going" thanks to a "very
good" International menu ("delicious duck strudel"), a
"cool bar", a "nice view of the skyline" and piano music;
critics find the food "good, but not memorable."

Remi's Cafe   18 17 18 $23
141 Kings Hwy. E. (Haddon Ave.), Haddonfield, NJ, 856-795-7232
☑ A "nice, neighborhood" Italian in Haddonfield that's
"pleasant" enough for "getting together with an old
friend" for an "intimate lunch", though it "could use a
breath of creativity."

Rhapsody's   ▽ 20 20 21 $35
25 S. Broad St. (Jenkins Ave.), Lansdale, 215-362-5669
☑ Anglophiles unite! – there's "tea with scones on Sunday"
at this "charming" and "frumpy" Victorian-decorated
Continental in Lansdale; "personal service" and "very
good" edibles make it "well worth the trip."

Rib Crib ●⇄   ▽ 25 9 16 $15
6333 Germantown Ave. (bet. Duval St. & Washington Ln.),
215-438-6793
■ Charged up reviewers shout "damn the cholesterol, full
speed ahead" for the "best BBQ on the planet" at this
Germantown Soul Fooder with "great ribs"; as the decor
rating suggests, it's "perfect for takeout."

Ristorante Alberto S   21 16 20 $36
1415 City Ave. (Haverford Ave.), Wynnewood, 610-896-0275
☑ Connoisseurs claim they have the "best veal chop" in the
city at this "still reliable" Wynnewood Italian; but on the
downside it's a little "too expensive for Haverford" and "you
might have to wait even with a reservation."

Ristorante Fieni's S ▽ 22 17 21 $25
800 S. Burnt Mill Rd. (next to Echelon Mall), Voorhees, NJ, 856-428-2700
■ This "quiet" Northern Italian BYO in a "revamped ranch" in Voorhees offers "fine food" at "reasonable" prices and has a "great staff and host/owner."

Ristorante Gallo Nero 21 22 19 $39
(nka Ristorante San Marco)
504 N. Bethlehem Pike (Dager Rd.), Spring House, 215-654-5000
☑ Despite a post-*Survey* ownership change, this Montco Italian still has the same chef turning out "high quality" Tuscan and regional dishes; some find it "overpriced" with "pretentious service", and add that it's "not what it was on 15th street" in Center City, but it's still "one of the better suburban restaurants."

Ristorante La Buca 23 19 23 $38
711 Locust St. (bet. 7th & 8th Sts.), 215-928-0556
■ Though "they favor regulars" at this "true old-world" Italian seafooder in a "cellar" off Washington Square, insiders insist that "they're true artists", offering "delicious" food and "pampering" service; there is disagreement over decor, however – while some say it's "elegant", others sniff "dark and dreary" and caution "bring a flashlight."

Ristorante Laceno S ▽ 22 16 19 $27
Echelon Village Plaza, White Horse Rd. (bet. Burnt Mill Rd. & I-561), Voorhees, NJ, 856-627-3700
■ There's a "lot of great choices" at this "high-quality, BYO Italian seafooder, an interesting place to "take out-of-town guests and watch their reactions", from "strip mall – yuck" to "food fabulous."

Ristorante Mediterraneo S 22 20 20 $33
303 Horsham Rd. (Rte. 611), Horsham, 215-672-5595
■ The "singing waiters are a plus" at this "upscale", "surprise" Italian, perhaps the "only place with tablecloths" in Horsham; expect "very good" food that seems "pricey for the area", that is, until the "evening is topped off by the man with the dessert cart."

Ristorante Ottimo (CLOSED) 16 14 15 $30
218 S. 16th St. (bet. Locust & Walnut Sts.), 215-985-4844
☑ Some think this Center City Italian "shows promise" especially on the "romantic" "second floor", but others contend it's "disappointing", though staff is "pleasant."

RISTORANTE PANORAMA S 23 21 20 $37
Penn View Hotel, 14 N. Front St. (Market St.), 215-922-7800
■ Oenophiles exclaim that the "wine flights are the attraction" ("outrageous selection"), but the pasta is also "always great" at this "sleek and trendy" Old City Italian, with a "romantic" bar that's the "nicest in town"; overall, "Philly needs more like this one."

Ristorante Positano S   22   20   21 $33
21 W. Lancaster Ave. (bet. Ardmore & Cricket Aves.),
Ardmore, 610-896-8298
801 W. Sproul Rd. (¼ mi. north of Rtes. 1 & 320),
Springfield, 610-543-6644
■ "Homey" Italian twins on the Main Line and in Delco
that will "quickly become your favorites" for "authentic",
"magnifico" cuisine, "old-Italy" atmosphere" and "funny,
attentive" waiters who are "always a treat"; N.B. Springfield
is BYO, Ardmore has a decent wine list.

Ristorante Primavera S   21   18   19 $29
148 South St. (bet. Front & 2nd Sts.), 215-925-7832 ⊟
384 W. Lancaster Ave. (Conestoga Rd.), Wayne, 610-254-0200
■ This Italian duo in Wayne ("huge", "a bit loud" and
packed with Main Liners) and on South Street ("small and
intimate") are both known for "consistent", "better than
average" food; pasta is the standout.

Ristorante San Carlo S   21   17   20 $30
214 South St. (bet. 2nd & 3rd Sts.), 215-592-9777
■ "The antipasti in the window draws you into" this
"intimate" somewhat "cramped" Italian on South Street
that wins raves for its "consistently exceptional" food ("the
stuffed squid is to die for"), "eager to please manager" and
"articulate", though occasionally "overattentive" staff;
some are "surprised it isn't higher rated."

Ritz-Carlton Grill S   24   24   25 $44
Ritz-Carlton, Chestnut & 17th Sts. (Liberty Pl.), 215-563-1600
☑ The Ritz-Carlton's "elegant" Contemporary American–
Mediterranean is a "businessman's hangout" ideal for
entertaining "important clients" on an expense account with
"delicious", "creative" food and "inspired wine dinners";
the "great dinner tables and chairs" are perfect "when in
the mood for the *Lifestyles of the Rich and Famous*"; N.B.
the hotel's name will change to the St. Regis in mid-1999.

River City Diner ◗S   13   17   15 $18
UA Complex, 3720 Main St. (Ridge Ave.), 215-483-7500
☑ "Lots of parking" and a "clever" "stage set out of the
'50s" are the draws of this "fancy" retro diner in Manayunk;
surveyors acknowledge that it's a "fun", "great concept",
but the food's "mediocre"and "overpriced for what it is";
at press time, it was about to close and be remade into a
midpriced seafooder called Fish on Main; stay tuned.

Rizzo's S   18   9   16 $13
21 E. Glenside Ave. (Easton Rd.), Glenside, 215-887-2909
■ "Great pizza and everything else slightly better than
adequate" is the line on this Glenside neighborhood
"standby", popular with families thanks to a Tuesday
night AYCE; service is generally "friendly" and "best
when you get a waitress who's old enough to vote."

Rock Lobster [S] 14 | 18 | 14 | $26

221 N. Delaware Ave. (Vine St.), 215-627-7625

■ A seasonal seafooder with a deck overlooking the Delaware; most "go for sitting outdoors on a nice summer night, not for the food"; those with their eyes on bigger fish say "pick up a meal or a single."

ROCOCO [S] 22 | 26 | 19 | $38

123 Chestnut St. (2nd St.), 215-629-1100

■ This "hip", "New York–like" Contemporary American is "the place to see and be seen" in Old City; expect everything to be "beautiful", from the food ("fantastic" "nouvelle" treats) to the people ("wear black, be thin") to the decor ("breathtaking room", "sexy cigar" lounge and "happening bar"); the only drawback is that it can get "so loud that it's difficult to hold a conversation."

Roller's [S]≠ 22 | 12 | 18 | $28

Top of the Hill Shopping Ctr., 8705 Germantown Ave. (Bethlehem Pike), 215-242-1771

■ Paul Roller's reputation is "well-deserved", declare fans of this "long-standing" Eclectic "contender" at the top of Chestnut Hill; despite a seriously "deafening", "cramped" room and "no decor", it's a "favorite" for "consistently good", "innovative" home cooking at "a fair price" (four nightly $10 specials); bring cash (no cards) and don't leave without trying at least one of the "great desserts."

Ron's Ribs [S] 19 | 7 | 12 | $14

1627 South St. (bet. 16th & 17th Sts.), 215-545-9160

■ Reviewers think this "Philadelphia institution" that's been around for 65 years is "worth a trip" to South Street West for "great ribs and cornbread" and "still great chicken"; since the neighborhood can get a little hairy, and there's "no decor", you might want to "get takeout."

Roscoe's Kodiak Cafe [S] 23 | 21 | 21 | $38

4425 Main St. (Carson St.), 215-483-7108

■ An "exotic", "creative" Alaskan-Northwestern menu ("imaginative fish"), "rugged" decor, an open kitchen and "friendly" service that "tries hard" are the attractions of this "surprise" in the northern exposure of Manayunk; solid ratings across the board indicate it's "great for a change of pace."

ROSELENA'S COFFEE BAR [S] 24 | 27 | 22 | $18

1623 E. Passyunk Ave. (Tasker St.), 215-755-9697

■ This "soothing" South Philly "fantasy land" dishes "divine" desserts and Eclectic food in a Victorian setting that oozes "old-world" warmth; it's the "ultimate date place" and "may be the most romantic spot around", plus the buffet brunch is a "bargain."

ROSE TATTOO CAFE 23 | 22 | 20 | $31
1847 Callowhill St. (19th St.), 215-569-8939
■ "Sit upstairs" on the balcony of this plant-filled New American near the Free Library, a "place to get away from it all" with "gorgeous flowers" and a real "New Orleans look"; the food's "always excellent" and the staff "polite", so "from beginning to end expect a satisfying experience."

Rose Tree Inn [S] 23 | 21 | 22 | $35
1243 Providence Rd. (Rtes. 1 & 252), Media, 610-891-1205
■ A "quiet" "special occasion" Franco-American in Media that's "always a treat" for "top-drawer" (if "a little pricey") food and "attentive" service in a "sophisticated" ambiance.

Rouge 99 ◐[S] – | – | – | M
Rittenhouse Claridge Apt. Bldg., 205 S. 18th St. (bet. Locust & Walnut Sts.), 215-732-6622
Neil Stein, of Striped Bass fame, has turned the wine shop in the Rittenhouse Claridge into a sexy, '20s Paris salon with a comfy bar; delicious Euro-American food from chef Peter Dunmire keeps the crowd around into the wee hours.

Ruby's [S] 14 | 17 | 15 | $13
Suburban Sq., 5 Coulter Ave. (Anderson Ave.), Ardmore, 610-896-7829
Plaza at King of Prussia, 160 N. Gulph Rd. (Rte. 202), King of Prussia, 610-337-7829
◪ "Just like *Happy Days*" sizes up this minichain of '50s-themed "concept joints"; the "long waits" and "redefined *Romper Room*" atmosphere irk some ("don't go without earplugs"), but parents rave about the "juicy" burgers.

Ruhling's Seafood [S] 17 | 14 | 17 | $22
7210 Rising Sun Ave. (Cottman Ave.), 215-745-0202
◪ A "neighborhood" seafooder near Five Points in the Northeast that's a "step back in time" for "good", "no-frills" food ("many fried dishes") and a "family atmosphere"; a recent renovation helps, but some think the place is still "not up to its past performance."

Russell's 96 West [S] ▽ 21 | 18 | 19 | $42
96 W. State St. (Main St.), Doylestown, 215-345-8746
◪ This "romantic" New French with Asian influences in Doylestown crafts "painstakingly prepared" food (from a "limited menu"), and has "attentive" service and a "great garden"; the monthly art shows and cigar bar are also pluses.

Ruth's Chris Steak House ◐[S] 23 | 21 | 20 | $47
260 S. Broad St. (Spruce St.), 215-790-1515
◪ An "expense-account" steakhouse chain outpost in the heart of Center City that's praised for "generous portions" of "excellent" steaks"; despite solid ratings, service comments are a tossup with some getting the "royal treatment" and others noting miscues from an "indifferent" staff.

Saffron   _ _ _ M
121 S. 19th St. (Sansom St.), 215-564-6070
An often overlooked International near Rittenhouse Square
in a "cozy", "beautiful, old" Victorian home with lots of dark
wood paneling; the food, cooked by a veteran of the Frog/
Commissary, is well thought-out and presented.

SAGAMI S   27 17 21 $29
*37 Crescent Blvd. (1 block north of Collingswood Circle),
Collingswood, NJ, 856-854-9773*
■ Hordes "happily make the trek" to Collingswood to put
up with "long waits", a "basement setting" and seating
that's "as tight as a phone booth" for "impeccably fresh"
"sublime" sushi served by a "helpful", "efficient" staff; it's
"the best Japanese restaurant in the area" ("by a large
stretch") and No. 1 in the *Survey*.

Sage Diner ● S   15 11 16 $16
1170 Rte. 73 (Church Rd.), Mt. Laurel, NJ, 856-727-0770
■ "Another Jersey diner" is the line on this "friendly" Mount
Laurel "quickie", "a place to meet the relatives" for "decent"
but "nothing special" food from an "endless menu."

Saigon S ⊄   22 12 20 $17
935 Washington Ave. (bet. 9th & 10th Sts.), 215-925-9656
■ It's one of the granddaddies of Vietnamese cuisine, but
this "family-run" South Philadelphian is "still a bargain" with
"fabulous" food and the "nicest waitresses in town"; old-
timers urge newcomers to "tell chef Ha to surprise you."

Sakura Spring S   _ _ _ M
*Heritage Sq. Shopping Ctr., 1871 Rte. 70 E. (east of Rte. 295),
Cherry Hill, NJ, 856-489-8018*
A hospitable Asian BYO in Cherry Hill that ably handles
Chinese, Japanese, Thai and Vietnamese treats; the warmly
lit atmosphere, complete with sushi bar, is suitable for
families earlier in the evening and couples later on.

Sala Thai S (CLOSED)   19 14 17 $20
700-702 S. Fifth St. (Bainbridge St.), 215-922-4990
☑ An "upscale Thai in a downscale" setting off South
Street; there are "creative" dishes and the usual standards
("chicken satay and cucumber salad are tops") plus "good
recommendations" from the staff; patience is required –
"if you have an entire evening to wait, it's fine."

SALOON   25 23 23 $48
*750 S. Seventh St. (bet. Catharine & Fitzwater Sts.),
215-627-1811*
☑ The "rich, masculine atmosphere is unrivaled" at this
South Philadelphia Italian where patrons "dine like
kings" on "big portions" of "wonderful" steaks and "great"
veal served by "attractive waitresses"; dissenters growl
"overrated" and "resting on their laurels" and warn "watch
the specials – expensive."

Samosa [S] 18 | 11 | 17 | $11
1214 Walnut St. (bet. 12th & 13th Sts.), 215-545-7776
■ This "decent if modest", extremely "affordable" vegetarian Indian buffet with the "nicest" service impresses Center City lunchers who arrive "before noon" to beat the crowd; while a few say "dishes look different but taste the same", the majority praises food that's a "riot of tastes and spices."

Samuel Adams Brew House (CLOSED) 16 | 15 | 16 | $18
1516 Sansom St., 2nd fl. (bet. 15th & 16th Sts.), 215-563-2326
◪ Barflies "go for the beer" at this "fun" Center City brewpub that's also a "good place to grab a burger" and "hang out with friends"; foodies find the grub "average" and note that the atmosphere's "smoky."

Samuels [S] 22 | 23 | 21 | $39
Spread Eagle Village, 503 W. Lancaster Ave. (Eagle Rd.), Wayne, 610-687-2840
◪ A "pretty" New American that caters to the Main Line's "upper crust"; foodwise, reviewers like it for the "best brunches in the area", but find that other meals can be "inconsistent" and "overpriced"; check out the cigar bar.

Sang Kee Peking Duck House [S]⊄ 21 | 6 | 17 | $16
238 N. Ninth St. (Vine St.), 215-925-7532
■ "Ooh, that duck!" and "needs a good scrubbing" are the two most frequently mentioned comments for this Chinatown Chinese known for attracting connoisseurs, including "many Asians"; in addition to the eponymous dish, they're also revered for "the best won ton noodle soup" and anything with eggplant.

Sansom Street Oyster House 20 | 15 | 19 | $25
1516 Sansom St. (bet. 15th & 16th Sts.), 215-567-7683
◪ A "classic", "always dependable" Center City seafooder with the "largest selection" of "top-notch" oysters and "good", "old-style, nothing-fancy" fish at "fair prices"; the "oyster plates on the walls" are nice, but a few crab about "tables too close together" and an "unimaginative" menu.

Santa Fe Burrito Co. [S]⊄ 18 | 11 | 15 | $10
212 S. 11th St. (bet. Locust & Walnut Sts.), 215-413-2378
227 S. 20th St. (bet. Locust & Walnut Sts.), 215-563-4468
■ The "fabulous" burritos at these Center City "pit stops" "can stuff you for a year"; they're popular with the lunch crowd for their "eclectic" combos and "bargain" prices; only the stressed snarl "long waits" are "a crime."

Saranac [S] – | – | – | M
614 W. Lancaster Ave. (Penn St.), Bryn Mawr, 610-520-3430
This minuscule Main Line BYO has quickly drawn a following for its restful interior and Contemporary American cuisine that changes weekly, but is heavy on seafood and chops.

Sassafras Cafe ●S   17 | 17 | 18 | $20
48 S. Second St. (bet. Chestnut & Market Sts.), 215-925-2317
■ An "intimate", Old City bar with a "nifty tin ceiling" and "tile walls and floor"; it's "still a favorite" as a "romantic spot" for "the best burgers" "by the fireplace."

SAVONA S   25 | 27 | 23 | $54
100 Old Gulph Rd. (Montgomery Ave.), Gulph Mills, 610-520-1200
■ This "trendy" Main Line Italian seems to have picked up where its highly rated predecessor, Tierra, left off; there's "incredible", "cosmopolitan" decor, "excellent" food, a "great wine list" and "efficient" service; but at these prices "take someone you want to impress but charge it to the firm."

Sawan's Mediterranean Bistro S   18 | 16 | 18 | $21
116 S. 18th St. (bet. Chestnut & Sansom Sts.), 215-568-3050
■ It's "wonderful when they open the streetside windows in summer" at this "pretty", if a bit "spare", Center City Mediterranean from the owners of Cedars; the "solid food" from an "interesting menu" is a "great value for the money" and service is "obliging."

Scampi Ristorante Italiano S   21 | 13 | 18 | $26
2312 Garrett Rd. (Lansdowne Ave.), Drexel Hill, 610-284-3333
☑ A rising food rating confirms suspicions that this Delco Italian is "improving", turning out "terrific" food "without any fanfare"; a few grumble that the "atmosphere needs improvement" and that "parking is a problem."

Scoogi's Classic Italian S   16 | 15 | 16 | $22
738 Bethlehem Pike (Valley Green Rd.), Flourtown, 215-233-1063
■ A Flourtown Italian "neighborhood place" "to bring your whole family" (even "your son-in-law's mother") for "basic", "middle of the road" food and "good thin-crust pizza"; the "new room and new walls help" the decor as does the "pretty" new porch.

Seafood Unlimited   18 | 6 | 15 | $18
270 S. 20th St. (bet. Locust & Spruce Sts.), 215-732-3663
■ Prepare yourself for "bright lights, paperbag tablecloths" and seating that's "elbow to elbow with strangers" when dining at this "absolutely unpretentious" Center City stop for "reasonably priced" "fresh seafood served straight up"; those looking for creature comforts say "your best bet is takeout."

Serrano S   19 | 16 | 18 | $26
20 S. Second St. (bet. Chestnut & Market Sts.), 215-928-0770
☑ There's "always some new dish to try" at this "homey" International in Old City with a "varied" and "creative" menu; while some detect "overspicing" and find the seating "cramped", most appreciate the "layers of flavor"; after dinner, "catch a show upstairs" at the Tin Angel.

Seven Stars Inn S   21 | 18 | 20 | $35
Hoeffecker Rd. & Rte. 23, Phoenixville, 610-495-5205
■ "Don't eat for two days before going" to this Chester
County "landmark" known far and wide for "startlingly
large" portions of prime rib that "would feed a third-world
country"; while a few blurt – "average", the overwhelming
majority insists the beef's "quality" stuff, even if there's
"too much" of it.

Shank's & Evelyn's ⊅   23 | 8 | 16 | $13
932 S. 10th St. (Carpenter St.), 215-629-1093
■ Despite "slam-it-down wait service", this Italian
breakfast-and-lunch "hole-in-the-wall" in South Philly is
"as good as anything anywhere"; "they should charge
admission" to watch "politicos" and locals chow down on
the "best" roast beef, pork and chicken cutlet sandwiches;
"it's worth the time it takes to park."

Ship Inn S   17 | 17 | 18 | $32
Rte. 30 & Ship Rd., Exton, 610-363-7200
◪ A "charming", "historic" Exton inn offering up "classic
American" dishes with a Continental touch; modernists
unimpressed with the "colonial" motif and traditional menu
say "this place could use an update into the '90s"; the
"extensive" Sunday brunch is a good deal.

Shiroi Hana S   23 | 15 | 18 | $25
222 S. 15th St. (bet. Locust & Walnut Sts.), 215-735-4444
■ A "quiet" "sushi heaven" ("second to Sagami") in
Center City that's "stayed consistent over the years"; a
planned spring '98 redecoration includes a balance of
tatami and western-style seating; the box lunch is "a deal."

Siam Cuisine I S   22 | 16 | 19 | $24
925 Arch St. (bet. 9th & 10th Sts.), 215-922-7135
Siam Cuisine II S
*Village at Newtown S., 2124 S. Eagle Rd., Newtown,
215-579-9399*
Siam Cuisine III S
*Buckingham Green, 4950 York Rd. (Rte. 202), Buckingham,
215-794-7209*
■ The "terrific" flambéed hen "makes quite a presentation"
at these "consistently excellent" Thai triplets that also
produce a "yum" winning herb cake and coconut ice
cream; Newtown is BYO.

Siggie's L'Auberge   23 | 20 | 21 | $42
Ford & Front Sts. (Rte. 23), West Conshohocken, 610-828-6262
◪ A "cozy" French-American right off the Expressway
and Blue Route in West Conshy, with "excellent" food
(remember Helen Sigel Wilson's?) and "sophisticated",
"elegant" decor; a few perceive "attitude" and find the
tab "expensive for the location."

Sign of the Sorrel Horse S   19 | 24 | 18 | $44
4424 Old Easton Rd. (Rte. 313), Doylestown, 215-230-9999
☑ Slippage has been noticed at this "out-of-the-way" Doylestown Continental; while the country inn setting remains "lovely", and the "serious" food is mostly "well-prepared", a number report "amateurish" service that mars the experience.

Silk & Spice S   ▽ 19 | 17 | 20 | $17
758 E. Rte. 70 (Cropwell Rd.), Marlton, NJ, 856-988-7714
■ An "upscale" Marlton BYO Chinese that those in the know rate one of the "best in the county"; patrons get "service with a smile" and "delicious" food ("try the dumplings and the bird's nest").

Silk City ◑S⊄   17 | 15 | 16 | $12
435 Spring Garden St. (5th St.), 215-592-8838
■ "Nightcrawlers" flock to this "friendly, fast and fun" diner in Northern Liberties for its "funky" atmosphere, "solid" food ("don't miss the chocolate bread pudding") and "bargain" prices; a few who aren't jazzed about this "jumpin' joint" say "gag me with a greasy spoon."

Silk Cuisine S   20 | 15 | 19 | $22
(fka Silk of Siam)
654 W. Lancaster Ave. (Old Lancaster Ave.), Bryn Mawr, 610-527-0590
■ Main Liners think this Bryn Mawr neighborhood BYO Thai's new location is "brighter" and "warmer" than the old digs; the food is still "better than average" ("super pad Thai") and the staff is still "friendly."

Singapore Kosher Vegetarian S   21 | 16 | 20 | $18
1029 Race St. (bet. 10th & 11th Sts.), 215-922-3288
219 Berlin Rd. (Hwy. 41), Cherry Hill, NJ, 856-795-0188
■ Mavens say you "can't go wrong" taking "wonderful" chef-owner Peter Fong's advice, or relying on one of his "helpful waiters", at this "unusual" kosher Southeast Asian in Chinatown, one of "the best vegetarians in the city"; the new Cherry Hill outpost opened post-*Survey*.

Siri's Thai French Cuisine S   24 | 20 | 21 | $28
Tracktown Mall, 2117-2119 Rte. 70 W. (opp. Garden State Race Track), Cherry Hill, NJ, 856-863-6781
■ World travelers say "if you can't go to Bangkok", try this "elegant" Thai-French "gem" "hidden" in a Cherry Hill strip mall; a visit is an "experience for the palate" with "sophisticated", "imaginative" food ("excellent desserts"), "beautiful", "tastefully decorated" surroundings and "always pleasant" service; if in Philly, "it would get the recognition it deserves."

Sitar India [S] 19 10 14 $14

60 S. 38th St. (bet. Chestnut & Market Sts.), 215-662-0818

■ This University City Indian BYO, a fave of "Penn people", is an "incredible bargain, even when you don't get the buffet", which, by the way, is definitely "one of the better ones in West Philly"; decor isn't great, but who cares?

Smokin' Sam's Italian Grill [S] 17 11 16 $18

417 Germantown Pike (Joshua Rd.), Lafayette Hill, 610-941-4652

◪ A "friendly" neighborhood Italian-BBQ in Montco that's "nothing fancy" but "decent for bar food", especially the "good ribs"; the "smoky" atmosphere can be a problem.

Snockey's Oyster & Crab House [S] 16 11 15 $21

1020 S. Second St. (Washington Ave.), 215-339-9578

◪ Fans of this "scruffy, bare-bones, but seaworthy shellfish joint" in Queen Village still consider it an "old standby", but newcomers insist it's "disappointing" and "past its prime."

Society Hill Hotel [S] 13 15 14 $18

301 Chestnut St. (3rd St.), 215-925-1919

■ Despite tepid ratings, many think this "lively" ("when the piano gets going"), *Cheers*-like" streetcorner American in the Historic District is a "good choice" for either Sunday brunch or a "quick sandwich and beer" "after the movies", especially "at a sidewalk table in summer"; the unimpressed shrug "adequate bar food."

Solaris Grille [S] – – – M

8201 Germantown Ave. (Highland Ave.), 215-242-3400

Weeks after its 1997 opening, this promising Chestnut Hill Eclectic burned down; newly reopened, its new chef (ex Striped Bass) is now serving Contemporary American bistro fare in an airy, simple setting.

Somsak Thai – – – M

Plaza 38, 2442 Rte. 38, Cherry Hill, NJ, 856-482-0377

Echo Shopping Ctr., 200 White Horse Pike (Broadmill Rd.), Voorhees, NJ, 856-782-1771 [S]

These "super" Camden County BYO twins (Voorhees is the original) are "excellent" time and again for "fresh and clean" Thai flavors, "reasonable prices" and decent service.

Sonoma [S] 19 17 16 $28

4411 Main St. (bet. Gay & Levering Sts.), 215-483-9400

◪ On weekends good looking yuppies stand "elbow to elbow" at the "seriously loud" upstairs vodka bar of Derek Davis' "futuristic", "high tech" Manayunk "Ital-ifornian", "still the place to be seen", if not to dine on "reliably good", "reasonably priced" food ("great mashed potatoes"); detractors dis "inattentive", "snooty" service and "long waits" and claim it "needs a new menu."

South St. Souvlaki 🛇⌀ | 21 | 12 | 17 | $18 |
509 South St. (bet. 5th & 6th Sts.), 215-925-3026
■ Tom Vasiliades' "cheap", "kick-ass" Greek food hits "Olympian peaks" at this "fun" South Street "institution" that's "survived fickle tastes" thanks to "great gyros" and the "best baba ghanoush"; even those who find the traditional fare a tad "greasy" acknowledge it's always "tasty"; P.S. the decor got a slight boost during a minor, post-*Survey* renovation.

Spaghetti Warehouse 🛇 | 11 | 15 | 14 | $16 |
1026 Spring Garden St. (bet. 10th & 11th Sts.), 215-787-0784
◩ Despite unimpressive ratings, many diners find this "cavernous", "inexpensive" warehouse Italian in Spring Garden "fine" for a "fun" meal "with the kids"; purists scoff, "I could cook better blindfolded" and recommend "boiling water and opening a jar of Ragu" instead.

SPIGA D'ORO 🛇 | 25 | 15 | 24 | $31 |
Providence Sq., 831 Providence Rd. (bet. Bishop Ave. & Oak Ln.), Secane, 610-284-2225
■ If it were a headline it would read: "Blue Collar Strip Mall Meets Excellence", in the form of "caring" owner Giovanni Di'Gironimo's "exquisite" Italian, "one of Delaware County's least-known treasures" for "fabulous" food ("best Caesar") and "warm and friendly" service; definitely "check it out!"

Spotted Hog 🛇 | 14 | 16 | 16 | $20 |
Peddler's Village Shopping Ctr., Rte. 202 & Street Rd., Lahaska, 215-794-4030
◩ "After a hard day shopping in Peddler's Village", this "cute", "always busy" Eclectic makes a "good place to pig out" and drink from a "great selection" of beers; but if not in the area most "wouldn't go out of the way" and say "stick to sandwiches"; "what's up with the fabric covered ceiling?"

Spring Mill Café 🛇 | 21 | 20 | 20 | $35 |
164 Barrenhill Rd. (bet. Ridge Pike & River Rd.), Conshohocken, 610-828-2550
◩ "Intriguing entrees" with international (French/North African/Asian) influences are the hallmark of this "getaway" in an "old stone farmhouse" in Conshy with "charming and whimsical" decor that appeals to the "romantically inclined"; there's also "beautiful" alfresco seating.

State Street Cafe 🛇   ▽ | 19 | 14 | 18 | $26 |
57 W. State St. (Hamilton St.), Doylestown, 215-340-0373
■ While not Doylestown's most popular BYO, this chef-owned Eclectic does "well-prepared" dishes from an "innovative" menu, notably at "lunch"; "get a window table" for the best people-watching, otherwise the decor might appear "plain."

Stazi Milano S
18 | 20 | 18 | $25

*Jenkintown Train Station, Greenwood & West Aves.
(Township Line Rd.), Jenkintown, 215-885-9000*

☑ The decor is definitely on track with surveyors at this
"bustling", "noisy" Italian in a "beautiful", "polished", "art
deco" "made-over train station" in Jenkintown; but while
most give a solid "good" to the food and service, there
are a lot of mixed comments, indicating "inconsistency."

Stephen's S (CLOSED)
18 | 16 | 17 | $32

105 Shurs Ln. (Main St.), 215-487-3136

■ A "pleasant" Manayunk Mediterranean/Thai (separate
dishes, no fusion) that recently reopened after a total
renovation closed it during the *Survey*; the food is generally
"solid" and service "cordial"; it's worth another look.

Stix S
19 | 17 | 18 | $25

2227 Pine St. (23rd St.), 215-985-3680

☑ For Dmitri's "top-notch grilled octopus" "without the
wait", this Fitler Square Mediterranean is "another good
one", though some find it "disappointing, considering the
owner's other places"; "there's more table space", but
"don't expect to carry on a conversation."

Stockton Inn S
20 | 23 | 20 | $37

*1 Main St./Rte. 29 (Bridge St./Rte. 263), Stockton, NJ,
609-397-1250*

■ "The small hotel" in Stockton that inspired Rodgers &
Hart is "alive and kicking" with American-Continental
cooking in a "romantic", "postcard" setting that includes
an outdoor patio ("ideal" in summer for brunch), waterfall,
wishing well and pond; the disenchanted say it "has the
history and the location", but the "food needs a lift."

STRIPED BASS S
26 | 28 | 24 | $56

1500 Walnut St. (15th St.), 215-732-4444

■ Neil Stein's "power heavy", "destination" seafooder in
the heart of Center City's Restaurant Row has a new chef,
Terence Feury (ex NYC's Le Bernardin), whose culinary
derring-do is only matched by the "knockout" old bank vault
decor; though the usually "stellar" service can occasionally
be "snotty" and you might holler "holy mackerel!" when
the check arrives, this place is "never dull", and remains
one of Philly's favorites.

Sugar Mom's
Church Street Lounge ◑S
15 | 17 | 14 | $16

*Sugar Refinery Bldg., 225 Church St. (bet. 2nd & 3rd Sts.),
215-925-8219*

■ "One of the best beer selections", an "excellent" jukebox
and "cheap bar food" ("decent sandwiches") make this
Old City "hangout" a fave among after-hours restaurant
workers and other "interesting" types.

SUSANNA FOO ◗🅢   27 | 26 | 25 | $49
1512 Walnut St. (bet. 15th & 16th Sts.), 215-545-2666
■ "The blending of Asian and French cuisines is a marriage made in heaven" at this Restaurant Row "favorite", where the "smashing", "understated" "new decor" (up four notches from the last *Survey*) now lives up to the "sublime", "sparkling" creations and "fine", "attentive" service; there's still some quibbling over the "skimpy portions" but overall, it's easily No. 1 in its genre.

SWANN LOUNGE & CAFE ◗🅢   27 | 27 | 26 | $38
Four Seasons Hotel, 1 Logan Sq. (bet. Benjamin Franklin Pkwy. & 18th St.), 215-963-1500
■ "Civilized" "relaxing" American-Continental in the Four Seasons singled out for the "lovely floral arrangements", lunch buffet, "best afternoon tea", Saturday night dessert bar and Sunday brunch; since it's "almost as good as the Fountain", it's (even at these prices) "a best value."

TACCONELLI'S PIZZA 🅢⌿   26 | 8 | 15 | $15
2604 E. Somerset St. (bet. Almond & Thompson Sts.), 215-425-4983
■ Where else but this incredibly popular, 50-year-old, cash-only Port Richmond parlor would patrons be required to reserve their dough in advance to get a piece of the "best pizza in the world" ("especially the white" version); but remember, since it's just pizza, period, you may want to "bring your own salad" and wine; P.S. it's dethroned DeLorenzo's as No. 1 in the *Survey*.

Taco House 🅢⌿   14 | 7 | 11 | $9
1218 Pine St. (bet. 12th & 13th Sts.), 215-735-1880
◪ This "quirky" Center City "hole-in-the-wall" is home to a "fast and tasty" Mexican that's definitely "better than the Bell"; it's a destination for "students", "slackers" and "characters" for its "cheap" ("eat here when you're broke") prices and hot sauce that "kills germs."

Tai Lake ◗🅢   23 | 11 | 18 | $21
134 N. 10th St. (bet. Cherry & Race Sts.), 215-922-0698
■ Insiders say some of the "best fish" in Chinatown comes out of the "live tanks" of this Chinese mainstay, "the real McCoy" that attracts "many Asian diners."

Taj Mahal 🅢   – | – | – | M
1903 Chestnut St. (19th St.), 215-575-1199
"Varied and tasty dishes" are the hallmark of the "excellent" buffet lunch at this fun (albeit somewhat tacky) Center City Indian that "fills you up past dinner"; it's more ammunition for those who say "you don't have to go to West Philly" for food this good.

117

Tandoor India S
21 11 16 $16
106 S. 40th St. (bet. Chestnut & Walnut Sts.), 215-222-7122
■ A University City Indian that's "not afraid to put spice in its offerings" and "stands out" from the pack thanks to "excellent", "low-cost" lunch and dinner buffets; when "warm hospitality" is factored in, diners "don't know if [they] love the cook or owner better."

Tang Yean
20 12 17 $19
220 N. 10th St. (bet. Race & Vine Sts.), 215-922-8636
■ This Chinatown Chinese BYO is "a place to feel good about stuffing oneself" since the menu has loads of "healthful", but flavorful, vegetarian dishes; there's "no atmosphere" but the "friendly owner" (a "character") makes up for it.

Taqueria Moroleon S
▽ 23 15 16 $17
New Garden Ctr., 15 New Garden Ctr. (Baltimore Pike), Kennett Square, 610-444-1210
■ For "large portions" of "authentic Mexican food at peso prices", it's "worth the drive" to this Kennett Square taqueria that "caters to the area's large Mexican community."

Taquet
24 21 22 $43
Wayne Hotel, 139 E. Lancaster Ave. (bet. Wayne Ave. & Waynewood St.), Wayne, 610-687-5005
▨ A "typical Main Line crowd" says sit "outside on the porch" in spring and summer when dining at Jean-Francois Taquet's Contemporary French in an "elegant" vs. "stuffy" room at the Wayne Hotel; it's "among the best suburban restaurants" so expect "classy presentations" of "quality" food; a few holdouts are still pining for the food and atmosphere of the old place in Radnor.

Tavern on Green S
14 13 14 $20
2047 Green St. (N. 21st St.), 215-235-6767
■ This Art Museum–area American "neighborhood bar" is "not sensational" but "priced right" and a "convenient" pit stop for a drink and "decent", if "unimaginative", "pub grub"; critics add that the staff can be "unreliable" and the setting "needs an overhaul."

Taxi S
– – – M
328 South St. (bet. 3rd & 4th Sts.), 215-413-8294
A welcoming International on South Street that's a decent, casual choice for lunch or dinner; the cool decor certainly fits in with the street.

Tenth St. Pour House S⊄
16 13 15 $11
262 S. 10th St. (Spruce St.), 215-922-5626
▨ The "academic environment" and "mellow service" at this Center City Cajun coffeehouse nurture "creative types" in need of java, though it's "more than just a coffeehouse" due to the "surprisingly varied menu"; over-caffeinated critics say "tables are wobbly and so is the food."

Tequila's Authentic Mexican   23 | 21 | 21 | $26
1511 Locust St. (bet. 15th & 16th Sts.), 215-546-0181
■ An "authentic", "haute" Mexican in Center City that's
moved up in ratings since the last *Survey*; amigos love the
affable waiters who "make you feel at home" as well as the
"consistently enjoyable" "creative dishes" with "complex
tastes"; even the "dim lighting" works.

Teresa's Cafe Italiano S   – | – | – | M
*124 N. Wayne Ave. (next to the train station off Lancaster Ave.),
Wayne, 610-293-9909*
This gorgeous contemporary brick-oven Italian bistro is
"what Wayne has needed for a long time"; there's pizza,
"yummy, plentiful" pasta and charming, informal service.

Tex Mex Connection S   17 | 14 | 16 | $22
*201 E. Walnut St. (bet. N. Wales Rd. & Sumneytown Pike),
North Wales, 215-699-9552*
◪ Watch the "potent margaritas" at this "good, suburban"
Tex Mex in North Wales, which despite being "ordinary
looking" is a "fun place to visit with friends"; a drop in
ratings since our last *Survey* supports those who claim
it's now "generic."

Thai Garden S   20 | 16 | 18 | $22
101 N. 11th St. (opp. Convention Ctr.), 215-629-9939
◪ Located across from the Convention Center, this Thai
continues to receive a solid food rating thanks to "excellent
steamed dumplings" and "outstanding pad Thai", though
atmosphere and service aren't quite in the same league.

Thai Orchard S   – | – | – | M
*Berwyn Shopping Ctr., 556 W. Lancaster Ave. (Rte. 30),
Berwyn, 610-651-7840*
A "first-class" Thai BYO in Berwyn run by "pleasant" people,
offering "authentic", "sophisticated" dishes in a "cozy"
atmosphere that even fussy Main Liners deem "lovely."

Thai Pepper S   19 | 16 | 18 | $22
64 E. Lancaster Ave. (Rittenhouse St.), Ardmore, 610-642-5951
*372 W. Lancaster Ave. (opp. Strafford Shopping Ctr.),
Wayne, 610-688-5853*
■ "Thai standards" are "done well" at this "mainstream"
Ardmore BYO that's "reliable" for "good food and service"; a
few quibble that it's "too tame" and "could use some menu
updates"; N.B. the new Wayne location opened post-
Survey and has a liquor license.

Thai Singha House S   22 | 16 | 19 | $22
3939 Chestnut St. (39th St.), 215-382-8001
■ A sibling of Pattaya Grill, this Thai is lauded as a real
"asset to University City" thanks to "interesting", "delicious"
food, a "bargain" lunch and "great early bird"; factor in a
"fine" staff and "extremely nice" owners and it's not hard
to see why in its category it's one of "Philly's best."

Philadelphia

F | D | S | C

30th Street Station Market 🕒   16 | 16 | 14 | $11
Amtrak Station, 30th & Market Sts., 215-349-1821
◪ "Chew! Chew!" exclaim happy Amtrak travelers and
commuters who praise the "bonanza" of food stalls offering
"great quick bites" and a "variety of ethnic foods" at the
city's main rail station ("one more reason not to fly"); though
some feel it "suffers from comparison with Reading
Terminal", most say "take it aboard."

Thomas' 🕒   20 | 17 | 19 | $28
4201 Main St. (Pennsdale St.), 215-483-9075
◪ Thanks to the "coziest bar in Manayunk" (with lots of
"local taproom flavor") and "excellent crab cakes" this
American-Eclectic is usually "worth the parking hassle";
those just looking to imbibe should consider the "great hot
drinks on a winter evening"; a post-*Survey* chef change
and renovation is not reflected in the ratings.

Tierra Colombiana 🕒   ▽ 23 | 17 | 21 | $20
4535-39 N. Fifth St. (3 blocks from Roosevelt Blvd.), 215-324-6086
◼ Brush up on your Spanish then head to this "overlooked"
Colombian-Cuban "ethnic experience" "in the barrio" of
North Philadelphia, where "monstrous portions" of "heavy"
dishes ("the best paella I ever had") give you the energy
to dance the night away in the "don't miss" disco upstairs.

Tira Misu Ristorante 🕒   22 | 20 | 19 | $36
528 S. Fifth St. (bet. Lombard & South Sts.), 215-925-3335
◪ A "dark" but "pretty" Italian off South Street with a
"novel" Jewish-Roman menu; reviewers find most of the
dishes "top-notch", especially the "delicious, home-baked
matzohs" and "wonderful artichokes"; but despite solid
ratings there's a lot of kvetching about the staff's "attitude."

TONY CLARK'S 🕒 (CLOSED)   24 | 22 | 22 | $49
121 S. Broad St. (Sansom St.), 215-772-9238
◪ The "beautiful people" and other "fast living types" say
the "cutting edge" Eclectic fare continues to be a winner at
this "sophisticated" Center City stop, where the change to a
"warmer" decor was "for the better", though it's anyone's
guess what will happen since chef Tony Clark himself
left at press time.

Tony Luke's
Old Philly Style Sandwiches ⊄   23 | 6 | 14 | $9
39 E. Oregon Ave. (Front St.), 215-551-5725 ◐
118 S. 18th St. (Sansom St.), 215-568-4630
◼ For "awesome" "sammidges wit attytude" it's hard
to beat this "inspired", "no-ambiance" sandwich duo,
where broccoli rabe and the "best roast pork" are available
for a song; besides, "they treat you like a human, even if
you're not from South Philly"; the original at Front and
Oregon is a modified truck stop, but the new location in
Center City has tables.

TOSCANA CUCINA RUSTICA S   24 | 20 | 21 | $38
Bryn Mawr Mews, 24 N. Merion Ave. (bet. Montgomery Ave. & Rte. 30), Bryn Mawr, 610-527-7700
■ Perhaps more "elegant than rustic", this "attractive" Italian "hidden" off the main drag is "one of the best on the Main Line" with "consistently" "delicious" Tuscan entrees and a "classy but unpretentious" staff; on the downside the tables are "much too close together" and you may have to put up with "table-hopping", "yuppie" "schmoozers."

Totaro's Ristorante   23 | 13 | 20 | $38
729 E. Hector St. (parallel to Spring Mill Ave.), Conshohocken, 610-828-9341
■ It's ok with regulars if you can't find this "diamond in the rough" located in a "renovated" bar in Conshy, since it's "getting too crowded already" thanks to "outstanding", "ambitious" Italian-International food; while the room's "undistinguished", the "hostess gives it a homey touch."

Trattoria San Nicola   23 | 19 | 21 | $28
666-668 Lancaster Ave. (Main Ave.), Berwyn, 610-296-3141
■ A "very crowded" but "cozy" and "inexpensive" Italian in Berwyn with "solid", "well-prepared" food ("great soups"); "make reservations early", but if it's booked, "sit at the bar."

Treetops S   22 | 24 | 22 | $38
Rittenhouse Hotel, 210 W. Rittenhouse Sq. (19th & Walnut Sts.), 215-790-2533
■ Surveyors "go out on a limb" to praise this "quiet", "airy" New American in the Rittenhouse Hotel with an "excellent view", an "unobtrusive" staff and "gorgeously" presented dishes from chef Jim Coleman; Sunday brunch "is best."

Tre Scalini S   23 | 13 | 21 | $29
1533 S. 11th St. (Tasker St.), 215-551-3870
■ Those looking to enter "mushroom heaven" should try this "true mom-and-pop" Italian BYO with "incredible", "carefully prepared", "made-to-order" classics ("great spaghetti with clam sauce") served by a "sweet" staff; as ratings suggest, there's a "typical South Philly ambiance."

Triangle Tavern ●S   16 | 10 | 16 | $17
1338 S. 10th St. (Reed St.), 215-467-8683
■ A "dingy" South Philadelphia "cliché red sauce" Italian where the Friday and Saturday night floor show by the "geriatric rock band" is such "a hoot" "beyond description" that some forget to eat ("who notices the food?"); if hungry, the mussels are the way to go.

Trinacria   ▽ 21 | 16 | 22 | $37
1016 DeKalb Pike (1 mi. east of Rte. 476), Center Square, 610-275-0505
■ While "unnoticed", even on busy DeKalb Pike, this "fancy" Southern Italian in Center Square delivers "terrific" Sicilian dishes served by elegant "waiters in tuxes."

Tulipano Nero S   22 | 19 | 19 | $31
Princeton Pl. Shopping Ctr., 3747 Church St. (bet. Fellowship Rd. & Kings Hwy.), Mt. Laurel, NJ, 856-235-6955
■ The wood-burning grill makes for "unbelievable" seafood at this BYO Italian "tucked" "out of the way" in Mount Laurel; aesthetes say the decor is "lovely", "sophisticated" and "out of character" for the strip mall setting; overall, a solid choice "when you don't want to go to the city."

UMBRIA S⌀   25 | 16 | 21 | $34
7131 Germantown Ave. (bet. Mt. Airy & Mt. Pleasant Aves.), 215-242-6470
■ "They're serious about food" (especially the "wonderful steaks"), at this "unassuming, "intimate" Eclectic BYO in a "tough neighborhood" of Mount Airy; while the "limited" chalkboard menu "could be updated" more often, it's "all very good"; check out the art for sale.

United States Hotel Bar & Grill S   16 | 14 | 15 | $24
4439 Main St. (Green Ln.), 215-483-9222
◩ A Manayunk "neighborhood" pub with a "good looking" cherrywood bar that's "cool for a drink" or for a "hamburger after a ride" on the canal.

Upstares at Varalli S   19 | 18 | 19 | $29
1345 Locust St. (Broad St.), 215-546-4200
■ "Get a seat by the window" at this "underrated", "up-energy", muraled Italian across from the Academy of Music and enjoy "people-watching", "terrific risotto" and a "pleasant" staff that "knows curtain time"; some call the climb upstairs an "aerobic" workout.

Valley Forge Brewing Co. S   13 | 12 | 15 | $19
Gateway Shopping Ctr., 267 E. Swedesford Rd. (Rtes. 202 & 252), Wayne, 610-687-8700
■ "Good beer" but "pedestrian food" is the word on this "cavernous" strip mall brewpub near Valley Forge; if you're going to chow down, the "simpler preparations [such as burgers] work the best."

Valley Green Inn S   18 | 22 | 17 | $28
Springfield Ave. & Wissahickon Creek, 215-247-1730
■ Surveyors say this city-owned, Fairmount Park Eclectic's "bucolic" "streamside setting" "in the heart of the woods" is worth the two-mile walk, especially if you go "for Sunday brunch" "out on the veranda"; N.B. while ratings aren't bad, a new management team and chef were hired post-*Survey* to bring the food and service up to the setting.

Valley Stream Inn S   20 | 19 | 21 | $24
748 Bridgetown Pike (Rte. 413), Langhorne, 215-750-1994
■ "Come for the crab cakes, stay for Art Brown at the piano", at this "out of the way" Traditional American "along a stream" in Lower Bucks; make sure to "arrive early on the weekends", otherwise prepare for "long waits."

Van's Garden [S] (CLOSED) 21 | 8 | 16 | $15
121 N. 11th St. (bet. Arch & Cherry Sts.), 215-923-2438
■ "Feast on a great variety of food for practically no money" at this "popular" Vietnamese BYO in Chinatown with "no atmosphere" but "delicious" fare, such as "hauntingly perfect vegetables with oyster sauce" and "fabulous pho."

Vega Grill ◐ [S] 23 | 17 | 19 | $30
4141 Main St. (Jamestown Ave.), 215-487-9600
■ The "colorful", "artfully presented", "terrific food" (the "Chilean sea bass is one of the best dishes in town") is so "daring" and "challenging" at this "cramped but convivial" Manayunk Nuevo Latino that diners think the "chef must never sleep"; pump some iron before handling the "20-pound metal menus", but otherwise, for once "the hype was right."

Vickers Tavern 23 | 24 | 22 | $44
192 E. Welsh Pool Rd. (Gordon Dr.), Exton, 610-363-7998
◪ "Lots of fireplaces" are part of the "warm", "romantic" atmosphere at this "lovingly restored" inn "hidden away" in Exton; admirers say they have "some of the best French-Continental food in Chester County" and service that makes you "feel like a V.I.P."; detractors find it "not worth the price."

Victor Café [S] 18 | 21 | 21 | $32
1303 Dickinson St. (bet. Broad & 13th Sts.), 215-468-3040
◪ "Puccini and pasta" come together at this South Philly Italian, a "fun place to take out-of-town friends" thanks to "talented" singing waiters and waitresses who break into arias; while the food is "not the high note", it's still "good."

Vietnam Palace [S] 21 | 9 | 17 | $16
222 N. 11th St. (bet. Race & Vine Sts.), 215-592-9596
■ The "overwhelming menu" "shows many sides of Vietnamese cuisine" at this "always good" Chinatown stop with "friendly" servers; N.B. from Vietnam food war vets: this is the one on the west side of 11th Street.

Vietnam Restaurant [S] 24 | 11 | 19 | $17
221 N. 11th St. (bet. Race & Vine Sts.), 215-592-1163
■ "Spectacular squid", "divine spring rolls" and "pho that will make you a friend" are some of the "amazing food" at this, "no-frills" Vietnamese, the top-rated in the *Survey*; "cheap prices" and "quick service" add to its popularity but the "newly enlarged" quarters only slightly budged the decor rating; N.B. it's the one on the east side of 11th Street.

Villa Di Roma [S] ⊘ 20 | 10 | 17 | $23
932-36 S. Ninth St. (bet. Christian St. & Washington Ave.), 215-592-1295
■ "The original blackboard menu still exists" at this "predictable but dependable" Italian Market Italian "known for" a "wonderful" chicken Neapolitan and a "don't miss" Ziti Francis; the decor is "no frills" and it's "cash only, hon."

Village Porch Bistro 🆂
16 | 12 | 16 | $19

Olde Sproul Shopping Village, 1178 Baltimore Pike (Rte. 320), Springfield, 610-544-3220

■ A "cutesy" New American in a Delco strip mall that doesn't rack up high ratings, but has a following as an "honest", "affordable" bistro with an outstanding ice cream selection; it's a place to "catch up with the girls" over "dessert after the play."

Villa Strafford
22 | 21 | 22 | $40

115 Strafford Ave. (Rte. 30), Wayne, 610-964-1116

■ A "comfortable", "well-serviced" Continental in Wayne with "very good food" ("Horst's Weiner schnitzel is to die for") that's "remained consistent over the years"; fans tout "great jazz in the bar on Friday and Saturday."

Vincent's
▽ 21 | 19 | 21 | $31

10 E. Gay St. (bet. High & Walnut Sts.), West Chester, 610-696-4262

■ Denizens of this "green-walled", "cozy" and "friendly" West Chester Continental applaud the "good" food, but give a standing ovation for the "the great jazz club upstairs" (Thursday–Saturday), ideal after dinner.

Waldorf Café 🆂
21 | 18 | 20 | $30

500 S. 20th St. (Lombard St.), 215-985-1836

■ With "consistently good food" and a certain "non-hurried charm", this "underappreciated" Center City Eclectic "deserves to be more crowded"; "romantics" think it's "a bit of Paris off Rittenhouse Square", and there's no arguing that prices are "reasonable."

Warmdaddy's ⦿🆂
16 | 19 | 17 | $27

4 S. Front St. (Market St.), 215-627-8400

■ There's "excellent" (if "deafening") blues, jazz and soul music and "fattening Southern cuisine" at this "dark and mysterious" Old City club, which "feels like Beale Street in Memphis"; it's clear the "decent" food "plays second fiddle to the music."

Warsaw Cafe
20 | 17 | 20 | $27

306 S. 16th St. (Spruce St.), 215-546-0204

■ "After all these years" this "very small", but "couldn't be cuter", Eastern European in Center City "still turns out wonderful" if "heavy" standards such as pierogi, potato pancakes and sauerbraten; some would like to "keep old favorites on the menu, but add delicious new items", especially "more healthier choices."

Washington Crossing Inn 🆂
17 | 19 | 17 | $28

Rtes. 32 & 532, Washington Crossing, 215-493-3634

■ Though not reflected in ratings, surveyors say this Bucks Continental has "lots of potential" and is "consistently improving" and "drawing new crowds"; it's recommended for the "tasty brunch."

Washington House 🆂   – | – | – | M
136 N. Main St. (Temple Ave.), Sellersville, 215-257-3000
"They know they are in the hospitality business" at this
"gem" in Upper Bucks serving "well-prepared" American
food out of an "old", "romantic" Victorian hotel; making
its debut in the *Survey*, indignant reviewers say, "how did
you miss this longtime favorite?"

WHITE DOG CAFE 🆂   24 | 21 | 20 | $32
3420 Sansom St. (34th St.), 215-386-9224
■ Even if you "don't like her politics" (what some call a
"politically correct atmosphere") "your tail won't stop
wagging" after sampling Judy Wicks' "consistently
creative" and "delish" New American food; the dog-
themed, "eclectic" Penn campus setting has "cozy little
rooms" that get "noisy" and "crowded", but everyone
agrees this is a "unique Philadelphia restaurant."

Wild Onion   15 | 14 | 16 | $25
Restaurant & Brasserie 🆂
900 Conestoga Rd. (Garrett Ave.), Rosemont, 610-527-4826
◪ A "fun", hearty American bistro "tucked away" in
Rosemont that's "not bad for a Main Line college town";
those expecting more say the "menu gets you excited"
but sometimes the "food is a letdown ("quality varies"); a
"blasé" staff is balanced by "bartender Walt, who makes
this place come alive."

William Penn Inn 🆂   22 | 24 | 23 | $34
Rte. 202 & Sumneytown Pike, Gwynedd, 215-699-9272
■ A "senior crowd" "still wears jackets" when dining at
this "spacious" Montco Continental with a "marvelous
Sunday brunch" and early bird; the "gorgeous" colonial
decor is especially "spectacular" around the holidays
when "they really go all out"; hipsters find the place a
little "stodgy", even though there's "always one or two
large celebratory parties."

Willistown Grille   22 | 19 | 21 | $32
4 Manor Rd. (Lancaster Ave.), Paoli, 610-695-8990
■ The "wonderful" fireplace "adds a nice touch" at
this "consistently good" Continental in Paoli with "very
congenial host-owners" and an "accommodating" staff;
respondents like it "for lunch."

Wolfgang's Cafe 🆂   19 | 14 | 20 | $23
32 Rittenhouse Pl. (Lancaster Ave.), Ardmore, 610-896-2850
■ The sauerkraut, "sausages and desserts are particularly
good" at this "reasonably priced" storefront German-
Austrian BYO off the main drag in Ardmore that "shows
that the suburbs can match at quality"; to those who think
the "crowded" space "needs improving", a spring '98
renovation is in progress.

Wrap Planet 🆂 (CLOSED) | – | – | – | I |
220 S. 16th St. (bet. Locust & Walnut Sts.), 215-546-5990
A mod-looking Center City cornershop run by Chanterelles'
Philippe Chin; the whopping, flavorful wrap sandwiches,
each "an adventure and a delight", are rolled by an eager
staff that compensates for occasional lines.

Wycombe Inn 🆂 | 19 | 19 | 19 | $30 |
1073 Millcreek Rd. (Rte. 413), Wycombe, 215-598-7000
◪ "There's no hurry to eat" at this "comfortable" Bucks
County Continental with "country charm" and the "best beef
Wellington"; thrill-seekers find the menu "unexciting."

Xando Coffee & Bar ◖🆂 | 16 | 21 | 14 | $12 |
1128 Walnut St. (12th St.), 215-413-1608
325 Chestnut St. (4th St.), 215-399-0214
235 S. 15th St. (Locust St.), 215-893-9696
3601 Walnut St. (36th St.), 215-222-4545
8605 Germantown Ave. (Evergreen Ave.), 215-753-1707
Bryn Mawr Plaza, 761 Lancaster Ave., Bryn Mawr, 610-520-5208
■ "Stylish", "crowded" "oases" for "coffee, conversation
and relaxation" that are like "the set of *Friends*", where folks
"hang out" on comfy sofas and nibble "yummy" cook-your-
own s'mores (cocktails start in late afternoon); impressions
of the staff range from "friendly" to "slacker."

YANGMING 🆂 | 24 | 22 | 22 | $31 |
1051 Conestoga Rd. (Haverford Rd.), Bryn Mawr, 610-527-3200
■ This "bustling" Bryn Mawr nouvelle Chinese that's "still
the best on the Main Line" and "almost as good as Susanna
Foo"; "lovely presentations" and "beautiful", "authentic
surroundings" make long- deprived suburbanites declare –
"at last, gourmet Asian cuisine in suburbia."

Yellow Springs Inn 🆂 | 23 | 24 | 21 | $41 |
1701 Art School Rd. (Rte. 113 & Yellow Springs Rd.),
Chester Springs, 610-827-7477
■ For a "good country experience", day-trippers endorse
this "romantic" Chester Springs Continental set in a
historical inn; a "beautiful Victorian setting", "awesome"
French-influenced food and "no-rush service" explain
why it's a "destination."

Ye Olde Temperance House 🆂 | 17 | 19 | 18 | $30 |
5 S. State St. (Rte. 413), Newtown, 215-860-0474
◪ "Sunday brunch is a blast" for jazz at this "historic"
Newtown Continental that's also a B&B; some say that
the kitchen can't keep pace with the "better music."

Yorktown Inn 🆂 | 14 | 17 | 16 | $26 |
8121 Old York Rd. (Church Rd.), Elkins Park, 215-887-0600
■ While it "pleases a finicky older crowd", most think this
Elkins Park American was "much better in the past", before
the fire, and now serves "unimaginative", "mediocre"
dishes; N.B. the food rating has fallen since our last *Survey*.

Zanzibar Blue ◐ S
21 | 23 | 20 | $35

Park Hyatt at the Bellevue , 200 S. Broad St. (Walnut St.),
215-732-5200

■ A "chic" crowd gathers at this "sexy", "classy", '50s-
looking Contemporary American supper club beneath the
Park Hyatt, *the* place to listen to "the greatest jazz" and
"surprisingly good" food ("love the noisy Sunday brunch"); a
few insist it "was better at the original location."

Zocalo S
22 | 19 | 19 | $29

3600-04 Lancaster Ave. (36th St.), 215-895-0139

☑ "Don't expect tacos and burritos" or margaritas from
a pitcher at this "innovative", "alta cucina" Mexican in
University City where "they make tortillas before your eyes"
and whip up a "plethora of great flavors"; a few say "used to
be good" but others want to give the new owners a chance;
N.B. the post-*Survey* return of original chef Jackie Pestka
has regulars rejoicing.

ZuZu S
15 | 11 | 13 | $11

Swedesford Plaza, 416 W. Swedesford Rd., Berwyn,
610-695-9400

☑ This "Boston Market of Mexican food" in Berwyn is
a "good kids place" offering "inexpensive", "quick",
"wholesome" grub; bashers say "better than Taco Bell, if
that's saying much."

Lancaster/Berks

Top Food
26 Log Cabin
25 Green Hills Inn
24 Gracie's
   Market Fare
23 Rest. at Doneckers

Top Decor
24 Log Cabin
   Gracie's
23 Green Hills Inn
   Rest. at Doneckers
22 Olde Greenfield Inn

Top Service
25 Log Cabin
24 Green Hills Inn
23 Groff's Farm
22 Rest. at Doneckers
21 Gracie's

Top Value
   Isaac's
   Windmill
   Bird-in-Hand
   Zinn's Diner
   Hoss's

F	D	S	C

Alois at Bube's Brewery S ▽ | 19 | 23 | 19 | $25 |
102 N. Market St. (bet. Market & Old Market Sts.), Mt. Joy,
717-653-2057
Bottling Works at Bube's Brewery S
102 N. Market St. (bet. Market & Old Market Sts.), Mt. Joy,
717-653-2160
Catacombs at Bube's Brewery S
102 N. Market St. (bet. Market & Old Market Sts.), Mt. Joy,
717-653-2056
☑ "A great place to experience, even if once" because of its "unique" atmosphere, this 19th-century brewery in Mount Joy houses three restaurants: Alois, offering Eclectic food from a prix fixe menu, the Catacombs (set 43-feet below street level) serving New American cuisine, and the Bottling Works, a more casual spot for light meals and sandwiches.

Bird-in-Hand Family Restaurant | 18 | 16 | 19 | $15 |
2760 Old Philadelphia Pike (Ronks Rd.), Bird-In-Hand,
717-768-8266
■ Definitely worth more than two in the bush, indicate fans of this huge, Lancaster County Pennsylvania Dutch stop, claiming it's "great for the family" for "plenty" of "good", if "heavy", "home cooking" that's an "excellent value."

Brewery Inn ⌀ | – | – | – | M |
546 S. Ninth St. (Laurel St.), Reading, 610-375-9412
Most surveyors aren't familiar with this humble corner bar in Reading where the Italian "food just keeps coming" for a budget prix fixe; it's a "fun place with a large group", but since it only serves dinner Wednesday, Friday and Saturday nights, it seems to take "a year to get a reservation."

Good N' Plenty 20 | 14 | 20 | $19

Rte. 896 (1 mi. north of Rte. 30), Smoketown, 717-394-7111

■ "The name says it all" insist visitors to this huge, all-you-can-eat Lancaster County Pennsylvania Dutchery, where it pays to "wear your elastic waistband pants" to make room for "the best fried chicken" and other homespun fare; lonely hearts may enjoy the communal seating "at tables with hordes of unknowns."

GRACIE'S 24 | 24 | 21 | $43

Manatawny Rd. (Rtes. 100 & 422), Pine Forge, 610-323-4004

■ "Take your passport" to this "otherworldly" Eclectic outside of Pottstown with "superb", "avant-garde" food and "the most unusual" decor ("check out the ladies room"); it's an "oasis in the middle of nowhere" that also serves up live jazz on weekends.

GREEN HILLS INN 25 | 23 | 24 | $45

2444 Morgantown Rd. (9 mi. north of Pennsylvania Tpke., exit 22), Reading, 610-777-9611

■ This "charming" Classic French–American, set in an "elegant" inn near Reading, is "still a winner" and "more than worth the drive" for "excellent" haute preparations ("oh, those quenelles!") and "friendly, professional" service; a recent redo may lift decor scores even higher.

Groff's Farm Restaurant [S] 22 | 20 | 23 | $28

650 Pinkerton Rd. (1 mi. south of Mt. Joy Ctr.), Mt. Joy, 717-653-2048

■ "The chicken and beef are good" at this family-style spot that's "like having dinner at mom's", thanks to "sociable" owners and a "warm, friendly" staff; a few nostalgic types gripe that it's "not like the old days" before the 18-hole golf course was built.

Haydn Zug's 22 | 21 | 20 | $31

1987 State St. (Rte. 72), East Petersburg, 717-569-5746

■ A "solid value" American in East Petersburg that's a "wonderful find"; there's a "homey" atmosphere, "accommodating" service and an award-winning wine list.

Historic Revere Tavern [S] ▽ 19 | 20 | 19 | $28

3063 Lincoln Hwy. E. (Rte. 896), Paradise, 717-687-8601

◪ Seven fireplaces contribute to the "charming" atmosphere at this Traditional American outside of Lancaster, once owned by President James Buchanan and later an old stagecoach stop; the old-time menu includes a 40-ounce porterhouse for two and snapper soup.

Hoss's Steak & Sea House [S] 17 | 15 | 18 | $16

1693 Oregon Pike (Rte. 30), Lancaster, 717-393-9788

■ Diners suggest this Lancaster steakhouse "when you're really hungry" because of the "good old American" AYCE buffet; the "plain" food's "not gourmet", but it's "a bargain."

Isaac's Restaurant & Deli <u>21</u> <u>13</u> <u>16</u> <u>$12</u>

Cloister Shopping Ctr., 120 N. Reading Rd. (Rte. 272 N.), Ephrata, 717-733-7777 S

Central Mkt. Mall, 44 N. Queen St. (King St.), Lancaster, 717-394-5544

Granite Run Sq., 1559 Manheim Pike (Rte. 72 N.), Lancaster, 717-560-7774 S

Sycamore Ct., 245 Centerville Rd. (Rte. 30 W.), Lancaster, 717-393-1199 S

Shoppes at Greenfield, 555 Greenfield Rd. (Rte. 30 E.), Lancaster, 717-393-6067 S

Shops at Traintown, Rte. 741 E., Strasburg, 717-687-7699 S

◪ The "many choices" of "yummy" grilled sandwiches are the attraction at this American deli chain, a "fun", "casual" place that's "great for the kids."

JOE'S BISTRO 614 (CLOSED) <u>23</u> <u>19</u> <u>21</u> <u>$35</u>

614 Penn Ave. (bet. 5th & 6th Sts.), Reading, 610-371-9966

◪ While ratings remain strong at this "charming" West Reading American bistro, surveyors are on the fence about the new ownership; some say it's "still worthwhile", with a "lovely environment" and "delicious" food that can even "make a bad outlet shopping day worthwhile"; dissenters insist it's "not the same" since Jack (also once the owner of the "legendary", but now closed, Joe's) "moved on."

Lemon Grass Thai <u>21</u> <u>16</u> <u>19</u> <u>$22</u>

2481 Lincoln Hwy. E. (Rte. 30W), Lancaster, 717-295-1621

See review in Philadelphia directory.

LOG CABIN S <u>26</u> <u>24</u> <u>25</u> <u>$36</u>

11 Lehoy Forest Dr. (Rte. 272), Leola, 717-626-1181

■ For "an old-fashioned, grand dining experience" on a "romantic special occasion", head to this "intimate" Traditional American in a former speakeasy north of Lancaster; since it's known for serving up "delicious beef", "vegetarians beware!"

MARKET FARE RESTAURANT S <u>24</u> <u>20</u> <u>20</u> <u>$31</u>

50 W. Grant St. (Market St.), Lancaster, 717-299-7090

■ When "visiting Downtown Lancaster", this cigar-friendly New American is a "surprise" for "very good" edibles; brunch is the specialty.

Miller's Smorgasbord S <u>18</u> <u>16</u> <u>18</u> <u>$20</u>

2811 Lincoln Hwy. E. (2 mi. east of Rtes. 30 & 896), Ronks, 717-687-6621

■ There are "tons of various dishes" on the "classic smorgasbord" of this "always packed" Pennsylvania Dutch stop east of Lancaster with a "commissary style" set-up ideal for families and "tour buses"; some think "good in quantity, fair in quality."

Moselem Springs Inn 🅂   17 | 18 | 17 | $28
Rtes. 222 & 662, Fleetwood, 610-944-8213
◪ This Pennsylvania Dutch landmark in Berks is a "nice Sunday dinner place" that's "perfect for Grandma", although some find the food "bland"; the on-premises smokehouse means you should expect a lot of dishes made with sausage and ham.

Nav Jiwan International Tea Room   – | – | – | I
240 N. Reading Rd. (bet. Martin Ave. & Trout Run Rd.), Ephrata, 717-721-8418
There's a different cuisine every week at this Lancaster County International with a "great chef who knows how to cook everything"; at a minimum it offers a "break from Pennsylvania Dutch food"; N.B. it's lunch-only on weekdays, with dinner also offered on Friday.

Olde Greenfield Inn 🅂   22 | 22 | 20 | $27
595 Greenfield Rd. (William Penn Way), Lancaster, 717-393-0668
■ Dining in "the wine room makes the night" at this "peaceful" Traditional American with "attentive service"; overall, "another Lancaster discovery – delightful."

Plain & Fancy Farm 🅂   17 | 13 | 18 | $17
3121 Olde Philadelphia Pike (2 mi. west of Rte. 340), Bird-In-Hand, 717-768-4400
■ "All plain, no fancy" is the verdict on this Pennsylvania Dutch spot serving "huge helpings of bread, fruit and fried chicken" family style – "pass the mashed potatoes."

Red Caboose 🅂   ▽ 15 | 18 | 17 | $18
Paradise Ln. (Rte. 741), Strasburg, 717-687-5001
■ "A favorite place for kids and the young at heart", this casual Pennsylvania Dutch–Traditional American is set up in two cars of an old train in Strasburg; most consider the "very Lancaster" food "ok" but think the "service and setting are better" ("the caboose made the experience").

Restaurant at Doneckers   23 | 23 | 22 | $35
318-409 N. State St. (Walnut St.), Ephrata, 717-738-9501
■ "Part of the Doneckers store complex" (which offers "superb shopping"), this "stylish" New French makes "a neat day trip from Philadelphia" for "very good", if "trendy", food; "it may be the only fine dining in the area", so consider it as "a place to take visitors for lunch."

Stockyard Inn   20 | 16 | 17 | $29
1147 Lititz Pike (Rtes. 222 & 501), Lancaster, 717-394-7975
■ "A throwback to an earlier time", this Lancaster Traditional American (where "beef is No. 1") has "hearty food" but "plain decor"; some think the grub's "not what it used to be."

Stoltzfus Farm ▽ | 23 | 14 | 24 | $17 |
3716-A E. Newport Rd. (Rte. 772), Intercourse, 717-768-8156
■ "Grandma loves" this AYCE Pennsylvania Dutchery
down on the farm in Intercourse where "simple and
simply delicious" "homey" vittles are the order of the day;
N.B. closed January–March.

Stoudt's Black Angus S | 19 | 19 | 19 | $29 |
Rte. 272, Adamstown, 717-484-4386
☑ "The beer brewed on premises is sublime", as is the
"beautiful antique Packard", at this Traditional American
in Adamstown that's convenient before antiquing; some
say "great meat, good all-around meal", while others
grouse the grub's "plain" and "disappointing."

Willow Valley Resort | 17 | 15 | 17 | $19 |
Family Restaurant S
*Willow Valley Resort, 2416 Willow St. Pike (Rte. 222),
Lancaster, 717-464-2711*
■ "You'll overeat at the buffet" at this Pennsylvania Dutch
stop in Lancaster with "polite" staff and a "lovely view
of the pond"; "bus trippers and retirees" find it a "good
value" for lunch.

Windmill S | 20 | 15 | 20 | $14 |
Rtes. 10 & 23, Morgantown, 610-286-5980
■ A "hilarious lighted windmill" beckons hungry travelers
to this Route 23 chow house with "hearty" ("try the corn
chowder") "all-American and Pennsylvania Dutch food"
and a take-out ice cream bar; servers "go out of their way
to make sure you're pleased."

Zinn's Diner S | 16 | 11 | 18 | $14 |
Rte. 272 (Pennsylvania Tpke., exit 21), Denver, 717-336-1774
☑ "Obnoxious billboards lead you" to this traditional
Amish diner on Route 272, known as "Lancaster County's
eating institution" for "plentiful", "cheap", "starch-o-ganza"
food that's fine "if you want to look like Big Amos", the
20-foot Amish man outside; but sniping aside, be ready for
"long lines in summer."

Atlantic City/Cape May

Top Food
27 Le Palais
Washington Inn
26 410 Bank Street
White House
Capriccio

Top Service
27 Le Palais
26 Washington Inn
25 Medici
24 Capriccio
Brighton Steakhouse

Top Decor
27 Le Palais
26 Capriccio
Ram's Head Inn
Washington Inn
25 Medici

Top Value
White House
Green Cuisine
Tony's Baltimore
Little Saigon
Planet Hollywood

F | D | S | C

A Ca Mia [S] ▽ 22 | 15 | 20 | $29
524 Washington Mall (Ocean St.), Cape May, 609-884-6661
◪ While not well known, this Cape May Northern Italian yearling's decent scores back up those who call it a "solid touch in a gorgeous town", with praise for the "impressive food presentation, interesting menu" and "great service"; although a few growl it's an "overpriced disappointment", its convenient mall setting is another reason to give it a try.

A.C. Station Steakhouse [S] ▽ 18 | 17 | 17 | $30
Tropicana, Boardwalk & Brighton Ave. (2nd fl., South Tower), AC, 609-340-4050
■ Recently reopened after a post-*Survey* renovation, Tropicana's paean to beef also offers mesquite-grilled chicken and seafood; if past comments are any indication, it's not bad as "casino fare" goes, and has a "nice view."

Aleathea's [S] 21 | 20 | 20 | $29
Inn of Cape May, 601 Beach Dr. (Ocean Dr.), Cape May, 609-884-5555
◪ It's "romantic Cape May at its best" when you "eat on the porch" of this seasonal beachside American; while comments center on the "outstanding atmosphere", the food rating indicates the vittles must be quite "good" as well.

Alexander's Inn [S] 25 | 24 | 23 | $37
653 Washington St. (bet. Franklin St. & Ocean Dr.), Cape May, 609-884-2555
■ It's hard not to "love the service with waiters wearing white gloves" at this Cape May Continental that's an "elegant escape" and "step back in time" ("lovely Victorian decor"); there's a "great Sunday brunch" and "BYO helps alleviate the cost."

Alfe's ◐ [S] ▽ 25 | 19 | 23 | $29

3401 New Jersey Ave. (Oak St.), Wildwood, 609-729-5755

■ Despite "stereotypical" decor and music ("Sinatra's always on"), Zagateurs are "pleasantly surprised" at the "good food" and "reasonable prices" at this "homestyle" Italian in Wildwood; try the "quiet" patio in warm weather.

Andreotti's [S] ▽ 23 | 22 | 23 | $43

Harrah's, 777 Harrah's Blvd. (Illinois Ave.), AC, 609-441-5576

■ Though surveyors have little to say about this Italian in Harrah's, it's generally regarded as a solid choice with "large portions" of "very good food"; a strolling guitarist contributes to the atmosphere.

Angeloni's II ◐ [S] 17 | 13 | 17 | $25

2400 Arctic Ave. (Georgia Ave.), AC, 609-344-7875

◩ The award-winning wine list is the draw at this long-standing, waterside "red sauce Italian"; overall, reactions range from "always reliable" to "nothing special, except some of the clientele."

Angelo's Fairmount Tavern [S] 20 | 13 | 18 | $23

2300 Fairmount Ave. (Mississippi Ave.), AC, 609-344-2439

■ This "noisy", traditional Italian "institution" in an iffy part of AC (give "your car to the attendant") is "as honest as they come" for "consistent", "stick-to-the-ribs" food, "reasonable prices" and outstanding "homemade wine."

A Touch of Italy [S] 19 | 17 | 19 | $24

6629 Black Horse Pike (bet. Hamilton & Shore Malls), Cardiff, 609-646-1855

■ An inland "family" Italian on Black Horse Pike with a "large menu" and "large portions"; the "heavy" food's "not gourmet" but certainly "decent"; a few nostalgists still pine for the old place in Pleasantville.

Axelsson's Blue Claw [S] 21 | 19 | 20 | $33

991 Ocean Dr. (Wildwood Crest Toll Bridge), Cape May, 609-884-5878

◩ This "dependable", year-round, family-run Cape May stop at the foot of the Wildwood Crest toll bridge is "packed in the summer" with diners chowing down on "very good", if a tad "overpriced", seafood; N.B. they removed the piano.

Brighton Steakhouse [S] 23 | 23 | 24 | $40

Sands Hotel & Casino, Brighton Park & Indiana Ave., AC, 609-441-4300

◩ The Sands' steakhouse gets strong ratings across the board, especially for the "excellent" namesake entrees and the "superb" Sunday brunch; though high rollers note that "without an entertainment book or a comp", "prices are out of sight."

Brittany Cafe S ⊘   23 | 8 | 20 | $27
4313 Ventnor Ave. (Delancey St.), AC, 609-348-8741
■ "Cult patrons" ("named my daughter after the joint") of this "innovative" Continental–coffee shop laud the "great food", but the uninitiated find it "too cramped to pay the cost for dinner."

Busch's S   20 | 15 | 18 | $30
8700 Landis Ave. (87th St.), Sea Isle City, 609-263-8626
◪ A "popular", family-owned Shore seafooder with the "best she-crab soup ever" and "huge portions" ("share a platter"); dissenters moan about "too much fried food" and say it's "living on its reputation."

Cafe 8 South S   21 | 10 | 18 | $30
8 S. Essex Ave. (bet. Atlantic & Ventnor Aves.), Margate, 609-822-6363
■ The "young chef" at this BYO Continental in Margate "looks 12 years old but cooks like he's had 100 years of experience"; reviewers say there's "lots of nicely prepared fish" and the prix fixe and early-bird meals are a "good value"; on the downside the "atmosphere's claustrophobic" and "you're still eating in the Downbeach deli."

California Pizza Kitchen (CLOSED)   19 | 16 | 18 | $17
Resorts Casino Hotel, 1133 Boardwalk (North Carolina Ave.), AC, 609-340-8820
■ The pizza topping combos may be "a bit off the wall", but this "innovative" chain "off the casino floor" in Resorts is a "pleasant snack spot" "in the land of buffets"; the "cheerful" ambiance and "ocean view" outweigh "sluggish" service.

Camelot S   22 | 22 | 23 | $41
Resorts Casino Hotel, Boardwalk & North Carolina Ave., AC, 609-340-6450
■ A highly-rated casino steakhouse in Resorts with "nice strolling" guitarists, "excellent food" and ambiance; some are "surprised to find this setting within a casino."

CAPRICCIO S   26 | 26 | 24 | $42
Resorts Casino Hotel, Boardwalk & North Carolina Ave., AC, 609-340-6789
■ "Watch for the high-stakes characters" soaking up the "delicious" food, "super service" and Boardwalk views at this "classy" Italian in Resorts; perhaps they're the same patrons who sometimes "sing with the roving musician" who strolls through the "beautiful surroundings."

Caruso's ◗ S   23 | 25 | 21 | $44
Hilton, Boardwalk & Boston Ave. (Pacific Ave.), AC, 609-340-7400
■ Even with terrific ratings, this "romantic" Italian at the AC Hilton may be "underappreciated"; it's "pretty in a glitzy way", has "exceptional service" and "very good" food, but like its casino competitors it's "outrageously expensive."

Casa DiNapoli [S] – – – E

Showboat Hotel Casino, 801 Boardwalk (Delaware Ave.), AC, 609-343-4000

A Showboat Italian with Gothic-Byzantine decor and "great antipasti and appetizers"; those not getting comped like to take advantage of the three-course dinner for $35.

Casa Nicola [S] – – – E

Trump Taj Mahal, 1000 Boardwalk (Virginia Ave.), AC, 609-449-1000

Formerly Marco Polo, this big-ticket Italian in the Taj has a large menu of pasta, meat ("terrific veal chops") and fish entrees, plus pizzas baked in a wood-burning oven.

Cedar Creek Brewery [S] – – – M

236 Philadelphia Ave. (opp. Post Office), Egg Harbor City, 609-965-6367

A fun Egg Harbor City brewpub with "excellent" unusual beers and a "small menu" of pub grub that's "better than expected" ("great beer-battered onions").

Center Point Deli [S] 14 8 12 $14

Flamingo Motel, 3105 Pacific Ave. (bet. Chelsea & Montpelier), AC, 609-347-5000

Dave's Center Point Rest. [S]

World Gym Shopping Ctr., Cresson Ave. & Tilton Rd., Northfield, 609-641-2000

◪ They might not "compare to New York's Carnegie", but these "bright" nosheries serving "basic" "bagel and lox bargains" are "all right", though they can be too "sterile."

Charlie's Bar & Restaurant ◐ [S] ⊄ 18 12 15 $20

800 Shore Rd. (bet. Delaware & New Jersey Aves.), Somers Point, 609-927-3663

■ The "corner bar atmosphere" seems to work just right at this "crowded and noisy" Somers Point Traditional American where a "good mix of people" recommend the burgers, chowder, "best wings" and "Wes' special sandwich."

Chef Vola's [S] ⊄ 24 11 23 $39

111 S. Albion Pl. (Pacific Ave.), AC, 609-345-2022

◪ "You practically have to submit a resume" to get a reservation at this Italian BYO in the "cramped" "basement of an old house" in Atlantic City; most find the Espositos' home cooking "superb" and say you'll take home a "shopping bag full of leftovers"; negativists insist it "thrives on its mystique of inaccessibility"; N.B. bring cash.

China Moon [S] ▽ 20 20 20 $33

Sands Hotel & Casino, Brighton Park & Indiana Ave., AC, 609-441-4300

■ The Sands take on Chinese is "good", especially with a new chef from Hong Kong, but try to "win at the tables before you get the bill"; the nifty decor and snazzy looking waiters mean this place won't be confused with Chinatown.

Cousins Country House S
19 | 22 | 19 | $31

3373 Bargain Town Rd. (bet. Fire & Zion Rds.), Egg Harbor Township, 609-927-5777

■ While this "old-fashioned" Continental might be "a ride from the beach" in Egg Harbor Township, the "crowds" manage to make the trek; its popularity is due to the 150-year-old farmhouse setting, "enjoyable", "creative" food in "large portions" and a soothing piano bar; the less-enthused say "nothing special" but "better than most in the AC area."

Cousin's Restaurant S
20 | 14 | 19 | $26

104 Asbury Ave. (1st Ave.), Ocean City, 609-399-9462

◪ This "family-oriented" Ocean City Italian seafooder compensates for a "low ceiling" ("if over six feet, don't straighten up") and "uncomfortable" chairs with "extra-rich" food at "reasonable prices"; try the "good early bird."

Crab Trap S
20 | 16 | 18 | $25

Circle (May's Landing Rd.), Somers Point, 609-927-7377

◪ "Blue-haired" afish-ionados and families say prepare to "wait" at this Somers Point landmark known for "large helpings" of "basic" but "excellent seafood"; for the full effect, "wear old clothes, roll up your sleeves" and "dig in to crabs and a pitcher of beer."

Cucina Rosa S
21 | 18 | 20 | $26

Washington St. Mall, 301 Washington St. Mall (Perry St.), Cape May, 609-898-9800

■ "Make reservations or you'll never get into", or sit outside of ("limited outdoor seating"), this Cape May Italian BYO with "above-average" food, including "always good" veal; once seated, patrons "always feel welcome."

Cucina Rustica S
23 | 19 | 21 | $31

9407 Ventnor Ave. (bet. Adams & Jefferson Aves.), Margate, 609-823-2700

■ "A welcome addition" and "Margate's answer to good food" reflect the chorus of approval for this new BYO International-Italian in a "crowded, noisy, anything but rustic" setting; it's already being viewed as "one of the few shore restaurants with Philadelphia quality" cuisine.

Culinary Garden, The S
18 | 16 | 18 | $22

841 Central Ave. (9th St.), Ocean City, 609-399-3713

■ Closed November–February, this Ocean City New American offers a "great brunch" and "good breakfast" ("delicious corned beef hash"), though surveyors are silent on dinner; winos beware, Ocean City is dry.

Deauville Inn S
15 | 16 | 15 | $25

201 Willard Rd. (Ocean Dr.), Strathmere, 609-263-2080

◪ This Strathmere Continental, with a "great" deck and view, is "better known for its entertainment and waterside bar" than its "adequate" food; if looking to dine, critics say "stick with sandwiches."

Dock's Oyster House [S] 20 17 19 $31
2405 Atlantic Ave. (Georgia Ave.), AC, 609-345-0092
◪ A "crowded", "mom-and-pop", AC seafooder/steakhouse with "a lot of history" (circa 1897), a pleasant piano bar and a large selection of "quality" ocean edibles, including the "best oyster stew"; nonetheless, a contingent still feels it's "not as good as yesteryear."

Doc's Place [S] 18 18 19 $29
646 Bay Ave. (on the Marina), Somers Point, 609-926-0404
◪ "The pleasant owner is always there" at this seasonal Somers Point American seafooder, a "shore favorite" for its "very nice outdoor deck" ("wonderful place for a small party") and Sunday brunch.

Dry Dock Ice Cream Bar & Grille [S] 💳̸ – – – I
1440 Texas Ave. (Pittsburgh Ave.), Cape May, 609-884-3434
This "friendly" little American fast-fooder with table seating is a local secret for inexpensive, "imaginative lunches and light meals"; "owner-run" by the former proprietors of the Manor House, its highlights include "great cheese steaks", grilled veggie sandwiches and a child's fantasy selection of ice cream and toppings.

Ebbitt Room [S] 26 25 23 $44
Virginia Hotel, 25 Jackson St. (bet. Beach Dr. & Carpenter's Ln.), Cape May, 609-884-4358
■ Still one of the "best of Cape May" is the line on this "destination" for "inventive" New American cuisine using "local produce" as part of a seasonally changing menu; the "beautiful" Victorian hotel is "very romantic", and, as always, "Stevie LaManna is wonderful on the piano."

Fantasea Reef Buffet [S] ▽ 18 24 20 $19
Harrah's, 777 Harrah's Blvd., AC, 609-441-5576
■ As casino buffets go, this "well-organized" spread at Harrah's might be the "best bargain in AC"; the regular menu has a "bountiful" selection of International and seafood dishes, and the "gorgeous, beneath-the-sea" room contains an aquarium.

Fedeli's [S] 14 11 14 $24
9403 Ventnor Ave. (Adams Ave.), Margate, 609-822-1293
◪ "You have to know what to order" at this Margate Italian known for "big portions" of "ok" food; some find it "lost in the '50s."

Fork's Inn [S] ▽ 19 26 19 $32
4800 Pleasant Mills Rd. (Rte. 542), Sweetwater, 609-567-8889
■ This Sweetwater New American in an 18th-century privateers inn has a "beautiful" (and newly enlarged) waterside patio that makes a "nice spot for a summer evening meal" or Sunday brunch; while there may be "some rough spots", it's "so pretty that it's worth the trip."

Fortune's S   – | – | – | E
Trump Plaza, Boardwalk & Mississippi Ave., AC, 609-441-6000
"The window tables have great views of the ocean" at
this Trump Plaza Chinese, where "yummy" seafood goes
directly from tank to table; N.B. like most high-end AC
restaurants, it's open for dinner only.

410 BANK STREET S   26 | 20 | 23 | $39
410 Bank St. (Lafayette St.), Cape May, 609-884-2127
■ A "convivial", if "cramped", Cape May Eclectic BYO
that gets tons of votes as "the best restaurant on the
shore" thanks to "excellent", "creative" Cajun-Creole-
Caribbean combinations ("incredible sauces"); service is
"nifty", and the only real quibble is that the waits are "too
long, even with reservations."

Freda's Cafe S⊅   24 | 16 | 21 | $31
210 Ocean St. (Carpenter's Ln.), Cape May, 609-884-7887
■ "The best deal is lunch" at this "cute" bistro in Cape
May with "tasty", "imaginative" International food that
makes fans forget the "simple" surroundings and tables
too "close together"; BYO helps keep it affordable.

Frescos S   24 | 20 | 22 | $34
412 Bank St. (Lafayette St.), Cape May, 609-884-0366
■ This upscale, "just as good" sister to 410 Bank Street,
located in a restored Victorian cottage, is a contender for
"best Italian at the shore"; expect "great service" and
excellent food, though, as you might also expect, "long lines."

Gary's Little   24 | 15 | 20 | $32
Rock Cafe S (CLOSED)
*5214 Atlantic Ave. (bet. Little Rock & Weymouth Aves.),
Ventnor, 609-823-2233*
■ It's "hard to get a reservation", there are "long waits" and
it's "cramped" and "too noisy", but this Ventor Eclectic BYO
continues to reign as one of the "best noncasino restaurants
on the island", with an "inspired", "creative menu" packed
with "amazing flavors – try the warm duck salad."

Girasole S   21 | 19 | 18 | $36
*Ocean Club Condos, 3108 Pacific Ave. (bet. Bally's Grand
& Tropicana), AC, 609-345-5554*
■ "People-watchers" congregate over "innovative pizzas"
at this "beautifully decorated" AC Ocean Club Condos
Italian; a shore branch of the Philadelphia favorite, it's a
standout for "casual elegance in a place known for glitz."

Golden Inn S   15 | 16 | 17 | $28
Dune Dr. & 78th St., Avalon, 609-368-5155
◪ Critics say the "average age of diners is 80" ("should
be called golden oldies") at this Avalon inn with a "great
location", but "plain" seafood and a "worn" environment.

Green Cuisine S🗗   23 14 18 $13
302 96th St. (3rd Ave.), Stone Harbor, 609-368-1616
■ There are "no corn dogs" served at this "unshorelike" Stone Harbor health fooder, where "giant-sized portions" of "great salads" and "creative soups" and sandwiches are served by "always courteous yuppies"; it's a rare combination of being "so good, and good for you."

Gregory's ◖S   15 11 15 $22
900 Shore Rd. (Delaware Ave.), Somers Point, 609-927-6665
■ "Typical bar fare with a crowd to match" is the analysis of this Somers Point Eclectic with a menu ranging from Jersey Shore seafood ("great soft-shell crabs") to Mexican.

Hard Rock Cafe ◖S   14 19 16 $22
Trump Taj Mahal, 1000 Boardwalk (Virginia Ave.), AC, 609-441-0007
☑ "Go for the shirts, not the food" is the familiar refrain about this "fun" Taj Mahal outpost of the "trendy" chain that serves Traditional American eats in a memorabilia-laden atmosphere; the star-struck enjoy the burgers and the "interesting stuff" on the walls, while critics croon "been there, done that."

Hatteras Coastal Cuisine S   20 19 15 $34
801 Bay Ave. (New Jersey Ave.), Somers Point, 609-926-3326
☑ Surveyors appreciate the "good", "creative" New American food (especially the "great prix fixe dinners") at this waterside BYO "hideaway" in Somers Point; however, complaints about the service, ranging from problems with reservations to staff "attitude", hold down this rating.

Henny's S   16 13 17 $25
9626 Third Ave. (Garden State Pkwy., exit 10), Stone Harbor, 609-368-2929
☑ This "crowded" "blast from the past" in Stone Harbor is a "consistent", "family-style" seafooder with "big portions" and "delicious crab cakes"; modernists complain that the preparation style "hasn't changed since I was a teenager."

Il Verdi   ▽ 26 25 26 $53
Tropicana, Boardwalk & Brighton Ave., AC, 609-340-4070
■ A "beautifully appointed" Italian in the Tropicana with "excellent food" and "great European service" from a "meticulous, dedicated" staff.

Inn at Sugar Hill S   22 24 22 $34
Inn at Sugar Hill, 5704 Mays Landing-Somers Point Rd. (Rtes. 40 W. & 559), Mays Landing, 609-625-2226
■ "Great porch dining" in warm weather makes this waterside American-Continental in Mays Landing a sweet choice for a "romantic" evening; the "innovative" menu changes seasonally and the rendezvous package (dinner for two, lodging and continental breakfast for $65 above the room rate) is a deal.

Jackson Mountain Cafe S   13 | 10 | 14 | $18
Washington St. Mall, 400 Jackson St., Cape May,
609-884-5648
■ While not the highest-rated joint in Cape May, this pub
in the Washington Street Mall is fine for "sitting outside
and watching shoppers go by" while chowing down on
"reliable" burgers and chugging beers.

Joe Italiano's Maplewood Inn S   22 | 11 | 19 | $23
470 White Horse Pike (Rte. 30), Hammonton, 609-561-9621
■ "Garlic lovers" stop at this "homespun" Hammonton
Italian (when heading "to or from Atlantic City") for "simple
but fabulous" "giant portions of pasta and salad"; so what if
there's "no atmosphere"? – the staff calls everyone "hon."

Joe Italiano's Maplewood II S   23 | 11 | 20 | $23
6126 Black Horse Pike (Rte. 322), Mays Landing,
609-625-3923
■ This "no-frills" "spaghetti house" on the "way to the
shore" in Mays Landing is a "winner" for "fabulous",
"reasonably priced" "good gravy" Italian amidst a "fun",
carefree atmosphere; like it's sibling, it "gets really crowded
in the summer" and "you will take home half" your portion.

Johan's (CLOSED)   20 | 16 | 21 | $34
1200 Atlantic Ave. (North Carolina Ave.), AC, 609-441-1200
■ Chef Johan Vroegop continues to impress patrons of
his American–Classic French BYO in AC, whipping up
"fabulous food" in an "interesting setting"; while service
is "attentive", the lack of parking can be a drawback.

LE PALAIS S   27 | 27 | 27 | $47
Resorts Casino Hotel, Boardwalk & North Carolina Ave.,
AC, 609-340-6400
■ Merv's really cooking at his "gorgeous", classy New
French at Resorts, where "exquisite", "luscious" food
("best foie gras and chocolate soufflé") and an "elegant"
ambiance are complemented by an "outstanding" staff that
"treats you royally every time"; Sunday brunch is "beautiful."

Little Brat's Haus S   – | – | – | M
615 E. Moss Mill Rd. (Rte. 9), Smithville, 609-652-9377
An "unexpected", "real" German brathaus in sleepy
Smithville with "good food" and reasonable prices; outdoor
dining comes with a view of Lake Meone.

Little Saigon S⊘   23 | 11 | 22 | $20
Arctic & Iowa Aves., AC, 609-347-9119
■ This Vietnamese BYO in AC has finally been "discovered"
as a "wonderful alternative to casino rip-offs" since the
"terrific" food is a "shore bargain" – "little in name,
grand in quality."

Lobster House 🅂   21 | 18 | 19 | $30
Fisherman's Wharf, Rte. 9 & Schellanger's Landing Rd., Cape May, 609-884-8296
☑ "It wouldn't be summer without a trip" to this "classic" Cape May seafooder at Fisherman's Wharf; diners recommend "sitting outside" and taking in the "scenic marina views" while chowing down on "large portions" of usually "very good" food; detractors insist it's an "overpriced, tourist trap" that's "not worth braving the wait"; some opt for "takeout."

Lobster Loft 🅂   17 | 14 | 15 | $28
318 42nd Pl. (Park Rd.), Sea Isle City, 609-263-3000
■ "If you can stand the din", this "touristy" waterside seafooder in Sea Isle City is a "decent" choice for "good lobsters" or fried shrimp.

Los Amigos 🌙🅂   15 | 11 | 18 | $19
1926 Atlantic Ave. (bet. Michigan & Ohio Aves.), AC, 609-344-2293
☑ Many surveyors think this "dark" AC Tex-Mex with an "updated" menu is "cheaper and better than the casinos" (and it's open 'til dawn); nevertheless, ratings have slipped in recent years.

Louisa's Cafe ⊄   25 | 16 | 22 | $26
104 Jackson St., Cape May, 609-884-5882
■ Foodies say "don't tell anyone" because it's already very "hard to get a reservation" at this BYO seafooder in Cape May, a "wonderful little hole-in-the-wall" with "lovingly prepared food" ("try the crab cakes"); prepare to make new friends, as "close seating leads to congeniality."

Mac's 🅂   18 | 15 | 19 | $28
908 Shore Rd. (Somers Point Circle), Somers Point, 609-927-2759
☑ This "plain Jane" Italian seafooder in Somers Point, owned for over 50 years by the same family, is "consistent, if nothing else", with lots of good crab dishes and a "friendly" staff; negativists say it's "getting by on its reputation."

Mad Batter, The 🅂   22 | 20 | 19 | $27
Carrol Villa Hotel, 19 Jackson St. (bet. Beach Dr. & Lafayette St.), Cape May, 609-884-5970
■ "People-watchers" observe that there's "no better place for a hearty breakfast" ("great French toast" and breads) than the porch of this "relaxed" Eclectic BYO in a Victorian B&B in Cape May; a few are driven mad by the hype and claim it's "overpriced" and "not what it used to be."

Maloney's Beef & Beer 🌙🅂⊄   18 | 12 | 17 | $22
23 S. Washington Ave. (bet. Atlantic & Ventor Aves.), Margate, 609-823-7858
☑ The "great bar crowd" at this Margate pub with "bare walls and full plates" insists it's "more than beef and beer", declaring it a "legendary" "summer fun" stop; dissenters beg to differ, invoking the "typical bar" refrain.

Mama Mia 🅂   23 | 18 | 22 | $28
Cedar Sq. Shopping Ctr., Rte. 9 (Rte. 50), Seaville, 609-624-9322
■ Located on Route 9, this strip mall Italian packs 'em in for "large portions" of "varied" standards that its admirers call the "best for miles around."

Max's Steak House 🅂   ▽ 25 | 25 | 25 | $51
Trump Plaza, Boardwalk & Mississippi Ave., AC, 609-441-6000
■ A "high roller's dream steaks" are offered at this Trump Plaza surf 'n' turfer, showcasing a "comfortable" ambiance that's perfect for a "break" before heading back to the tables.

Medici   24 | 25 | 25 | $44
Sands Hotel & Casino, Brighton Park & Indiana Ave., AC, 609-441-4300
■ This Sands high-end Italian offers one of AC's lovelier rooms, with superb food and dazzling ocean view, though you might hanker for a comp to foot the tab.

Melissa's Bistro 🅂   23 | 14 | 18 | $34
9307 Ventnor Ave. (bet. Decatur & Washington Aves.), Margate, 609-823-1414
■ In high season, this Margate BYO New American is packed with diners tolerating a "too cramped" and "incredibly noisy" setting for "creative", "consistently excellent food"; while it's "becoming an old standby", it's "better off-season" when things calm down; P.S. Melissa's daughter makes all the desserts.

Merion Inn 🅂   21 | 21 | 20 | $32
106 Decatur St. (Columbus Ave.), Cape May, 609-884-8363
◪ Dating back to 1885, this "quiet" bit of the "Main Line in Cape May" features a "great bar" and solid American-Continental fare amidst "comfortable" dining rooms; some claim it's "seen better days."

Mirage, The 🅂   ▽ 17 | 16 | 16 | $27
79th St. & 3rd Ave., Avalon, 609-368-1919
■ A seasonal, "friendly" Avalon Continental seafooder that's "a great value for its early bird" and weekend piano music.

Mississippi Steak & Seafood Co. 🅂   – | – | – | E
Showboat Hotel Casino, 801 Boardwalk (Delaware Ave.), AC, 609-343-4000
Surveyors don't have much to say about this seafooder/steakhouse, but it gets a generally good response, is appropriately showy (this is the Showboat, after all) and the pianist in season sets the right tone.

Oaks, The ⬤🅂   ▽ 20 | 22 | 20 | $43
Hilton, Boardwalk & Boston Ave. (Pacific Ave.), AC, 609-340-7400
■ The "salad bar is gone but the food is still good" at Hilton's seafooder/steakhouse, serving dinner only amidst English tavern decor.

Obadiah's S · 17 | 15 | 17 | $28
321 Roosevelt Blvd. (Garden State Pkwy., exit 25), Marmora, 609-390-3574
☑ Expect "average Jersey shore fare" and "long waits" at this Marmora seafooder/steakhouse with Buster the crab perched invitingly on the roof; while some claim it's still a "good Friday night seafood and beer place", others think it's "something of a tourist trap" that's "resting on its past."

Oceanfront Restaurant and Lounge S · ▽ 18 | 19 | 20 | $30
1400 Ocean Ave. (14th St.), Brigantine, 609-266-7731
■ "Ask for a window seat and watch the sunset" at this warm and casual Eclectic on the beach in Brigantine; the "soup and salad bar are a meal unto themselves."

Official All Star Cafe ◑S · ▽ 16 | 19 | 17 | $25
Trump Taj Mahal, 1000 Boardwalk (Virginia Ave.), AC, 609-347-8326
☑ This Hard Rock Cafe–like, sports-theme restaurant in the Taj Mahal has an "informative" staff and food that's "ok, if you're hungry" and looking to catch a game with the kids ("gotta love those TVs"); as with most themeries, it's "way too loud" for some.

Old Waterway Inn S · 18 | 18 | 18 | $32
1700 W. Riverside Dr. (Rte. 30), AC, 609-347-1793
☑ "Sit on the deck in season" when visiting this "serene" Continental with a "beautiful view" overlooking AC; the food and service are "usually good", though not as consistent as the vista.

Orsatti's · 18 | 16 | 18 | $28
22-24 S. North Carolina Ave. (bet. Atlantic & Pacific Aves.), AC, 609-340-8557
☑ The "gracious" "Mr. O himself watches over" this legendary Italian in AC, which some regard as a "friendly, classy" favorite with the "best pasta anywhere"; critics call it "sometimes good, sometimes not" and a "mere shadow" of its former self.

Peaches at Sunset S · 22 | 22 | 22 | $34
1 Sunset Blvd. (Broadway), West Cape May, 609-898-0100
■ "A little BYO gem that tries hard to please" is the consensus on this "very reliable", year-round Californian-Thai in West Cape May; expect "charming" decor, a "nice porch", an "orgasmic" garlic Gilroy and "the best veal"; P.S. don't miss "nice early-bird prices."

Peregrines S · ▽ 26 | 27 | 24 | $67
Hilton, Boardwalk & Boston Ave. (Pacific Ave.), AC, 609-340-7400
■ This Hilton New American has "exquisite", "first-class" food, "top-notch" service and a "great wine selection"; while the five-course tasting menu is $60 ($90 with wine), for some it's "the only place in AC worth the price."

Peter Shields 🅂   22 | 24 | 22 | $37
1301 Beach Dr. (Trenton Dr.), Cape May, 609-884-9090
■ There's "a great ocean view from the porch" of this BYO "anniversary spot" in a "stately" Cape May mansion; toss in "large portions" of "excellent" Eclectic fare "served very elegantly" and it's "another one vying for my favorite."

Pier 7   ▽ 27 | 18 | 24 | $35
Tropicana, Boardwalk & Brighton Ave., AC, 609-340-4090
■ This casual Tropicana fish house, while not the biggest draw in AC, is one of the "best casino seafood restaurants"; though the "food is wonderful, especially the soups", the location "needs an ocean view" to match the menu.

Pilot House ◑🅂   14 | 13 | 16 | $23
142 Decatur St. (Carpenter's Ln.), Cape May, 609-884-3449
■ Your "basic shore place" turning out hot roast beef sandwiches, burgers and other pub grub for a "swinging" Cape May crowd, especially on Fridays at happy hour.

Planet Hollywood ◑🅂   15 | 21 | 17 | $20
Caesars, 2100 Pacific Ave. (Boardwalk), AC, 609-347-7827
◪ Fans love the "trendy" "glitz" at this AC outpost of the Hollywood themer off the Caesars lobby; though there are "no surprises" and only "decent" American food, admirers give four stars to ogling the "cool movie props" and buying souvenirs; "if you don't want a hearing loss, stay out."

Portofino   ▽ 24 | 25 | 23 | $44
Trump Marina, Brigantine & Huron Aves., AC, 609-441-8342
■ "Exceptionally classy" Italian in Trump Marina with food that "melts in your mouth"; the strolling guitars and violins play off the outstanding "view overlooking the ocean."

Primavera 🅂   ▽ 24 | 21 | 21 | $35
Caesars, 2100 Pacific Ave. (Arkansas Ave.), AC, 609-348-4411
■ "You almost forget you're in a casino" at this Italian in Caesars, enjoying a bump in ratings since our last *Survey*; there's "awesome food" in a "comfortable" atmosphere, and the 11 PM seating suits night owls.

Prime Place 🅂   ▽ 27 | 26 | 25 | $44
Bally's Park Pl., Boardwalk & Park Pl., AC, 609-340-2350
■ It's prime all right, is the line on this Bally's steakhouse that satisfies carnivores with top-notch beef and a winning salad bar and Sunday brunch; the "classy decor" (20-foot high picture windows) is augmented by a harpist.

Ram's Head Inn 🅂   23 | 26 | 23 | $40
9 W. White Horse Pike (Garden State Pkwy. & Rte. 30), Absecon, 609-652-1700
■ A "favorite for many years", this "good place to spend an entire evening" is an "old-fashioned, dressy" American in Absecon that "continues to hold its own" with "superb" food, "elegant" atmospherics and "fine" service.

Ravioli House [S] ▽ 23 | 14 | 17 | $18
102 E. Bennett Ave. (New Jersey Ave.), Wildwood, 609-522-7894
■ This smoke-free, family-owned Italian in Wildwood is just the thing for excellent pastas "after a day at the beach"; the jury is out on whether it's "reasonable" or "overpriced."

Regent Court [S] – | – | – | E
Tropicana, Boardwalk & Brighton Ave., AC, 609-340-4080
Boosters of this New American in Tropicana insist it has "excellent food" "served appetizingly", "the best brunch" and "elegance far exceeding" the norm, in the form of dark, English manor decor; wallet-watchers hint: "get a comp."

Renault Winery [S] 20 | 23 | 21 | $31
72 N. Breman Ave. (Moss Mill Rd.), Egg Harbor City, 609-965-2111
■ The "very good Sunday brunch" is the favored meal when visiting this Egg Harbor City winery with a Traditional American–Italian menu; a few find that the "lovely vineyard setting" and "pretty restaurant" overshadow the food.

Rio Station ◐ [S] ▽ 15 | 14 | 16 | $25
3505 Rte. 9 S. (Rte. 47), Rio Grande, 609-889-2000
■ Even though it may be "one of the better places in the Wildwood area", this seafooder/steakhouse still receives tepid ratings, suggesting the food is basically "decent"; live music and dancing are the main draws, anyway.

Roberto's [S] ▽ 24 | 26 | 23 | $47
Trump Plaza, Boardwalk & Mississippi Ave., AC, 609-441-6000
■ This long-running Italian in Trump Plaza continues to pull strong ratings all around, especially by brunchers who take in the enormous spread and ocean view.

Sabatini's [S] ▽ 15 | 14 | 15 | $25
2210-14 Pacific Ave. (bet. Caesars & Trump Plaza), AC, 609-345-4816
■ Located between Caesars and Trump Plaza, this relaxing, family-owned AC Southern Italian features an early bird and free buffet bar on football nights.

Safari Steakhouse [S] ▽ 23 | 23 | 22 | $44
Trump Taj Mahal, 1000 Boardwalk (Virginia Ave.), AC, 609-449-1000
■ The jungle motif might strike some as "tacky" (leopard skin–style chairs, faux trees with lights), but the beef and potatoes at this Taj steakhouse are "excellent"; it's another favorite of those with comps.

Savaradio [S] 🚫 25 | 16 | 21 | $30
5223 Ventnor Ave. (Little Rock Ave.), Ventnor, 609-823-2110
■ Just "try to get in" to this Ventnor BYO "gem" during high season when everyone's clamoring for the "delicious", "beautifully served", "cutting-edge" Eclectic food; even if the "comfort level is low", it's "worth going back to again."

Scannicchio's S   14 | 10 | 15 | $27

119 S. California Ave. (bet. Boardwalk & Pacific Ave.), AC, 609-348-6378

☑ Surveyors are split on this AC Italian that touts its homemade pastas and 45 wines; while ratings have plunged, some insist the food is still "ok"; as the decor rating suggests, the basement setting needs work.

Scheherazade S   – | – | – | VE

Trump Taj Mahal, 1000 Boardwalk (Virginia Ave.), AC, 609-449-1000

Most reviewers aren't familiar with this Continental–Classic French in the Taj; the restaurant's view of the casino floor is perfect for gamblers who like to keep one eye on their plates and the other on the tables.

Schooners & C.B.'s Galley ◑S   ▽ 21 | 17 | 21 | $22

Massachusetts Ave. & New Rd., Somers Point, 609-927-1117

■ A "dark", spirited bar and Eclectic restaurant in Somers Point with 24 microbrews, 22 appetizers (the "best clams casino"), live bands and an early-bird special.

Screnci's S   20 | 15 | 19 | $24

6208 Landis Ave. (63rd St.), Sea Isle City, 609-263-2217

☑ "Another after-the-beach must", this "underrated" Sea Isle City BYO Italian has "fried eggplant and a liquored dessert that are worth the trip."

Sea Grill S   19 | 18 | 16 | $27

225 21st St. (bet. Dune & Ocean Drs.), Avalon, 609-967-5511

☑ Tell the chef how you want it done at this "fun" Avalon seafooder/steakhouse where you place your order directly with the kitchen; the "good salad bar" is another example of how "they do a good job for a formula type restaurant."

Spiaggi S (CLOSED)   22 | 20 | 21 | $38

Beach & Decatur Sts., 2nd fl., Cape May, 609-884-3504

☑ While some call this Cape May high flyer's change from Restaurant Maureen "a mistake", others embrace Stephen and Maureen Horn's "imaginative", "well-prepared", "light" Italian creations; the interior's now more colorful and no longer Victorian, and those seeking the same "beautiful beachfront location" can still "sit on the front porch."

Steakhouse, The S   ▽ 25 | 23 | 23 | $43

Harrah's, 777 Harrah's Blvd., AC, 609-441-5575

■ With "great martinis and beef", this steakhouse in Harrah's is an excellent "place to celebrate, if you're winning"; the "piano music" provides a relaxing touch.

Steak House, The S   – | – | – | E

Trump Marina, Brigantine & Huron Aves., AC, 609-441-8355

Both the Frederic Remington–inspired decor and the "very good" beef are riding high at this Trump Marina steakhouse; reservations are a must because hours change monthly.

Sutor's Owl Tree ◖ⓢ   18 | 16 | 18 | $23
2323 New Rd., Northfield, 609-645-0066
■ This Eclectic in Northfield is known for its "loud, smoky" happening happy hour and late-night bar scene on weekends; "reasonable" prices make it a nice choice for lunch as well.

Sweetwater Casino ⓢ   15 | 18 | 18 | $28
2780 Seventh Ave. (Rte. 643), Sweetwater, 609-965-3285
■ Captains suggest that on a sunny afternoon "when you don't know what to do", go by boat up the Mullica River to this Traditional American in a "beautiful setting"; however, while new owners have spruced up the decor, ratings haven't budged and surveyors report the food is still "about average."

Tisha's Fine Dining ⓢ   ▽ 22 | 20 | 16 | $31
714 Beach Dr. (Gurney St.), Cape May, 609-884-9119
■ "Pretty oceanside dining" with a "great view" and a "limited but excellent" Contemporary American–seafood menu mean this Cape May stop "could be fine if service gets it together."

Tomatoes ⓢ   17 | 16 | 16 | $26
9210 Ventnor Ave. (Decatur St.), Margate, 609-822-7535
☑ Picky eaters take note: this Italian-Eclectic BYO in Margate has such a large selection, including brick-oven pizzas, that "if you can't find something to eat there's something wrong."

Tony's Baltimore Grill ◖ⓢ⊄   19 | 9 | 18 | $15
2800 Atlantic Ave. (Iowa Ave.), AC, 609-345-5766
■ "It's a time warp" say nostalgists about this "cheap", "dependable" red sauce Italian in AC "where locals meet"; it's known for the best pies "in the western hemisphere", "fast" service and, unfortunately, "screaming kids."

Top of the Marq ⓢ   18 | 21 | 19 | $32
Marquis de Lafayette, 501 Beach Dr. (bet. Decatur & Ocean Sts.), Cape May, 609-884-3500
■ Respondents note that the "stunning view" from this "romantic" American in the Marquis de Lafayette in Cape May overshadows the good food; nonetheless, the "great early-bird specials" get some applause, as does the live music.

Tre Figlio ⓢ   24 | 19 | 22 | $36
500 W. White Horse Pike (bet. Manheim Ave. & Rte. 30), Egg Harbor, 609-965-3303
☑ "Slow down or you'll drive right by" this family Italian that's "a must" on the way to the shore; while "outstanding dishes are enhanced by great service", some quibble that the "tables are too close" together.

Tuckahoe Inn **S**   18 | 20 | 18 | $29

1 Harbor Rd./Rte. 9 (Beesley's Point Bridge), Beesley's Point, 609-390-3322

■ While the "great view from the porch" hasn't changed at this long-standing, "romantic" American near Ocean City, there are now "new chef-owners" and, while not reflected in ratings, some insist the food's "much improved"; P.S. the waterside dock is a boon to boaters.

Ugly Mug ◗ **S**   15 | 14 | 17 | $18

426 Washington St. Mall, Cape May, 609-884-3459

■ A Cape May "favorite informal, drop-in spot" with "jolly" atmosphere and "average" pub grub; in warm weather "sit outside and watch the tourists"; overall, "a joint, and that's a compliment."

Union Park Dining Room **S**   ▽ 26 | 23 | 26 | $37

Hotel Macomber, 727 Beach Ave. (Howard St.), Cape May, 609-884-8811

■ This classically inspired New American BYO in Cape May's Hotel Macomber is "pricey but worth it" for "imaginative" food, "comfortable seating" and "waiters who know how to wait on you"; this is "fine dining" all the way.

Urie's Waterfront Restaurant **S**   17 | 18 | 17 | $21

588 Rio Grande Ave. (Susquehanna St.), Wildwood, 609-522-7761

■ A long-running, waterside Wildwood seafooder with an AYCE buffet in July and August; it's best "on a nice day", but there's a good chance "you'll have a solid, but lightly priced meal" any time.

Van Scoy's Bistro **S**   – | – | – | M

Carpenter's Sq. Mall, 312 Carpenter's Ln. (bet. Jackson & Perry Sts.), Cape May, 609-898-9898

They bake their own breads and desserts at this Eclectic BYO in Cape May's Carpenter's Square Mall that's "good for an inexpensive, creative meal" or "delicious" sandwiches; "indifferent service" can be an occasional drawback.

Ventura Greenhouse ◗ **S**   17 | 16 | 16 | $25

106 S. Benson Ave. (Atlantic Ave.), Margate, 609-822-0140

■ A two-level, AC Italian next to Lucy the elephant: upstairs is a "dolled-up" "place to meet everyone" at dinner, with lots of "fresh fish choices"; downstairs is a cafe with "excellent" pizza and cheese steaks at "reasonable prices"; diners stress that "it's fun to eat outside on the deck" at lunch.

WASHINGTON INN **S**   27 | 26 | 26 | $41

801 Washington St. (Jefferson St.), Cape May, 609-884-5697

■ Ratings and comments indicate this American is "undoubtedly" the "top-dog", "best overall restaurant on Cape May", with "charming" Victorian surroundings ("nifty porch"), a "wide selection" of "fantastic" food, a world class wine cellar and "wonderful staff and management"; in sum, "it could be great in Manhattan."

Waterfront, The ◗🅂　　　　|14|19|16|$26|
998 Bay Ave. (Goll Ave.), Somers Point, 609-653-0099
■ Twentysomethings say this "informal" waterside
Somers Point American seafooder has a "great deck for
wasting away summer days and nights"; while some
patrons "go for the beer and the youth", a number praise
"good food" as well.

Waters Edge 🅂　　　　|26|22|23|$39|
Beach Dr. & Pittsburgh Ave. (Atlantic Ocean), Cape May,
609-884-1717
■ "Still a sleeper", this "relaxed yet sophisticated"
American overlooking the ocean in Cape May offers a
"nice wine list" and "cutting-edge" food served "without
a hint of the pomposity" some find elsewhere in town.

WHITE HOUSE 🅂⊄　　　　|26|9|16|$10|
2301 Arctic Ave. (Mississippi Ave.), AC, 609-345-1564
■ "Ultimate" "hoagies to die for" draw crowds (including
Philadelphians who willingly "travel 55 miles") to this "noisy"
institution off the AC casino track; aficionados who "wish
the D.C. White House was as dependable" assert that the
secret to these "cheap" treats is "the bread."

William Fisk Seafood 🅂　　▽ |19|20|20|$32|
Harrah's, 777 Harrah's Blvd., AC, 609-441-5126
☒ The casino comp crowd says this American seafooder in
Harrah's is a quiet, efficient spot for some good, if pricey, fish.

W.L. Goodfellows ◗🅂　　▽ |13|14|15|$19|
310 E. White Horse Pike (6th Ave.), Absecon, 609-652-1942
☒ To some, this "fun" American-Continental on the mainland
near AC "looks better than it is" ("run-of-the-mill, chain
quality"), but if it's "bar food" in the Bennigan's mold you're
after, it could be ok.

Yesterday's ◗🅂　　　　|18|14|18|$20|
316 Roosevelt Blvd. (Garden State Pkwy., exit 25),
Marmora, 609-390-1757
■ This "noisy" American near Ocean City is a "typical
shore" joint with "good food for the money" and a
happening bar with live jazz; despite (or because of) a
200-item menu ranging from peanut butter and jelly to
lobster thermidor, some like to play it safe ("stick with
sandwiches and appetizers").

Wilmington/
Nearby Delaware

Top Food
26 Green Room
   Brandywine Room
25 Tavola Toscana
   Positano
24 Vincente's

Top Decor
28 Green Room
27 Brandywine Room
21 Columbus Inn
   Silk Purse
   Positano

Top Service
26 Green Room
   Brandywine Room
23 Vincente's
22 Tavola Toscana
   Positano

Top Value
   Charcoal Pit
   Iron Hill Brewery
   Mrs. Robino's
   Caffe Bellissimo
   La Tolteca

F	D	S	C

Back Burner 🖪 | 24 | 19 | 22 | $34 |

425 Hockessin Corner (Mill Creek Rd. & Old Lancaster Pike),
Hockessin, 302-239-2314
◼ A "creative chef whips up fresh and innovative" Regional American food, including "souper" soups and vegetarian dishes, at this Hockessin "best" bet where an "open kitchen" and "comfortable" surroundings make for an atmosphere of "casual elegance"; since diners are "always" assured of "a good meal and a good time", they're moving this one up to the front burner.

Bangkok House 🖪 | ▽ 20 | 14 | 16 | $23 |

104 N. Union St. (bet. Lancaster & 2nd Aves.), Wilmington,
302-654-8555
◼ It's a shame this "unassuming", "authentic" Thai in Downtown Wilmington is "largely undiscovered", because the "sophisticated" food is "beautifully done"; the setting may be "hash house" but the service is "gentle" and the price is right.

Brandywine Brewing Co. ◑🖪 | 15 | 17 | 15 | $20 |

Greenville Ctr., 3801 Kennett Pike (Buck Rd.), Greenville,
302-655-8000
◪ "Yuppies" flock to this "lively", "noisy" Greenville microbrewery with American fare for decent beers, sandwiches and "awesome" pretzels; naysayers find it a "paragon of mediocrity" with a "frat house atmosphere."

BRANDYWINE ROOM S   26 | 27 | 26 | $43
Hotel du Pont, 11th & Market Sts., Wilmington, 302-594-3156
■ "Ah! to dine among the Wyeth paintings" at this "classy", "special-occasion" Traditional American in the Hotel du Pont; the "old-world elegance" and "carefully prepared" food are matched by "correct" (some say "stuffy") service.

Buckley's Tavern S   17 | 17 | 17 | $27
5812 Kennett Pike (south of Rte. 1), Centreville, 302-656-9776
■ "Decent roadhouse" with a "colonial atmosphere" just south of Route 1 that's a "popular neighborhood hangout" "where the du Ponts rub shoulders with the rest of us" over good "bar food that doesn't pretend to be anything else"; it's "best for lunch, drinks or a snack."

Caffe Bellissimo S   17 | 14 | 18 | $20
Depot Shopping Ctr., 3421 Kirkwood Hwy. (bet. Rtes. 2 & 41), Wilmington, 302-994-9200
☑ This "high-volume" Italian in Depot Shopping Center is known for "mountainous portions" of pasta served by "teenagers in a big room that is bedlam"; while fans feel the food is "tasty", foes call it "mediocre", but all agree it's "reasonably priced."

Carucci ◐   22 | 20 | 21 | $38
Wawasett Plaza, 506 Greenhill Ave. (5th St.), Wilmington, 302-654-2333
☑ Loyalists "love the opera singers", "innovative cuisine" and "personal" service at this "unprepossessing" but "festive" Classic French–Italian in Wawasett Plaza and say they'll "always return"; however, a number of naysayers whine it's "overpriced" and "a far cry from its heyday" – a slip in ratings supports this point of view.

Charcoal Pit ◐S⌿   18 | 13 | 17 | $11
240 Fox Hunt Dr., Bear, 302-834-8000
5200 Pike Creek Ctr. Blvd. (Limestone Rd.), Wilmington, 302-999-7483
2600 Concord Pike (Rte. 202), Wilmington, 302-478-2165
■ Aficionados call these "classic, *Flintstones*-era" "drive-in" burger joints a "Delaware institution" "worthy of a side trip" for "thick shakes", sundaes and the "best burgers in the mid-Atlantic" region; in short, "it's a fine pit."

Columbus Inn S   22 | 21 | 21 | $34
2216 Pennsylvania Ave. (Woodlawn Ave.), Wilmington, 302-571-1492
■ "They're trying to liven up" the "old-money", "men's club atmosphere" at this "reliable" New American "meat emporium" on Pennsylvania Avenue and it's paying off in stronger ratings; many feel the food is "delicious" and it's "good for a business dinner, though service can be slow."

DiNardo's 🅂 (CLOSED) `22` `11` `17` `$26`
405 N. Lincoln St. (4th St.), Wilmington, 302-656-3685
■ "Crabs, fries and coleslaw to die for" are the draws at this "fun" Downtown Wilmington seafood "dive"; "be prepared to wait – it's worth it though."

Feby's Fishery 🅂 `17` `12` `16` `$24`
3701 Lancaster Pike (bet. Rtes. 100 & 141), Wilmington, 302-998-9501
■ A downscale Wilmington "family fish place" serving "good selections" of decent seafood that are a "good buy"; some surveyors who find the surroundings too "cheap" may want to try takeout.

Fox Point Grill `24` `16` `19` `$35`
321 E. Lea Blvd. (Philadelphia Pike), Wilmington, 302-762-5655
◪ Fans feel this American-Eclectic off I-495 features "wonderful" food; however, the more aesthetically inclined warn about the "weird decor", and suggest patrons "squint and eat."

GREEN ROOM 🅂 `26` `28` `26` `$49`
Hotel du Pont, 11th & Market Sts., Wilmington, 302-594-3154
◪ This "gracious", "expensive" Classic French in the Hotel du Pont, which is the No. 1 ranked Delaware restaurant across the board, makes "you think you're dining in another century", with a balcony harpist and gold-plated chandeliers lending "old-world" charm; while a few critics claim the "food is too conservative", most maintain it's a "can't-miss" for "special occasions"; Sunday brunch features "more food than any human should ever eat."

Harry's Savoy Grill ◑🅂 `22` `20` `21` `$33`
2020 Naaman's Rd. (Foulk Rd.), Wilmington, 302-475-3000
■ A "bustling", "cigar-friendly" American in Northern Wilmington that's mainly a "prime spot for red meat"; "it's "nothing spectacular", but "a good standby" for a "relaxing night out" and the "wine tasting dinners are reasonable and delicious."

Hibachi Japanese 🅂 `17` `16` `18` `$24`
5607 Concord Ave. (Rte. 202), Wilmington, 302-477-0194
■ "Grill cooking is a real show" at this Concord Pike Japanese where "they throw food at you and you pay for it" – "bring your catcher's mitt"; while it's "fun for groups" and "kids love it", more sophisticated surveyors sniff "very average."

India Palace 🅂 `–` `–` `–` `M`
101 N. Maryland Ave. (New Point Rd.), Wilmington, 302-655-8772
The few respondents who frequent this humble Indian at Five Points say the "food is good"; but when it comes to decor, they suggest this ain't no palace.

Iron Hill Brewery & Restaurant 🅞🅢
20 19 18 $19

Traders Alley, 147 E. Main St. (bet. Chapel & Haines), Newark, 302-266-9000

■ Foam fans feel this "upscale" brewpub in Newark is "the best around", with "excellent" beers" and "imaginative" American food; a "striking" setting, live entertainment and "reasonable prices" lead loyalists to conclude "it has it all."

Krazy Kats 🅢
– – – E

Inn at Montchanin Village, Kirk Rd. & Rte. 100, Montchanin, 302-888-4200

There's clearly a sense of humor at work at this otherwise fancy, cat-themed Regional American in an upscale inn in the Brandywine Valley; the ever-changing menu includes duck, crab cakes and Angus beef, desserts are outstanding and the wine list is admirable; there's breakfast, too.

La Casa Pasta 🅢
22 17 22 $28

Four Seasons Pkwy. (Rte. 896), Newark, 302-738-9936

◪ You expect "Mama to serve you" at this "well-managed" Newark Southern Italian with "authentic", "tasty" food that's "trying for top-notch and almost making it"; but it's "pricey" for a setting that's "homey" to some, "low-down" to others.

La Tolteca 🅢
17 8 14 $16

4701 Concord Pike (Rte. 202), Wilmington, 302-778-4646

◪ Surveyors are of dos minds when it comes to this "fun" Mexican in a "converted Burger King" near Concord Mall: devotees deem the food "authentic" and "reasonably priced", but phobes feel it's merely "passable" and served in "the world's worst room."

L'Osteria Cucina Italiana
22 15 20 $35

407 Marsh Rd. (Philadelphia Pike), Wilmington, 302-764-5071

■ The "food's worth the trip" ("awesome gnocchi") to this Italian in a "bizarre location" in Northern Wilmington; it's an "up-and-comer" with "potential" where the "chef greets guests like family."

Luigi Vitrone's Pastabilities 🅢
– – – E

415 N. Lincoln St. (5th St.), Wilmington, 302-656-9822

"Good ingredients make for nicely prepared food" at this Eclectic-Italian in Wilmington; but what fans find "romantic and quaint", claustrophobics call "squished together."

Michele's (CLOSED)
22 19 21 $41

1828 W. 11th St. (bet. Lincoln & Scott Sts.), Wilmington, 302-655-8554

◪ Downtown Wilmington French–Northern Italian that pros praise as having "top-notch food and service" in a "lovely setting"; recent renovations have turned the first floor of this three-story home into a '60s retro space, while the second floor went contemporary and the third traditional.

Mikasa S   ▽ | 22 | 13 | 17 | $23 |
*Alpha Shopping Ctr., 3602 Kirkwood Hwy. (bet. Duncan Rd.
& Rte. 41), Wilmington, 302-995-8905*
■ Boosters claim this shopping center Japanese in
Wilmington has "without question" the "freshest sushi"
in Delaware; however, it can be "expensive" for a place
with such "plain decor."

Mrs. Robino's S | 17 | 10 | 17 | $16 |
*520 N. Union St. (bet. 5th & 6th Sts.), Wilmington,
302-652-9223*
■ "It is what it is" – a family-owned Italian in Downtown
Wilmington with "big portions" of "good", "inexpensive"
food; it's "dark, noisy", "homey" and hence the "epitome
of a neighborhood restaurant."

Pala's Cafe   ▽ | 16 | 8 | 13 | $15 |
701 N. Union St. (7th St.), Wilmington, 302-658-2346
■ Well-worn Downtown Wilmington "neighborhood tavern"
and Italian stalwart for "quick", "consistent" "red sauce"
specialties and pizza; "like your old shoes", it's "comfy."

Piccolo Mondo | 22 | 18 | 19 | $30 |
3604 Silverside Rd. (Rte. 202), Wilmington, 302-478-9028
■ It's "worth the hunt" to find this Italian "surprise" in an
"unlikely setting" off Route 202, where the "good food"
includes "nice veal dishes"; surveyors find the decor and
service "above-average."

POSITANO RISTORANTE | 25 | 21 | 22 | $44 |
*Devon, 2401 Pennsylvania Ave. (bet. Greenhill &
Riverview Aves.), Wilmington, 302-656-6788*
■ This "tiny" French-Italian in the Devon, with a "wide
selection of food and wine" and excellent "extras", is an
"outstanding" choice for a "great lunch" or "special
occasion"; a "solicitous" owner and "romantic" ambiance
add to the appeal.

Ristorante Amalfi | 23 | 20 | 21 | $35 |
*Greenville Ctr., 3801 Kennett Pike (Rte. 52), Wilmington,
302-655-7719*
■ A Kennett Pike Italian "oasis in a shopping center"
offering "better than usual" "fresh" fare, such as seafood
and pasta, that the chef-owner "will cook to order"; most
maintain it's a "good little spot."

Ristorante Attilio S⌀ | 18 | 11 | 15 | $19 |
*1900 Lancaster Ave. (Lincoln St.), Wilmington,
302-428-0909*
■ "It's not a dining experience but it's consistently good"
declare devotees of this "smoky", "red sauce" Italian "joint"
on Lancaster Avenue; "homey service" and a "checkered
tablecloth" ambiance make it an "everyday-type restaurant."

Sal's ◐ ▽ 23 | 16 | 19 | $42

603 N. Lincoln St. (6th St.), Wilmington, 302-652-1200

◪ Fans of this long-standing French-Italian in Downtown Wilmington praise the "excellent", "original" "made-to-order" food with ingredients that are "sometimes homegrown in the local neighborhood"; wallet-watchers acknowledge the "flair", but call it "overpriced."

Shipley Grill [S] 19 | 16 | 18 | $33

913 Shipley St. (bet. 9th & 10th Sts.), Wilmington, 302-652-7797

◪ This Downtown Wilmington Traditional American with "good", "well-prepared" food is "a favorite before concerts and plays"; however, critics complain about "uneven" service, and what some find a "pleasant" setting, others call "cramped" and "uncomfortable."

Sienna [S] – | – | – | M

1616 Delaware Ave. (bet. Clayton & du Pont Sts.), Wilmington, 302-652-0653

Jeannine Mermet, Les Smith and Daniel Frank – all veterans of Old City's now-defunct La Truffe – have resurfaced at this dramatic, welcoming Mediterranean in Downtown Wilmington; the fare is memorable and magnificent, and decor glows in umbers, oranges and yellows.

Silk Purse 24 | 21 | 22 | $44

1307 N. Scott St. (bet. 13th & 14th Sts.), Wilmington, 302-654-7666

◪ A "boffo" New American in Downtown Wilmington with "exceptional" food (albeit from a rather limited menu) that's worth a try; however, while fans find the atmosphere "posh", for others it's just "strange."

Sow's Ear 23 | 21 | 21 | $40

1307 N. Scott St. (bet. 13th & 14th Sts.), Wilmington, 302-654-7666

■ Located upstairs from the Silk Purse, this "excellent", "innovative" New American shares the same chef and offers the same menu at the same prices as its sibling; the difference is the setting – this one's "light, bright and cheery."

Sullivan's Steakhouse – | – | – | M

Market Sq., 5525 Concord Pike, Wilmington, 302-479-7970

The classic, big-portioned steakhouse fare is tasty at this chain (an upper tier version of Lone Star) named after the famed boxer; the spare, handsome decor and interesting art deco bar are augmented by piped-in Sinatra and jazz.

TAVOLA TOSCANA [S] 25 | 20 | 22 | $35

Rockford Shops, 1412 N. du Pont St. (14th St.), Wilmington, 302-654-8001

■ What's this "noisy but nice" Northern Italian "doing in a strip mall?" ask the many fans of this "class act" in the Rockford Shops; chef Dan Butler's Tuscan cooking is "creative", the staff is "knowledgeable" and the "upscale" atmosphere is "sunny"; overall, "a winner."

Terrace at Greenhill [S] 18 | 18 | 17 | $26
800 N. du Pont Rd. (bet. Lancaster Ave. & Rte. 52), Wilmington, 302-575-1990
■ The "lovely golf course" view and "creative" food are above par at this Regional American on du Pont Road; it offers "good value" in an "elegant, old-money atmosphere."

Utage [S] 20 | 13 | 18 | $25
Independence Mall, 1601 Concord Pike (Rte. 202), Wilmington, 302-652-1230
■ Sushi fans say good things about this Japanese in the "middle of nowhere" (meaning Independence Mall); while the "decor needs an update" and it's a "little pricey", the food is "authentic."

VINCENTE'S 24 | 18 | 23 | $36
Independence Mall, 1601 Concord Pike (Rte. 202), Wilmington, 302-652-5142
■ The "walking menu" is the gimmick at this "house of cholesterol" in Independence Mall; the "waiter asks diners what they like to eat" (think Italian) and he takes it from there, including "tableside" preparation with "great personality" thrown in.

Walter's Steakhouse [S] 23 | 17 | 21 | $35
802 N. Union St. (8th St.), Wilmington, 302-652-6780
■ "When you feel like steak", this Downtown Wilmington chophouse is the place; the menu is "traditional" and the portions of prime beef are "huge."

Waterworks Cafe 14 | 18 | 16 | $30
French & 16th Sts. (Brandywine River), Wilmington, 302-652-6022
◪ If you're having "lunch with the ladies", this Continental has a "super" vista of the Brandywine River; unfortunately, since the food is only "so-so" and the service is "uneven", critics conclude "what a waste of a view."

Indexes to Restaurants

Special Features and Appeals

CUISINES*

Afghan
Benkady
Kabul

American (New)
Acacia
Alaina's
America B&G
Anton's at Swan
Astral Plane
Azalea Room
Black Bass
Black Walnut
Blue in Green
Bottling Works/LB
Brandywine Brewing/DE
Bridget Foy's
California Cafe
Carambola
Carversville Inn
Catacombs/LB
Circa
Clayton's
Columbus Inn/DE
Coppermill Harvest
Culinary Garden/CM
Cutters
David's Yellow Brick
Dilworthtown Inn
Ebbitt Room/CM
Ebenezer's
Edge
Epicurean, The
Evermay on Del.
Food for Thought
Forager
Fork
Fork's Inn/CM
Founders
Fox Point Grill/DE
Friday, Sat., Sun.
Full Moon
Garden, The
Goat Hollow
Green Hills Inn/LB
Hadley's Bistro
Hatteras Coastal/CM
Herb Garden
Inn at Sugar Hill/CM

Inn of the Hawke
Inn on Blueberry Hill
Inn Philadelphia
Iron Hill Brewery/DE
Jake's
Joe's Bistro 614/LB
Johan's/AC
John Harvard's
Lambertville Station
Latest Dish
Liberties
Little Fish
London Grill
Mainland Inn
Main-ly Desserts
Marathon Grill
Market Fare/LB
Melissa's Bistro/CM
Mendenhall Inn
Montserrat
More Than Ice Cream
Odette's
Painted Parrot
Passerelle
Pepper's Cafe
Peregrines/AC
Philadelphia Fish
Philly Crab & Steak
Planet Hollywood/AC
Regent Court/AC
Ritz-Carlton Grill
Rococo
Roller's
Rose Tattoo Cafe
Rose Tree Inn
Rouge 98
Samuels
Saranac
Siggie's L'Auberge
Silk Purse/DE
Sow's Ear/DE
Swann Lounge
Taxi
Thomas'
Tisha's Fine Din./CM
Treetops
Union Park/CM
Valley Forge
Village Porch

---

* Restaurants are in the Philadelphia metropolitan area unless
  otherwise noted (AC=Atlantic City, CM=Cape May, DE=Delaware
  and LB=Lancaster/Berks).

Washington Inn/CM
Waterfront/CM
Waters Edge/CM
White Dog Cafe
Wild Onion Rest.
Zanzibar Blue

American (Regional)

Back Burner/DE
Bird-in-Hand/LB
California Cafe
Deetrick's Cafe
Good N' Plenty/LB
Groff's Farm/LB
Haydn Zug's/LB
Jack's Firehouse
Kimberton Inn
King George II
Krazy Kats/DE
Landing, The
Miller's Smorgasbord/LB
Moselem Springs/LB
Opus 251
Ortlieb's Jazzhaus
Pace One
Plain & Fancy/LB
Pompano Grille
Red Caboose/LB
Red Hot & Blue
Roscoe's Kodiak
Stoltzfus Farm/LB
Terrace at Greenhill/DE
Tuckahoe Inn/CM
Willow Valley Rst./LB
Windmill/LB
Zinn's Diner/LB

American (Traditional)

Abbey Grill
Academy Cafe
A.C. Station/AC
Aleathea's/CM
Alexander's Cafe
Allie's American
Artful Dodger
Arugula!
Bay Pony Inn
Blue Bell Inn
Braddock's Tavern
Brandywine Room/DE
Broad Axe Tavern
Buckley's Tavern/DE
Cedar Creek/CM
Century House
Chadds Ford Inn
Champion's

Champps Amer.
Charlie's Bar/CM
Chart House
Chestnut Grill
City Tavern
Cock 'n Bull
Concordville Inn
Cresheim Cottage
Cuttalossa Inn
Dave & Buster's
Dick Clark's
D'Ignazio's
Doc's Place/CM
Downey's
Down Home Diner
Dry Dock Ice Cream/CM
Fireside Room
Four Dogs Tavern
General Lafayette
Gourley's
Hank's Place
Hard Rock Cafe
Hard Rock Cafe/AC
Harry's Savoy Grill/DE
Hartefeld National
Historic Revere Tav./LB
Hoss's Steak/LB
Hunt Room
Ingleneuk Tea Hse.
Isaac Newton's
Isaac's/LB
Jackson Mountain/CM
Joseph Ambler
Kaminski's
Kaufman House
King George II
Lamb Tavern
Log Cabin/LB
Lucy's Hat Shop
Mace's Crossing
Manayunk Brewing
Marshalton Inn
Mayfair Diner
Meil's
Merion Inn/CM
Michael's Family
Moriarty's
Morning Glory Diner
Moselem Springs/LB
Mother's
Nick's B&G
Nifty Fifty's
Official All Star/AC
Old City Coffee
Olde Greenfield Inn/LB

Old Guard House
Old Mill Inn
Olga's Diner
Pilot House/CM
Pineville Tavern
Ponzio's Kingsway
Poor Henry's
Prime Rib
Pub Rest.
Ram's Head Inn/CM
Red Caboose/LB
Regatta B&G
Renault Winery/CM
Samuel Adams Brew
Sassafras Cafe
Ship Inn
Shipley Grill/DE
Society Hill Hotel
Stockton Inn
Stockyard Inn/LB
Stoudt's Black Angus/LB
Sugar Mom's
Sweetwater Casino/CM
Tavern on Green
Top of the Marq/CM
Ugly Mug/CM
United States Hotel
Valley Stream Inn
Washington House
William Fisk/AC
W.L. Goodfellows/CM
Yesterday's/CM
Yorktown Inn

Asian

Alisa Cafe
Bentley's Five
Chanterelles
Gourmet Rest.
Joseph Poon
Ly Michael's
Manila Bay B&G
Orfèo
Russell's 96 West
Sakura Spring
Singapore Kosher
Susanna Foo

Austrian

Wolfgang's Cafe

Bar-B-Q

Bentley's Five
Bomb Bomb BBQ
Fat Jack's
Mama Rosa

Red Hot & Blue
Rib Crib
Ron's Ribs
Smokin' Sam's
Warmdaddy's

Belgian

Bridgid
Cuvee Notredame
Monk's Café

Brazilian

Brasil's

Burmese

Rangoon

Cajun/Creole

Abilene
410 Bank St./CM
La Familia Sonsini
New Orleans Cafe
New Orleans Cafe II
Ortlieb's Jazzhaus
Tenth St. Pour Hse.

Californian

California Cafe
Food for Thought
Pacific Grille
Peaches at Sunset/CM
Sonoma

Caribbean

Chef Tell's
410 Bank St./CM
Jamaican Jerk Hut
Katmandu
Vega Grill

Cheese Steaks/Hoagies

Dalessandro's
Geno's Steaks
Jim's Steaks
Pat's King Steaks
Tony Luke's
White House/AC

Chinese

Abacus
Beijing
Charles Plaza
Cherry St. Chinese
China Castle
China Moon/AC
Chung Hing
CinCin

Elena Wu
Fortune's/AC
Garnian Wa
Golden Pond
Golden Sea
Harmony Vegetarian
H.K. Golden Phoenix
House of Chen
Hunan Rest.
Imperial Inn
Jannie
Joe's Peking
Joy Tsin Lau
Kimono Sushi Bar
Kingdom Vegetarians
Lai Lai
Lee Ho Seafood
Lee How Fook
Long's Gourmet
Mandarin Garden
Margaret Kuo's
Mustard Greens
Noodle Heaven
North Sea
Peking Rest.
Ray's Cafe
Sang Kee
Silk & Spice
Susanna Foo
Tai Lake
Tang Yean
Yangming

Coffeehouses/Desserts

Anthony's
Capriccio Cafe
Cassatt Tea Rm.
Dry Dock Ice Cream/CM
Ebenezer's
LionFish
Mademoiselle Paris
Main-ly Desserts
More Than Ice Cream
Old City Coffee
Painted Parrot
Pink Rose Pastry
Roselena's Coffee
Tenth St. Pour Hse.
Xando Coffee

Coffee Shops/Diners

Brittany Cafe/AC
Country Club
Down Home Diner
Little Pete's
Mayfair Diner

Melrose Diner
Michael's Family
Morning Glory Diner
Nifty Fifty's
Olga's Diner
Ponzio's Kingsway
Ray's Cafe
River City Diner
Ruby's
Sage Diner
Silk City
Zinn's Diner/LB

Colombian

Tierra Colombiana

Continental

Academy Cafe
Alexander's Inn/CM
Bay Pony Inn
Between Friends
Brittany Cafe/AC
Cafe 8 South/CM
Cafe Gallery
Centre Bridge Inn
Cousins Country/CM
Crier in Country
Deauville Inn/CM
Duling-Kurtz House
Evviva
Fountain Rest.
Four Dogs Tavern
Friday, Sat., Sun.
Gourley's
Happy Rooster
Harry's Bar & Grill
Inn at Sugar Hill/CM
Inn Philadelphia
Kennedy-Supplee
King George II
Lenape Inn
Lucy's Hat Shop
Merion Inn/CM
Mirage, The/CM
Museum Rest.
Nicholas Nickolas
Odette's
Old Mill Inn
Old Waterway Inn/AC
Orfèo
Plumsteadville Inn
Poor Henry's
Rhapsody's
Rose Tree Inn
Scheherazade/AC
Ship Inn

Sign of Sorrel Horse
Stockton Inn
Swann Lounge
Vickers Tavern
Villa Strafford
Vincent's
Washington Crossing
Waterworks Cafe/DE
William Penn Inn
Willistown Grille
W.L. Goodfellows/CM
Wycombe Inn
Yellow Springs Inn
Ye Olde Temp.

Cuban

Tierra Colombiana
Vega Grill

Delis/Sandwich Shop

Ben & Irv Deli
Center Point Deli/AC
Dave's Center Point Deli/CM
Famous 4th St. Deli
Hymie's
Isaac's/LB
Murray's Deli
New Corned Beef
Rachael's Nosheri

Dim Sum

Harmony Vegetarian
H.K. Golden Phoenix
Imperial Inn
Joy Tsin Lau
Kingdom Vegetarians

Eastern European

Warsaw Cafe

Eclectic/International

A Little Cafe
Alois/LB
Arpeggio
Azafran
Cafe Flower Shop
Cafe Noelle
Cafe Preeya
Cafette
Carman's Country Kit.
Cary Restaurant
Chambers
Chef Tell's
Continental
Cotton Club
Cucina Rustica/CM

Cuisines
Day by Day
Doylestown Inn
Edge
Fantasea Reef/AC
Five Spot
Flowing Springs
410 Bank St./CM
Fox Point Grill/DE
Frangelica
Freda's Cafe/CM
Gary's Little Rock/CM
General Warren
Gracie's/LB
Gregory's/CM
Gullifty's
Gypsy Rose
Haute To Trot
Havana
Homestead Rest.
Inn Philadelphia
Jake & Oliver's
Jefferson House
Judy's Cafe
Knave of Hearts
Lauren's
Le Bus
Liberties
LionFish
Loose Ends
Luigi Vitrone's/DE
Mad Batter/CM
Mama Palma's
Manayunk Farmer's Mkt.
Marbles
Marco's
Marco's Cafe
Marker, The
Martine's
Martini Café
Martini's Lounge
Melting Pot
Mirna's Cafe
Moshulu
Mrs. London's Cafe
Nav Jiwan Tea Rm./LB
New World Cafe
North Star Bar
Oceanfront/CM
Palladium
Paradigm
Peacock Parkwy.
Peter Shields/CM
Philly Crab & Steak
Purple Sage

Reading Terminal Mkt.
Rembrandt's
Roller's
Roselena's Coffee
Saffron
Savaradio/CM
Schooners & C.B.'s/CM
Serrano
Solaris Grille
Spotted Hog
Spring Mill Café
State St. Cafe
Sutor's Owl Tree/CM
30th St. Station
Thomas'
Tomatoes/CM
Tony Clark's
Totaro's Ristorante
Umbria
Valley Green Inn
Van Scoy's Bistro/CM
Waldorf Café
Wrap Planet
Yangming

English

Artful Dodger
Best of British
Cassatt Tea Rm.
Dickens Inn
Elephant & Castle
Rhapsody's

Ethiopian

Dahlak

French

Alisa Cafe
Barrymore Room
Beau Monde
Beau Rivage
Cafe Arielle
Carucci/DE
Coventry Forge
Deux Cheminées
Dilworthtown Inn
Dock Street
Frenchtown Inn
Full Moon
Golden Pheasant
Gourmet Rest.
Green Hills Inn/LB
Green Room/DE
Hotel du Village
Jean Pierre's
Johan's/AC

La Bonne Auberge
La Cocotte
La Familia Sonsini
La Fourchette
Le Bec-Fin
Le Champignon
Le Petit Cafe
Michele's/DE
Positano Rist./DE
Sal's/DE
Scheherazade/AC
Siggie's L'Auberge
Vickers Tavern
Yellow Springs Inn

French Bistro

Beaujolais
Bistro St. Tropez
Bravo Bistro
Caribou Cafe
Church St. Bistro
Cibo
Frenchtown Inn
Inn at Phillips Mill
La Campagne
La Cocotte
La Terrasse
Le Bar Lyonnais

French (New)

Alaina's
Black Walnut
Brasserie Perrier
Bunha Faun
Cafe Gallery
Chanterelles
Chateau Silvana
Chef Charin
Ciboulette
CinCin
Crier in Country
Fountain Rest.
Gourmet's Table
Grasshopper
Isabella's
Le Palais/AC
Ly Michael's
Mademoiselle Paris
Nais Cuisine
Nan
Nonna's
Pattaya Grill
Provence
Rest. at Doneckers/LB
Rose Tree Inn
Rouge 98

Russell's 96 West
Siri's Thai French
Susanna Foo
Taquet

German

Blüe Ox Brauhaus
Little Brat's Haus/CM
Otto's Brauhaus
Villa Strafford
Wolfgang's Cafe

Greek

Athena
Athens Cafe
Cafe Zesty
Effie's
Hank's Place
South St. Souvlaki

Hamburgers

Champion's
Charcoal Pit/DE
Charlie's Bar/CM
Copabanana
Copa-Too!
Hard Rock Cafe
Hard Rock Cafe/AC
Jackson Mountain/CM
Kaminski's
Mace's Crossing
Melrose Diner
Nick's B&G
Nifty Fifty's
Official All Star/AC
Pilot House/CM
Ruby's
Samuel Adams Brew
Sassafras Cafe
Sugar Mom's
Ugly Mug/CM
United States Hotel
Valley Forge

Health Food

Green Cuisine/CM

Indian

India Palace/DE
Khajuraho
Minar Palace
New Delhi
Palace of Asia
Passage to India
Rajbhog Indian
Samosa

Sitar India
Taj Mahal
Tandoor India

Irish

Bards
Downey's
Fergie's Pub
Finnigan's Wake
McGillin's
Plough & the Stars

Italian

(N=Northern; S=Southern;
N&S=Includes both)
A Ca Mia/CM (N)
Alberto's (N)
Alfe's/CM (N&S)
Alfio's (N&S)
Andreotti's (N)
Andreotti's/AC (N&S)
Angeloni's II/AC (N&S)
Angelo's Fairmount/AC (S)
Arpeggio (N&S)
Assaggi Italiani (N&S)
A Touch of Italy/CM (N&S)
Bella Trattoria (S)
Bentley's Five (N&S)
Bertolini's (N)
Bertucci's (N&S)
Bistro Romano (N&S)
Bomb Bomb BBQ (N&S)
Bonaparte (N&S)
Brewery Inn/LB (N&S)
Cafe Giuseppe (S)
Cafe Michaelangelo (N&S)
Cafe Zesty (S)
Caffé Aldo Lamberti (N&S)
Caffe Bellissimo/DE (N&S)
Caffe La Bella (N)
California Pizza Kit. (N&S)
California Pizza Kit./AC (N&S)
Capriccio/AC (N&S)
Carambola (N&S)
Carucci/DE (N&S)
Caruso's/AC (N&S)
Casa DiNapoli/AC (N&S)
Casa Nicola/AC (N&S)
Cassano Italian (N&S)
Casselli's Rist. (S)
Catelli (N&S)
Cent'Anni (N&S)
Chateau Silvana (N)
Chef Vola's/AC (N&S)
Christopher's (S)

Cibo (N&S)
Coco Pazzo (N)
Cousin's/CM (N&S)
Cucina Rosa/CM (N&S)
Cucina Rustica/CM (N&S)
D'Angelo's (S)
Dante & Luigi's (N&S)
Diamond's (N&S)
D'Ignazio's (N&S)
DiLullo Centro (N&S)
Dinon's (N)
East Side Mario's (N&S)
Euro Cafe (N)
Fedeli's/CM (S)
Felicia's (N&S)
1521 Café (N)
Filomena Cuc. Italiana (N&S)
Filomena Cuc. Rustica (N&S)
Foggia (N&S)
Frankie's at Night (S)
Frankie's Seafood (N&S)
Frederick's (N&S)
Frescos/CM (N&S)
Gianna's (N&S)
Girasole/AC (N&S)
Girasole Rist. (N&S)
Giumarello's Rist. (N)
Gourmet's Table (N)
Graziella's (N&S)
Il Giardino (N&S)
Il Portico (N)
Il Sol D'Italia (S)
Il Tartufo (N)
Il Verdi/AC (N)
Io E Tu Rist. (N&S)
Isabella's (N&S)
Italian Bistro (N&S)
J.J.'s Grotto (N&S)
Joe Italiano's/Inn/CM (N&S)
Joe Italiano's/II/CM (S)
Joe's Tomato Pies (N&S)
Johnny Mott's (N&S)
Joseph's Italian (N&S)
Jow's Garden (N&S)
La Campagna (N&S)
La Casa Pasta/DE (S)
La Collina (N)
La Famiglia (N&S)
La Familia Sonsini (N&S)
La Forno (N&S)
La Grolla (N)
La Locanda (N)
Lamberti's Cucina (N&S)
La Padella (N)
La Veranda (N&S)

La Vigna (N)
L'Osteria Cucina/DE (N&S)
Luigi's Canal Hse. (N&S)
Luigi Vitrone's/DE (N&S)
Mac's/CM (N)
Malvern Meeting Hse. (S)
Mama Mia/CM (N&S)
Ma Ma Yolanda's (N)
Mamma Maria (N&S)
Marabella's (N&S)
Marco Polo (N)
Marra's (N)
Marsilio's (N&S)
Martini Café (N&S)
Medici/AC (N&S)
Mel's Italian (N)
Michael's Rist. (N&S)
Michele's/DE (N)
Monte Carlo (N&S)
Moonstruck (N&S)
Mr. Martino's Tratt. (N&S)
Mrs. Robino's/DE (N&S)
Nonna's (N)
Orsatti's/AC (S)
Ozzie's Tratt. (N&S)
Paganini (N)
Pala's Cafe/DE (N&S)
Pastaria Franco & Luigi's (N&S)
Pastavino Tratt. (N&S)
Piccolo Mondo/DE (N&S)
Pippo's Fantastico (N&S)
Pizzicato (N)
Pollo Rosso (N&S)
Porcini (N&S)
Portofino (N)
Portofino/AC (N&S)
Port Saloon (S)
Positano Rist./DE (N)
Primavera/AC (N&S)
Primavera Pizza Kit. (N&S)
Ralph's (N&S)
Ravioli House/CM (N&S)
Remi's Cafe (N&S)
Renault Winery/CM (N)
Ristorante Alberto (N)
Ristorante Amalfi/DE (N&S)
Ristorante Attilio/DE (N&S)
Ristorante Fieni's (N)
Ristorante Gallo Nero (N&S)
Ristorante La Buca (N&S)
Ristorante Laceno (S)
Ristorante Mediterraneo (N&S)
Ristorante Ottimo (N&S)
Ristorante Panorama (N&S)
Ristorante Positano (S)

Ristorante Primavera (N&S)
Ristorante San Carlo (N)
Rizzo's (N&S)
Roberto's/AC (N&S)
Sabatini's/AC (S)
Saloon (N)
Sal's/DE (N&S)
Savona (S)
Scampi Rist. (N&S)
Scannicchio's/AC (N)
Scoogi's Classic (S)
Screnci's/CM (N)
Shank's & Evelyn's (S)
Smokin' Sam's (N&S)
Sonoma (N&S)
Spaghetti Warehse. (N&S)
Spiaggi/CM (N&S)
Spiga D'Oro (N&S)
Stazi Milano (N&S)
Tavola Toscana/DE (N)
Teresa's Cafe (N&S)
Tira Misu Rist. (N&S)
Tomatoes/CM (N)
Tony's Balt. Grill/AC (S)
Toscana Cucina (N&S)
Totaro's Ristorante (N&S)
Trattoria San Nicola (N&S)
Tre Figlio/CM (N&S)
Tre Scalini (N&S)
Triangle Tavern (N&S)
Trinacria (S)
Tulipano Nero (N)
Upstares at Varalli (N)
Ventura Greenhse./CM (N)
Victor Café (N&S)
Villa Di Roma (N&S)
Vincente's/DE (N&S)

Japanese

Aoi
Asakura
August Moon
Fuji Mountain
Genji I
Genji II
Hibachi Japanese/DE
Hikaru
Jannie
Kawabata
Kimono Sushi Bar
Kobe Japanese
Le Champignon
Meiji-En
Mikasa/DE
Nul Bom

Sagami
Shiroi Hana
Utage/DE

Jewish
(* Kosher)
Ben & Irv Deli
Country Club
Famous 4th St. Deli
Hymie's*
La Pergola
Maccabeam*
Murray's Deli
New Corned Beef
Rachael's Nosheri
Rajbhog Indian*
Singapore Kosher*
Tira Misu Rist.

Korean
August Moon
Kim's
Korea House
Nul Bom

Lebanese
Cedars

Malaysian
Penang

Mediterranean
Al Dar
Andreotti's
Arpeggio
Audrey Claire
Cedars
Dmitri's
Hamilton's Grill
La Pergola
Mia's
Mirna's Cafe
Overtures
Peacock Parkwy.
Ritz-Carlton Grill
Sawan's Med. Bistro
Sienna/DE
Stephen's
Stix

Mexican/Tex-Mex
Copabanana
Copa-Too!
Coyote Crossing
El Azteca
El Mariachi

El Sombrero
Hot Tamales Cafe
La Tolteca/DE
Los Amigos/AC
Mad 4 Mex
Mexican Food
Mexican Post
Santa Fe Burrito
Taco House
Taqueria Moroleon
Tequila's Authentic
Tex Mex Connection
Zocalo
ZuZu

Middle Eastern

Al Dar
Alyan's
Bitar's
Maccabeam
Norma's Middle Eastern
Persian Grill

Moroccan

Al Khimah
Fez Moroccan
Marrakesh

Pizza

Arpeggio
Bertucci's
Cafe Michaelangelo
California Pizza Kit.
California Pizza Kit./AC
Casa Nicola/AC
Celebre's Pizzeria
Christopher's
DeLorenzo's
J.J.'s Grotto
Joe's Tomato Pies
La Cipolla Torta
La Forno
Mama Palma's
Marra's
Pietro's Pizzeria
Pizzicato
Primavera Pizza Kit.
Rizzo's
Scoogi's Classic
Tacconelli's Pizza
Tomatoes/CM
Tony's Balt. Grill/AC

Portuguese

Berlengas Island
Cafe Espresso

Seafood

Axelsson's/CM
Barnacle Ben's
Barnacle Ben's West
Bentley's Five
Big Fish
Big River Fish Co.
BLT's Cobblefish
Bobby's Seafood
Bookbinders
Busch's/CM
Casa Nicola/AC
Concordville Inn
Cousin's/CM
Crab Trap/CM
DiNardo's/DE
DiNardo's Seafood
Dmitri's
Dock's Oyster Hse./AC
Doc's Place/CM
Emerald Fish
Fantasea Reef/AC
Feby's Fishery/DE
Fisher's
Fisher's Tudor Hse.
Flying Fish
Frankie's Seafood
Golden Inn/CM
Gregory's/CM
Gypsy Rose
Hardshell Cafe
Henny's/CM
Hoss's Steak/LB
Hunt Room
Johnny Mott's
La Collina
La Veranda
Lee Ho Seafood
Little Fish
Lobster House/CM
Lobster Loft/CM
Louisa's Cafe/CM
Mac's/CM
Marco Polo
Max's Steak Hse./AC
Mel's Italian
Mirage, The/CM
Mississippi Steak/AC
Mrs. London's Cafe
Nicholas Nickolas
North Sea
Oaks, The/AC
Obadiah's/CM
Old Original Book
Pacific Grille

Philadelphia Fish
Philly Crab & Steak
Pier 7/AC
Rio Station/CM
Ristorante La Buca
Ristorante Laceno
Rock Lobster
Roscoe's Kodiak
Ruhling's Seafood
Sansom St. Oyster
Seafood Unlimited
Sea Grill/CM
Ship Inn
Snockey's Oyster
Stix
Striped Bass
Thomas'
Tisha's Fine Din./CM
Urie's Waterfront/CM
Ventura Greenhse./CM
Waterfront/CM
William Fisk/AC

South American
Azafran

Southern/Soul
Rib Crib
Ron's Ribs
Warmdaddy's

Southwestern
Abilene
Adobe Cafe
Arroyo Grille
Los Amigos' New Mexico
Santa Fe Burrito

Spanish
Cibo
La Paella Tio Pepe
Pamplona

Steakhouses
A.C. Station/AC
Bentley's Five
Brighton Steakhse./AC
Bugaboo Creek
Camelot/AC
Dock's Oyster Hse./AC
Engine 46 Steakhse.
Harry's Savoy Grill/DE
Hoss's Steak/LB
JW's Steakhse.
Kansas City Prime
Kobe Japanese

Log Cabin/LB
Lone Star Steakhse.
Maloney's Beef/CM
Max's Steak Hse./AC
Mississippi Steak/AC
Morton's of Chicago
Oaks, The/AC
Obadiah's/CM
Outback Steakhse.
Palm
Philly Crab & Steak
Prime Place/AC
Prime Rib
Pub Rest.
Rio Station/CM
Ruth's Chris
Safari Steakhse./AC
Sea Grill/CM
Seven Stars
Steakhouse/AC
Steak House/AC
Stockyard Inn/LB
Stoudt's Black Angus/LB
Sullivan's Steakhse./DE
Walter's Steakhse./DE

Thai
Amara Cafe
Bangkok City
Bangkok House/DE
Bunha Faun
Chef Charin
Jow's Garden
Lemon Grass
Lemon Grass/LB
My Thai
Nais Cuisine
Nan
Pattaya Grill
Peaches at Sunset/CM
Pho Xe Lua
Sala Thai
Siam Cuisine I
Siam Cuisine II
Siam Cuisine III
Silk Cuisine
Siri's Thai French
Somsak Thai
Stephen's
Thai Garden
Thai Orchard
Thai Pepper
Thai Singha Hse.

Vegetarian

(Most Chinese, Indian and Thai restaurants)
Cherry St. Chinese
Green Cuisine/CM
Harmony Vegetarian
Kingdom Vegetarians
Montserrat
Rajbhog Indian
Samosa
Singapore Kosher
Tang Yean

Vietnamese

Capital Vietnam
Le Colonial
Little Saigon/AC
Pho 75
Pho Xe Lua
Saigon
Van's Garden
Vietnam Palace
Vietnam Rest.

LOCATIONS

PHILADELPHIA

Center City
(West of Broad St.)
Amara Cafe
Astral Plane
Audrey Claire
Bards
Beaujolais
Bertucci's
Between Friends
Bistro St. Tropez
Bookbinders
Brasserie Perrier
Capriccio Cafe
Cary Restaurant
Cassatt Tea Rm.
Circa
Coco Pazzo
Copa-Too!
Cutters
D'Angelo's
Day by Day
Dock Street
Elephant & Castle
El Mariachi
1521 Café
Foggia
Fountain Rest.
Friday, Sat., Sun.
Fuji Mountain
Garden, The
Genji II
Happy Rooster
Harry's Bar & Grill
Hikaru
Hot Tamales Cafe
Il Portico
J.J.'s Grotto
Korea House
Le Bar Lyonnais
Le Bec-Fin
Le Bus
Le Colonial
Little Pete's
Mace's Crossing
Mademoiselle Paris
Mama Palma's
Marathon Grill
Mia's
Minar Palace
Monk's Café

Morton's of Chicago
My Thai
New Corned Beef
Nicholas Nickolas
Nick's B&G
Opus 251
Orfèo
Peacock Parkwy.
Pietro's Pizzeria
Porcini
Prime Rib
Rachael's Nosheri
Ristorante Ottimo
Ritz-Carlton Grill
Ron's Ribs
Rouge 98
Ruth's Chris
Saffron
Samuel Adams Brew
Sansom St. Oyster
Santa Fe Burrito
Sawan's Med. Bistro
Seafood Unlimited
Shiroi Hana
Stix
Striped Bass
Susanna Foo
Swann Lounge
Taj Mahal
Tequila's Authentic
Treetops
Waldorf Café
Warsaw Cafe
Wrap Planet
Xando Coffee

Center City
(East of Broad St.)
Allie's American
Aoi
Caribou Cafe
Champion's
Chanterelles
Deux Cheminées
Down Home Diner
Effie's
Fergie's Pub
Frangelica
Girasole Rist.
Hard Rock Cafe
Hardshell Cafe

Haute To Trot
Hot Tamales Cafe
Inn Philadelphia
JW's Steakhse.
Lai Lai
Maccabeam
Marathon Grill
McGillin's
More Than Ice Cream
Moriarty's
Old City Coffee
Pamplona
Passage to India
Portofino
Reading Terminal Mkt.
Ristorante La Buca
Samosa
Santa Fe Burrito
Taco House
Tenth St. Pour Hse.
Xando Coffee

Avenue of the Arts

Academy Cafe
Barrymore Room
Bonaparte
Ciboulette
DiLullo Centro
Founders
Italian Bistro
Jamaican Jerk Hut
Noodle Heaven
Palm
Tony Clark's
Upstares at Varalli
Zanzibar Blue

Chinatown

Capital Vietnam
Charles Plaza
Cherry St. Chinese
China Castle
Golden Pond
Harmony Vegetarian
H.K. Golden Phoenix
House of Chen
Imperial Inn
Joe's Peking
Joseph Poon
Joy Tsin Lau
Kingdom Vegetarians
Lee Ho Seafood
Lee How Fook
North Sea
Pho Xe Lua
Rangoon

Ray's Cafe
Sang Kee
Siam Cuisine I
Singapore Kosher
Tai Lake
Tang Yean
Thai Garden
Van's Garden
Vietnam Palace
Vietnam Rest.

South Philly

Anthony's
Assaggi Italiani
Bitar's
Bomb Bomb BBQ
Carman's Country Kit.
Celebre's Pizzeria
Cent'Anni
Dante & Luigi's
Felicia's
Frankie's at Night
Frankie's Seafood
Geno's Steaks
Gianna's
Io E Tu Rist.
Joseph's Italian
La Vigna
Little Fish
Ma Ma Yolanda's
Mamma Maria
Marra's
Melrose Diner
Michael's Rist.
Morning Glory Diner
Mr. Martino's Tratt.
Nifty Fifty's
Ozzie's Tratt.
Pastaria Franco & Luigi's
Pat's King Steaks
Pho 75
Ralph's
Roselena's Coffee
Saigon
Saloon
Shank's & Evelyn's
Tony Luke's
Tre Scalini
Triangle Tavern
Victor Café
Villa Di Roma

South St./ Society Hill/ Queen Village

Abilene
Alyan's
Artful Dodger
Azafran
Beau Monde
Bistro Romano
Bridget Foy's
Cedars
Cibo
City Tavern
Copabanana
Dickens Inn
Dmitri's
Downey's
Euro Cafe
Famous 4th St. Deli
Fez Moroccan
Frederick's
Hadley's Bistro
Hikaru
Hot Tamales Cafe
Jim's Steaks
Judy's Cafe
Knave of Hearts
La Grolla
Latest Dish
Le Champignon
Marrakesh
Martini Café
Monte Carlo
Montserrat
Mustard Greens
Old Original Book
Overtures
Pink Rose Pastry
Pompano Grille
Ristorante Primavera
Ristorante San Carlo
Sala Thai
Snockey's Oyster
South St. Souvlaki
Taxi
Tira Misu Rist.

Delaware Riverfront

Chart House
Dave & Buster's
Engine 46 Steakhse.
Katmandu
La Veranda
Meiji-En
Moshulu

Port Saloon
Rock Lobster

Old City

Azalea Room
Blue in Green
Brasil's
Continental
DiNardo's Seafood
El Mariachi
Five Spot
Fork
Jake & Oliver's
Kabul
La Cipolla Torta
La Famiglia
La Locanda
Lamberti's Cucina
Los Amigos' New Mexico
Lucy's Hat Shop
Marco's
Mexican Post
Old City Coffee
Painted Parrot
Paradigm
Philadelphia Fish
Pizzicato
Plough & the Stars
Ristorante Panorama
Rococo
Sassafras Cafe
Serrano
Society Hill Hotel
Sugar Mom's
Warmdaddy's
Xando Coffee

Northern Liberties/ Port Richmond

Finnigan's Wake
Liberties
LionFish
Ortlieb's Jazzhaus
Poor Henry's
Silk City
Spaghetti Warehse.
Tacconelli's Pizza

Art Museum

Bridgid
Cafe Flower Shop
Cuvee Notredame
Gourley's
Jack's Firehouse
London Grill
Long's Gourmet

Martini's Lounge
Museum Rest.
North Star Bar
Rembrandt's
Rose Tattoo Cafe
Tavern on Green

West Philly (University City)

Beijing
Benkady
Dahlak
Genji I
Jim's Steaks
Jow's Garden
La Terrasse
Le Bus
Lemon Grass
Mad 4 Mex
Nan
New Delhi
Palladium
Pattaya Grill
Purple Sage
Sitar India
Tandoor India
Thai Singha Hse.
30th St. Station
White Dog Cafe
Zocalo

Northwest Philly (Chestnut Hill/ Germantown/Mt. Airy)

Best of British
Cafette
Chestnut Grill
CinCin
Cresheim Cottage
Flying Fish
Goat Hollow
Melting Pot
Pollo Rosso
Rib Crib
Roller's
Solaris Grille
Umbria
Valley Green Inn

Manayunk/ Roxborough/ East Falls

Adobe Cafe
Arroyo Grille
Bella Trattoria

BLT's Cobblefish
Cafe Giuseppe
Cafe Zesty
Casselli's Rist.
Cotton Club
Dalessandro's
Edge
Grasshopper
Hikaru
Il Tartufo
Jake's
Kansas City Prime
Le Bus
Main-ly Desserts
Manayunk Brewing
Manayunk Farmer's Mkt.
River City Diner
Roscoe's Kodiak
Sonoma
Stephen's
Thomas'
United States Hotel
Vega Grill

Northeast Philly

Blüe Ox Brauhaus
Bugaboo Creek
Cafe Espresso
Cafe Michaelangelo
Country Club
El Azteca
Fisher's
Gourmet Rest.
Isabella's
Jannie
Jim's Steaks
Kawabata
Lamberti's Cucina
La Padella
La Paella Tio Pepe
Lone Star Steakhse.
Manila Bay B&G
Mayfair Diner
Moonstruck
Nifty Fifty's
Philly Crab & Steak
Pho 75
Rajbhog Indian
Ruhling's Seafood
Tony Luke's

North Philly

Berlengas Island
Kim's
Mama Rosa
Tierra Colombiana

PHILADELPHIA SUBURBS

City Line Ave.
Chung Hing
Ly Michael's
Marabella's
Marker, The

Main Line
Abbey Grill
Al Dar
Bertucci's
Big River Fish Co.
Bravo Bistro
Bunha Faun
Chef Charin
Evviva
Fuji Mountain
Garnian Wa
Gullifty's
Hunan Rest.
Hunt Room
Hymie's
Il Giardino
Jake & Oliver's
John Harvard's
Khajuraho
La Collina
La Fourchette
Malvern Meeting Hse.
Marbles
Murray's Deli
Old Guard House
Passerelle
Pepper's Cafe
Primavera Pizza Kit.
Provence
Ristorante Alberto
Ristorante Positano
Ristorante Primavera
Ruby's
Samuels
Saranac
Savona
Silk Cuisine
Taquet
Teresa's Cafe
Thai Orchard
Thai Pepper
Toscana Cucina
Trattoria San Nicola
Valley Forge
Villa Strafford
Wild Onion Rest.
Willistown Grille

Wolfgang's Cafe
Yangming

Montgomery County
Abacus
Alaina's
Alexander's Cafe
Alfio's
Arpeggio
Arugula!
Athena
August Moon
Barnacle Ben's West
Bay Pony Inn
Ben & Irv Deli
Bertolini's
Bertucci's
Big Fish
Big River Fish Co.
Blue Bell Inn
Broad Axe Tavern
Cafe Preeya
California Cafe
California Pizza Kit.
Carambola
Century House
Christopher's
Coppermill Harvest
Coyote Crossing
Deetrick's Cafe
Dick Clark's
East Side Mario's
El Mariachi
Fireside Room
General Lafayette
Golden Sea
Gypsy Rose
Homestead Rest.
Jefferson House
Johnny Mott's
Joseph Ambler
Kaufman House
Kennedy-Supplee
Kimono Sushi Bar
Kobe Japanese
La Pergola
Lone Star Steakhse.
Mainland Inn
Mandarin Garden
Marabella's
Marco Polo
Mel's Italian
Mirna's Cafe
Nul Bom

Old Mill Inn
Otto's Brauhaus
Outback Steakhse.
Palace of Asia
Persian Grill
Regatta B&G
Rhapsody's
Ristorante Gallo Nero
Ristorante Mediterraneo
Rizzo's
Ruby's
Scoogi's Classic
Siggie's L'Auberge
Smokin' Sam's
Spring Mill Café
Stazi Milano
Tex Mex Connection
Totaro's Ristorante
Trinacria
William Penn Inn
Yorktown Inn
ZuZu

Bucks County

Black Bass
Black Walnut
Cafe Arielle
Carversville Inn
Centre Bridge Inn
Chambers
Chef Tell's
Cock 'n Bull
Cuttalossa Inn
Doylestown Inn
El Sombrero
Evermay on Del.
Fisher's Tudor Hse.
Forager
Golden Pheasant
Hardshell Cafe
Havana
Hotel du Village
Il Sol D'Italia
Inn at Phillips Mill
Inn on Blueberry Hill
Isaac Newton's
Jean Pierre's
King George II
La Bonne Auberge
Lamberti's Cucina
Landing, The
La Pergola
Luigi's Canal Hse.
Martine's
Michael's Family

Mother's
Odette's
Outback Steakhse.
Paganini
Pineville Tavern
Pippo's Fantastico
Plumsteadville Inn
Russell's 96 West
Siam Cuisine II
Siam Cuisine III
Sign of Sorrel Horse
Spotted Hog
State St. Cafe
Valley Stream Inn
Washington Crossing
Washington House
Wycombe Inn
Ye Olde Temp.

Delaware County

Alberto's
Alisa Cafe
Asakura
Bobby's Seafood
Chadds Ford Inn
Concordville Inn
Crier in Country
Cuisines
D'Ignazio's
Hank's Place
Ingleneuk Tea Hse.
John Harvard's
La Campagna
La Forno
Lamb Tavern
Lauren's
Le Petit Cafe
Nais Cuisine
New Orleans Cafe
Nifty Fifty's
Outback Steakhse.
Pace One
Peking Rest.
Ristorante Positano
Rose Tree Inn
Scampi Rist.
Spiga D'Oro
Taqueria Moroleon
Village Porch

Chester County

America B&G
Coventry Forge
Dilworthtown Inn
Dinon's
Duling-Kurtz House

East Side Mario's
Epicurean, The
Flowing Springs
Four Dogs Tavern
General Warren
Gourmet's Table
Hartefeld National
Herb Garden
Kimberton Inn
La Cocotte
Lenape Inn
Margaret Kuo's
Marshalton Inn
Mendenhall Inn
Seven Stars
Ship Inn
Vickers Tavern
Vincent's
Yellow Springs Inn

New Jersey Suburbs

Acacia
A Little Cafe
Al Khimah
Andreotti's
Anton's at Swan
Athens Cafe
Bangkok City
Barnacle Ben's
Beau Rivage
Bentley's Five
Bertucci's
Braddock's Tavern
Cafe Gallery
Cafe Noelle
Caffé Aldo Lamberti
Caffe La Bella
Cassano Italian
Catelli
Champps Amer.
Chateau Silvana
Church St. Bistro
Clayton's
David's Yellow Brick
East Side Mario's
Ebenezer's
Elena Wu

Emerald Fish
Fat Jack's
Filomena Cuc. Italiana
Filomena Cuc. Rustica
Food for Thought
Frenchtown Inn
Full Moon
Giumarello's Rist.
Graziella's
Hamilton's Grill
Hardshell Cafe
Inn of the Hawke
Italian Bistro
Joe's Peking
Kaminski's
La Campagne
La Familia Sonsini
Lambertville Station
Lone Star Steakhse.
Loose Ends
Marco's Cafe
Meil's
Mexican Food
Mrs. London's Cafe
New Orleans Cafe II
New World Cafe
Nonna's
Norma's Middle Eastern
Olga's Diner
Outback Steakhse.
Pacific Grille
Pastavino Tratt.
Ponzio's Kingsway
Pub Rest.
Red Hot & Blue
Remi's Cafe
Ristorante Fieni's
Ristorante Laceno
Sagami
Sage Diner
Sakura Spring
Silk & Spice
Siri's Thai French
Somsak Thai
Stockton Inn
Tulipano Nero

OUTLYING AREAS

Lancaster/Berks County
Alois
Bird-in-Hand
Bottling Works
Brewery Inn
Catacombs
Good N' Plenty
Gracie's
Green Hills Inn
Groff's Farm
Haydn Zug's
Historic Revere Tav.
Hoss's Steak
Isaac's
Joe's Bistro 614
Lemon Grass
Log Cabin
Market Fare
Miller's Smorgasbord
Moselem Springs
Nav Jiwan Tea Rm.
Olde Greenfield Inn
Plain & Fancy
Red Caboose
Rest. at Doneckers
Stockyard Inn
Stoltzfus Farm
Stoudt's Black Angus
Willow Valley Rst.
Windmill
Zinn's Diner

Trenton
DeLorenzo's
Diamond's
Joe's Tomato Pies
Katmandu
Marsilio's

Atlantic City
A.C. Station
Andreotti's
Angeloni's II
Angelo's Fairmount
Brighton Steakhse.
Brittany Cafe
California Pizza Kit.
Camelot
Capriccio
Caruso's
Casa DiNapoli
Casa Nicola
Center Point Deli
Chef Vola's
China Moon
Dock's Oyster Hse.
Fantasea Reef
Fortune's
Girasole
Hard Rock Cafe
Il Verdi
Johan's
Le Palais
Little Saigon
Los Amigos
Max's Steak Hse.
Medici
Mississippi Steak
Oaks, The
Official All Star
Old Waterway Inn
Orsatti's
Peregrines
Pier 7
Planet Hollywood
Portofino
Primavera
Prime Place
Regent Court
Roberto's
Sabatini's
Safari Steakhse.
Scannicchio's
Scheherazade
Steakhouse
Steak House
Tony's Balt. Grill
White House
William Fisk

Cape May
A Ca Mia
Aleathea's
Alexander's Inn
Axelsson's
Cucina Rosa
Dry Dock Ice Cream
Ebbitt Room
410 Bank St.
Freda's Cafe
Frescos
Jackson Mountain
Lobster House
Louisa's Cafe
Mad Batter
Merion Inn
Peaches at Sunset
Peter Shields

Pilot House
Spiaggi
Tisha's Fine Din.
Top of the Marq
Ugly Mug
Union Park
Van Scoy's Bistro
Washington Inn
Waters Edge

Sweetwater Casino
Tomatoes
Tre Figlio
Tuckahoe Inn
Urie's Waterfront
Ventura Greenhse.
Waterfront
W.L. Goodfellows
Yesterday's

Jersey Shore

Alfe's
A Touch of Italy
Busch's
Cafe 8 South
Cedar Creek
Charlie's Bar
Cousin's
Cousins Country
Crab Trap
Cucina Rustica
Culinary Garden
Dave's Center Point Deli
Deauville Inn
Doc's Place
Fedeli's
Fork's Inn
Gary's Little Rock
Golden Inn
Green Cuisine
Gregory's
Hatteras Coastal
Henny's
Inn at Sugar Hill
Joe Italiano's/Inn
Joe Italiano's/II
Little Brat's Haus
Lobster Loft
Mac's
Maloney's Beef
Mama Mia
Melissa's Bistro
Mirage, The
Obadiah's
Oceanfront
Ram's Head Inn
Ravioli House
Renault Winery
Rio Station
Savaradio
Schooners & C.B.'s
Screnci's
Sea Grill
Sutor's Owl Tree

Wilmington/
Nearby Delaware

Back Burner
Bangkok House
Brandywine Brewing
Brandywine Room
Buckley's Tavern
Caffe Bellissimo
Carucci
Charcoal Pit
Columbus Inn
DiNardo's
Feby's Fishery
Fox Point Grill
Green Room
Harry's Savoy Grill
Hibachi Japanese
India Palace
Iron Hill Brewery
Krazy Kats
La Casa Pasta
La Tolteca
L'Osteria Cucina
Luigi Vitrone's
Michele's
Mikasa
Mrs. Robino's
Pala's Cafe
Piccolo Mondo
Positano Rist.
Ristorante Amalfi
Ristorante Attilio
Sal's
Shipley Grill
Sienna
Silk Purse
Sow's Ear
Sullivan's Steakhse.
Tavola Toscana
Terrace at Greenhill
Utage
Vincente's
Walter's Steakhse.
Waterworks Cafe

SPECIAL FEATURES AND APPEALS

Breakfast

(All hotels and the following standouts)
Andreotti's
Ben & Irv Deli
Blue in Green
Carman's Country Kit.
Center Point Deli/AC
Country Club
Culinary Garden/CM
Down Home Diner
Golden Inn/CM
Hank's Place
Hymie's
Kim's
Kingdom Vegetarians
Le Bus
Little Pete's
Mademoiselle Paris
Manayunk Farmer's Mkt.
Marathon Grill
Meil's
Melrose Diner
Michael's Family
Morning Glory Diner
Mother's
Murray's Deli
New Corned Beef
Nifty Fifty's
Old City Coffee
Olga's Diner
Pink Rose Pastry
Ponzio's Kingsway
Rachael's Nosheri
Reading Terminal Mkt.
Red Caboose/LB
River City Diner
Sage Diner
Shank's & Evelyn's
Silk City
Spotted Hog
Tenth St. Pour Hse.
30th St. Station
Windmill/LB

Brunch

(Best of many)
Alexander's Inn/CM
Andreotti's
Arroyo Grille
Azalea Room
Barrymore Room
Black Bass
Blue in Green
Cafe Gallery
California Cafe
Carman's Country Kit.
Caruso's/AC
Carversville Inn
Casa Nicola/AC
Chateau Silvana
Chef Tell's
Cousins Country/CM
Crier in Country
Cucina Rustica/CM
Dahlak
1521 Café
Fireside Room
Fork's Inn/CM
Founders
Fountain Rest.
Golden Pheasant
Green Room/DE
Hadley's Bistro
Harry's Savoy Grill/DE
Herb Garden
Hunt Room
Inn Philadelphia
Jack's Firehouse
Judy's Cafe
La Campagne
La Fourchette
Lambertville Station
La Terrasse
Le Bus
London Grill
Marker, The
Market Fare/LB
Meiji-En
Mendenhall Inn
Morning Glory Diner
Olde Greenfield Inn/LB
Opus 251
Palace of Asia
Plumsteadville Inn
Prime Place/AC
Regatta B&G
Regent Court/AC
Rembrandt's
Renault Winery/CM
Roselena's Coffee
Russell's 96 West
Samuels
Swann Lounge
Tavern on Green

Treetops
Warmdaddy's
White Dog Cafe
William Penn Inn
Yellow Springs Inn
Ye Olde Temp.

Buffet Served

(Check prices, days
and times)
Abbey Grill
Academy Cafe
Alberto's
Alexander's Cafe
Allie's American
Aoi
Azalea Room
Barrymore Room
Bay Pony Inn
Bentley's Five
Between Friends
Bird-in-Hand/LB
Black Bass
Bobby's Seafood
Brighton Steakhse./AC
Cafe Gallery
Cafe Michaelangelo
Caruso's/AC
Casa Nicola/AC
Chef Tell's
Cock 'n Bull
Coppermill Harvest
Cousins Country/CM
Crier in Country
Dahlak
David's Yellow Brick
Fantasea Reef/AC
Fez Moroccan
Finnigan's Wake
Fork's Inn/CM
Founders
Gianna's
Gourmet's Table
Graziella's
Green Room/DE
Harry's Savoy Grill/DE
Hartefeld National
Henny's/CM
Hibachi Japanese/DE
Hunt Room
Jake & Oliver's
Judy's Cafe
Katmandu
Khajuraho
Lambertville Station

La Padella
La Tolteca/DE
Lobster Loft/CM
Manayunk Brewing
Manila Bay B&G
Marrakesh
Meiji-En
Mendenhall Inn
Miller's Smorgasbord/LB
Moshulu
Nav Jiwan Tea Rm./LB
Odette's
Opus 251
Otto's Brauhaus
Passage to India
Prime Place/AC
Ravioli House/CM
Regatta B&G
Regent Court/AC
Renault Winery/CM
Roberto's/AC
Roselena's Coffee
Russell's 96 West
Samosa
Samuels
Sawan's Med. Bistro
Ship Inn
Swann Lounge
Sweetwater Casino/CM
Taj Mahal
Tre Figlio/CM
Urie's Waterfront/CM
Valley Stream Inn
Villa Di Roma
Waterfront/CM
William Penn Inn
Willow Valley Rst./LB
Ye Olde Temp.
Yorktown Inn

Business Dining

Angeloni's II/AC
Azalea Room
Between Friends
Brasserie Perrier
Coco Pazzo
Cutters
Duling-Kurtz House
Fountain Rest.
Garden, The
Harry's Bar & Grill
Il Portico
Kansas City Prime
Le Bec-Fin
Marker, The

Morton's of Chicago
Nicholas Nickolas
Old Guard House
Old Original Book
Palm
Ristorante La Buca
Ruth's Chris
Saloon
Shipley Grill/DE
Striped Bass
Susanna Foo
Tony Clark's
Treetops
Yangming

BYO

Abacus
Acacia
A Ca Mia/CM
Alaina's
Alexander's Inn/CM
Alisa Cafe
A Little Cafe
Al Khimah
Alyan's
Anthony's
Asakura
Athena
Athens Cafe
Audrey Claire
Azafran
Bangkok City
Barnacle Ben's
Beijing
Benkady
Best of British
Black Walnut
BLT's Cobblefish
Blue in Green
Brittany Cafe/AC
Bunha Faun
Cafe 8 South/CM
Cafe Flower Shop
Cafe Noelle
Cafe Preeya
Cafette
Caffe La Bella
Carambola
Carman's Country Kit.
Chef Charin
Chef Vola's/AC
Cherry St. Chinese
China Castle
Cucina Rosa/CM
Cucina Rustica/CM

Dahlak
DeLorenzo's
Dinon's
Dmitri's
Down Home Diner
Ebenezer's
Effie's
Elena Wu
El Sombrero
Emerald Fish
Fedeli's/CM
1521 Café
Food for Thought
410 Bank St./CM
Frankie's at Night
Freda's Cafe/CM
Frescos/CM
Full Moon
Garnian Wa
Gary's Little Rock/CM
Giumarello's Rist.
Golden Sea
Gourley's
Gourmet's Table
Green Cuisine/CM
Hamilton's Grill
Hardshell Cafe
Hatteras Coastal/CM
Haute To Trot
Herb Garden
Il Tartufo
Ingleneuk Tea Hse.
Inn at Phillips Mill
Jamaican Jerk Hut
Joe's Tomato Pies
Johan's/AC
Joseph Poon
Kabul
Khajuraho
Kimono Sushi Bar
Kim's
Kingdom Vegetarians
Korea House
La Campagne
La Cipolla Torta
La Cocotte
La Familia Sonsini
La Forno
La Locanda
Lamberti's Cucina
La Pergola
Lauren's
Lee How Fook
Lemon Grass/LB
Le Petit Cafe

LionFish
Little Brat's Haus/CM
Little Fish
Little Saigon/AC
Lobster Loft/CM
Loose Ends
Louisa's Cafe/CM
Maccabeam
Mad Batter/CM
Mademoiselle Paris
Main-ly Desserts
Mama Mia/CM
Mama Palma's
Mamma Maria
Marathon Grill
Marco's
Marco's Cafe
Margaret Kuo's
Meil's
Melissa's Bistro/CM
Michael's Family
Minar Palace
Mirna's Cafe
Morning Glory Diner
Mr. Martino's Tratt.
Mrs. London's Cafe
Nais Cuisine
Nan
New Orleans Cafe II
Nonna's
Noodle Heaven
Norma's Middle Eastern
Overtures
Pacific Grille
Painted Parrot
Pastaria Franco & Luigi's
Peaches at Sunset/CM
Pepper's Cafe
Peter Shields/CM
Pink Rose Pastry
Porcini
Purple Sage
Rajbhog Indian
Remi's Cafe
Ristorante Fieni's
Ristorante Laceno
Ron's Ribs
Roselena's Coffee
Sagami
Sage Diner
Sakura Spring
Santa Fe Burrito
Saranac
Savaradio/CM
Screnci's/CM

Shank's & Evelyn's
Singapore Kosher
Siri's Thai French
Sitar India
Somsak Thai
Spiga D'Oro
Spring Mill Café
State St. Cafe
Taco House
Taj Mahal
Tang Yean
Taqueria Moroleon
Tenth St. Pour Hse.
Teresa's Cafe
Thai Orchard
Thai Pepper
Tisha's Fine Din./CM
Tomatoes/CM
Tre Scalini
Tulipano Nero
Umbria
Union Park/CM
Van Scoy's Bistro/CM
Van's Garden
Village Porch
Wolfgang's Cafe
Wrap Planet
ZuZu

Caters
(Best of many)
Alaina's
A Little Cafe
Andreotti's
Anton's at Swan
Arpeggio
August Moon
Barrymore Room
Bay Pony Inn
Berlengas Island
Bistro St. Tropez
Bitar's
Black Walnut
BLT's Cobblefish
Cafe Arielle
Cafe 8 South/CM
Cafe Noelle
Carucci/DE
Cary Restaurant
Casselli's Rist.
Catelli
Century House
Charles Plaza
Cherry St. Chinese
Church St. Bistro

Cibo
Circa
Clayton's
Columbus Inn/DE
Cotton Club
Crier in Country
Cucina Rustica/CM
Cuisines
Dahlak
D'Angelo's
David's Yellow Brick
Day by Day
DiLullo Centro
Doc's Place/CM
Ebenezer's
Effie's
El Mariachi
Emerald Fish
Evviva
Famous 4th St. Deli
Filomena Cuc. Italiana
Filomena Cuc. Rustica
Food for Thought
Frankie's at Night
Frankie's Seafood
Fuji Mountain
Gary's Little Rock/CM
Genji I
Genji II
Girasole/AC
Golden Pheasant
Gourmet's Table
Gracie's/LB
Gregory's/CM
Hamilton's Grill
Harry's Savoy Grill/DE
Hartefeld National
Hatteras Coastal/CM
Haute To Trot
Herb Garden
Historic Revere Tav./LB
H.K. Golden Phoenix
Hymie's
India Palace/DE
Isaac's/LB
Isabella's
Jack's Firehouse
Jamaican Jerk Hut
Jannie
Joe Italiano's/Inn/CM
Joe Italiano's/II/CM
Joseph Poon
Joseph's Italian
Khajuraho
La Bonne Auberge

La Cocotte
Lamberti's Cucina
La Padella
Latest Dish
La Tolteca/DE
Lauren's
La Veranda
Lemon Grass/LB
Little Brat's Haus/CM
Log Cabin/LB
Los Amigos/AC
Los Amigos' New Mexico
Mademoiselle Paris
Mad 4 Mex
Main-ly Desserts
Mama Palma's
Mamma Maria
Market Fare/LB
Mendenhall Inn
Michele's/DE
Mirna's Cafe
Mrs. London's Cafe
Nav Jiwan Tea Rm./LB
New World Cafe
Nonna's
Obadiah's/CM
Oceanfront/CM
Old Guard House
Opus 251
Pace One
Pacific Grille
Painted Parrot
Palace of Asia
Paradigm
Passerelle
Pepper's Cafe
Pilot House/CM
Pink Rose Pastry
Pompano Grille
Port Saloon
Provence
Purple Sage
Ram's Head Inn/CM
Ravioli House/CM
Ristorante Amalfi/DE
Ristorante Mediterraneo
Rococo
Roller's
Roscoe's Kodiak
Russell's 96 West
Saffron
Sakura Spring
Sal's/DE
Saranac
Savona

Schooners & C.B.'s/CM
Shipley Grill/DE
Shiroi Hana
Siggie's L'Auberge
Silk Purse/DE
Siri's Thai French
Spring Mill Café
Stockton Inn
Tavola Toscana/DE
Taxi
Tex Mex Connection
Tomatoes/CM
Toscana Cucina
Totaro's Ristorante
Tre Figlio/CM
Van Scoy's Bistro/CM
Villa Strafford
Washington House
Washington Inn/CM
Waters Edge/CM
Waterworks Cafe/DE
Windmill/LB
Yellow Springs Inn
Yesterday's/CM

Cigar Friendly

Abilene
Alexander's Cafe
Allie's American
America B&G
Arroyo Grille
Arugula!
Assaggi Italiani
Bards
Barrymore Room
Beau Rivage
Benkady
Bentley's Five
Blue Bell Inn
Blüe Ox Brauhaus
Braddock's Tavern
Brandywine Brewing/DE
Brighton Steakhse./AC
Brittany Cafe/AC
Cafe Arielle
Cafe Giuseppe
Caffe Bellissimo/DE
Caruso's/AC
Casa Nicola/AC
Cassano Italian
Catelli
Champion's
Champps Amer.
Chef Tell's
Christopher's

Ciboulette
Circa
Clayton's
Columbus Inn/DE
Continental
Copabanana
Cotton Club
Coyote Crossing
Crier in Country
Cuisines
D'Angelo's
Deauville Inn/CM
Deetrick's Cafe
Diamond's
Dickens Inn
D'Ignazio's
Dock Street
Doc's Place/CM
Doylestown Inn
Edge
Elephant & Castle
Engine 46 Steakhse.
Epicurean, The
Euro Cafe
Fat Jack's
Fergie's Pub
Filomena Cuc. Rustica
Fireside Room
Five Spot
Flowing Springs
Fortune's/AC
Founders
Fox Point Grill/DE
Frankie's Seafood
Frederick's
Frenchtown Inn
Garden, The
General Lafayette
Girasole/AC
Golden Pheasant
Gracie's/LB
Gypsy Rose
Happy Rooster
Hard Rock Cafe
Harry's Savoy Grill/DE
Hartefeld National
Havana
Hibachi Japanese/DE
Hoss's Steak/LB
Il Giardino
Il Portico
Il Sol D'Italia
Inn at Sugar Hill/CM
Inn of the Hawke
Inn Philadelphia

Iron Hill Brewery/DE
Jake & Oliver's
Jean Pierre's
Johan's/AC
John Harvard's
Joseph Ambler
Joseph's Italian
JW's Steakhse.
Kaminski's
Kansas City Prime
Katmandu
Kaufman House
King George II
La Campagna
La Campagne
Lambertville Station
La Veranda
Le Bar Lyonnais
Le Colonial
Lenape Inn
Liberties
Lobster House/CM
Log Cabin/LB
London Grill
Mace's Crossing
Maloney's Beef/CM
Malvern Meeting Hse.
Mamma Maria
Manayunk Brewing
Marabella's
Marker, The
Marshalton Inn
Marsilio's
Martini's Lounge
Max's Steak Hse./AC
McGillin's
Medici/AC
Meiji-En
Mel's Italian
Mia's
Michele's/DE
Monte Carlo
Montserrat
More Than Ice Cream
Morton's of Chicago
Moselem Springs/LB
Nick's B&G
Nonna's
North Star Bar
Oaks, The/AC
Official All Star/AC
Old Guard House
Old Original Book
Otto's Brauhaus
Ozzie's Tratt.

Pace One
Pala's Cafe/DE
Palm
Paradigm
Peacock Parkwy.
Peregrines/AC
Pilot House/CM
Pineville Tavern
Pippo's Fantastico
Planet Hollywood/AC
Plough & the Stars
Pompano Grille
Poor Henry's
Port Saloon
Prime Rib
Provence
Purple Sage
Ram's Head Inn/CM
Renault Winery/CM
Rio Station/CM
Ristorante Mediterraneo
Ristorante Panorama
Ristorante Positano
Ritz-Carlton Grill
Roberto's/AC
Rococo
Rose Tree Inn
Ruhling's Seafood
Russell's 96 West
Ruth's Chris
Sal's/DE
Samuel Adams Brew
Samuels
Sansom St. Oyster
Scannicchio's/AC
Scoogi's Classic
Seven Stars
Ship Inn
Sienna/DE
Sign of Sorrel Horse
Smokin' Sam's
Snockey's Oyster
Society Hill Hotel
Sonoma
Spaghetti Warehse.
Stephen's
Stoudt's Black Angus/LB
Sugar Mom's
Sullivan's Steakhse./DE
Sutor's Owl Tree/CM
Sweetwater Casino/CM
Tavern on Green
Taxi
Thomas'
Tira Misu Rist.

Tony Clark's
Triangle Tavern
Tuckahoe Inn/CM
Union Park/CM
United States Hotel
Urie's Waterfront/CM
Villa Strafford
Vincente's/DE
Vincent's
Walter's Steakhse./DE
Washington Crossing
Washington Inn/CM
Waterfront/CM
Waterworks Cafe/DE
W.L. Goodfellows/CM
Xando Coffee
Yellow Springs Inn
Ye Olde Temp.
Zanzibar Blue

Dancing/Entertainment

(Check days, times and
performers for entertainment;
D=dancing; best of many)

Abbey Grill (D/DJ)
Abilene (D/varies)
Adobe Cafe (varies)
Alaina's (piano)
Alberto's (D/varies)
Al Dar (varies)
Alfe's/CM (D/varies)
Al Khimah (belly dancer)
Andreotti's (D/varies)
Andreotti's/AC (guitar)
Artful Dodger (varies)
Axelsson's/CM (piano)
Azalea Room (D/varies)
Bards (varies)
Barrymore Room (D/piano)
Bay Pony Inn (guitar/piano)
Beau Monde (accordion)
Between Friends (D/jazz/piano)
Bistro Romano (piano)
Bistro St. Tropez (jazz)
Black Bass (piano)
Blue Bell Inn (D/piano)
Bobby's Seafood (D/blues)
Bonaparte (piano)
Brandywine Brewing/DE (jazz)
Brandywine Room/DE (jazz)
Brasil's (D/jazz)
Brighton Steakhse./AC (piano)
Broad Axe Tavern (rock/swing)
Busch's/CM (vocals)
Cafe Espresso (flamenco)

Cafe Giuseppe (accordion/piano)
Cafe Zesty (D/varies)
Caffe La Bella (harp)
California Cafe (jazz)
Capriccio/AC (guitar/vocals)
Carucci/DE (opera singer/piano)
Carversville Inn (classical)
Casselli's Rist. (opera singer)
Catelli (bands)
Cedars (belly dancer)
Circa (D)
Coco Pazzo (D/jazz)
Columbus Inn/DE (piano)
Cotton Club (D/singer)
Cousins Country/CM (piano)
Coyote Crossing (guitar/Spanish)
Crab Trap/CM (D/bands)
Crier in Country (varies)
Cuttalossa Inn (D/rock)
D'Angelo's (serenade)
Dave & Buster's (bands)
Deauville Inn/CM (D/duo)
Deetrick's Cafe (jazz)
Dick Clark's (D)
D'Ignazio's (piano)
DiLullo Centro (piano)
Dock's Oyster Hse./AC (piano)
Dock Street (D/varies)
Downey's (jazz/piano)
Doylestown Inn (jazz)
Ebbitt Room/CM (piano)
Ebenezer's (varies)
Edge (D)
El Mariachi (mariachi)
Emerald Fish (guitar)
Epicurean, The (blues/jazz/rock)
Fat Jack's (blues)
Fergie's Pub (blues/rock)
Fez Moroccan (belly dancer)
Finnigan's Wake (D/Irish/rock)
Fireside Room (jazz/piano)
Five Spot (D/salsa/swing)
Foggia (cabaret)
Forager (vocals)
Founders (D/jazz/piano)
Four Dogs Tavern (folk/jazz)
Frankie's at Night (opera)
Frederick's (D/big band/piano)
General Lafayette (folk)
Goat Hollow (varies)
Golden Inn/CM (D/bands)
Gracie's/LB (jazz)
Graziella's (opera)
Green Room/DE (harp/jazz)
Hadley's Bistro (D/piano)

Hard Rock Cafe/AC (bands)
Harry's Savoy Grill/DE (piano)
Hartefeld National (bands/jazz)
Havana (jazz/karaoke/R&B)
Henny's/CM (bands)
H.K. Golden Phoenix (karaoke)
Homestead Rest. (varies)
Hunt Room (varies)
Il Sol D'Italia (D/jazz/rock)
Inn at Phillips Mill (vocals)
Inn Philadelphia (piano)
Iron Hill Brewery/DE (blues/jazz)
Jack's Firehouse (varies)
Jake & Oliver's (D/DJ)
Jamaican Jerk Hut (steel band)
J.J.'s Grotto (jazz)
John Harvard's (varies)
Joseph Ambler (jazz)
Joy Tsin Lau (karaoke)
Katmandu (D/bands)
Kaufman House (varies)
Kennedy-Supplee (piano)
Kimberton Inn (harp/piano)
Kimono Sushi Bar (varies)
Kingdom Vegetarians (varies)
King George II (D/piano)
La Campagna (D/varies)
La Cipolla Torta (jazz)
La Collina (D/varies)
Lambertville Station (D/jazz)
Landing, The (varies)
La Padella (D/piano)
La Terrasse (piano)
Lauren's (jazz)
La Veranda (piano)
Le Bec-Fin (classical/guitar)
Le Champignon (D/jazz)
Le Palais/AC (piano/vocals)
Liberties (jazz)
LionFish (acoustic)
Log Cabin/LB (piano)
London Grill (bands)
Luigi's Canal Hse. (jazz/piano)
Manayunk Brewing (blues/jazz)
Marker, The (piano)
Marrakesh (belly dancer)
Martini's Lounge (funk/jazz)
McGillin's (D)
Meiji-En (jazz)
Mel's Italian (jazz)
Mendenhall Inn (harp/piano)
Merion Inn/CM (jazz/piano)
Mia's (piano)
Mirage, The/CM (piano)
Mississippi Steak/AC (piano)

Monte Carlo (DJ)
Moshulu (D/jazz)
Nick's B&G (piano)
North Star Bar (varies)
Obadiah's/CM (classical/piano)
Odette's (cabaret/piano)
Old City Coffee (acoustic)
Olde Greenfield Inn/LB (piano)
Orsatti's/AC (varies)
Ortlieb's Jazzhaus (jazz)
Ozzie's Tratt. (piano)
Paradigm (bands)
Passage to India (piano)
Passerelle (jazz)
Pastaria Franco & Luigi's (opera)
Peter Shields/CM (guitar)
Pier 7/AC (bands)
Pippo's Fantastico (D/varies)
Plough & the Stars (D/Irish)
Pompano Grille (D/Latin)
Portofino/AC (varies)
Prime Place/AC (harp)
Prime Rib (piano)
Ram's Head Inn/CM (varies)
Red Hot & Blue (blues)
Regatta B&G (piano)
Rembrandt's (varies)
Renault Winery/CM (piano)
Rio Station/CM (D/varies)
Ristorante Gallo Nero (piano)
Ristorante Mediterraneo (piano)
Ristorante Ottimo (jazz)
River City Diner (jazz)
Rock Lobster (D/jazz/rock)
Rose Tree Inn (piano)
Ruhling's Seafood (D/bands/DJ)
Sal's/DE (guitar/Latin)
Samuels (D/jazz)
Schooners & C.B.'s/CM (bands)
Ship Inn (piano)
Sign of Sorrel Horse (piano)
Silk City (varies)
Society Hill Hotel (jazz/piano)
Stazi Milano (jazz/rock)
Steakhouse/AC (piano)
Stockton Inn (D/piano)
Sullivan's Steakhse./DE (jazz)
Sutor's Owl Tree/CM (D/duo)
Swann Lounge (jazz)
Taqueria Moroleon (mariachi)
Tex Mex Connection (bands)
Thomas' (blues/jazz)
Tierra Colombiana (D/Latin)
Tira Misu Rist. (piano)
Tony Clark's (jazz)

Top of the Marq/CM (D/varies)
Triangle Tavern (bands)
Trinacria (guitar)
Tuckahoe Inn/CM (D/jazz)
Tulipano Nero (vocals)
Ugly Mug/CM (D/bands/DJ)
United States Hotel (jazz)
Upstares at Varalli (piano)
Urie's Waterfront/CM (bands)
Valley Stream Inn (piano)
Vickers Tavern (piano)
Victor Café (opera)
Villa Strafford (jazz)
Vincent's (blues/jazz)
Warmdaddy's (blues)
Washington Crossing (D/piano)
Waterfront/CM (D/music)
White Dog Cafe (piano)
William Penn Inn (harp/piano)
Willistown Grille (jazz)
Wycombe Inn (duos/trios)
Yangming (piano)
Ye Olde Temp. (jazz)
Yesterday's/CM (D/jazz)
Zanzibar Blue (jazz)

Delivers*/Takeout

(Nearly all Asians, coffee
shops, delis, diners and
pasta/pizzerias deliver or do
takeout; here are some
interesting possibilities;
D=delivery, T=takeout; * call
to check range and charges,
if any)
Academy Cafe (T)
A Ca Mia/CM (T)
Adobe Cafe (T)
Alaina's (D,T)
Al Dar (T)
Alfe's/CM (T)
A Little Cafe (D,T)
Al Khimah (D,T)
Allie's American (T)
Alyan's (T)
America B&G (T)
Andreotti's (D,T)
Anton's at Swan (T)
Arroyo Grille (T)
Artful Dodger (T)
Arugula! (T)
Athena (T)
Athens Cafe (T)
Audrey Claire (T)
Azafran (T)

Back Burner/DE (T)
Barnacle Ben's (T)
Bay Pony Inn (D,T)
Beaujolais (T)
Benkady (D,T)
Berlengas Island (T)
Best of British (T)
Big Fish (T)
Big River Fish Co. (T)
Bird-in-Hand/LB (T)
Bistro Romano (D,T)
Bistro St. Tropez (T)
Bitar's (T)
Black Bass (T)
Black Walnut (T)
BLT's Cobblefish (T)
Blue in Green (T)
Blüe Ox Brauhaus (T)
Bobby's Seafood (T)
Bomb Bomb BBQ (T)
Bookbinders (T)
Brandywine Brewing/DE (T)
Brasil's (T)
Bravo Bistro (T)
Broad Axe Tavern (T)
Buckley's Tavern/DE (T)
Bugaboo Creek (T)
Busch's/CM (T)
Cafe 8 South/CM (T)
Cafe Espresso (D,T)
Cafe Flower Shop (T)
Cafe Noelle (D,T)
Cafe Preeya (T)
Cafette (D,T)
Caffe La Bella (T)
California Cafe (T)
Carambola (T)
Caribou Cafe (T)
Carman's Country Kit. (T)
Carucci/DE (D,T)
Catelli (T)
Cedars (D,T)
Century House (T)
Chambers (T)
Champps Amer. (T)
Charlie's Bar/CM (T)
Chef Tell's (T)
Chestnut Grill (D,T)
Cibo (D,T)
Circa (T)
Coco Pazzo (T)
Columbus Inn/DE (T)
Concordville Inn (T)
Continental (T)
Copabanana (T)

Copa-Too! (T)
Cotton Club (T)
Cousin's/CM (T)
Coyote Crossing (T)
Crab Trap/CM (T)
Cresheim Cottage (T)
Crier in Country (T)
Cucina Rustica/CM (T)
Cuisines (D,T)
Culinary Garden/CM (T)
Cutters (T)
Cuvee Notredame (T)
Dahlak (T)
David's Yellow Brick (T)
Day by Day (D,T)
Deauville Inn/CM (T)
Dick Clark's (T)
Dickens Inn (T)
D'Ignazio's (T)
DiNardo's/DE (T)
DiNardo's Seafood (T)
Dinon's (T)
Dock Street (T)
Doc's Place/CM (T)
Downey's (T)
Dry Dock Ice Cream/CM (T)
East Side Mario's (D,T)
Ebenezer's (T)
Effie's (D,T)
El Azteca (T)
Elephant & Castle (T)
El Mariachi (T)
El Sombrero (T)
Emerald Fish (T)
Engine 46 Steakhse. (T)
Epicurean, The (T)
Evviva (T)
Fat Jack's (T)
Feby's Fishery/DE (T)
Fergie's Pub (T)
1521 Café (T)
Filomena Cuc. Rustica (T)
Finnigan's Wake (T)
Fireside Room (T)
Fisher's (T)
Fisher's Tudor Hse. (T)
Flowing Springs (T)
Flying Fish (T)
Forager (T)
Fork's Inn/CM (T)
Four Dogs Tavern (T)
Frankie's Seafood (D,T)
Freda's Cafe/CM (T)
Frenchtown Inn (T)
Friday, Sat., Sun. (T)

General Lafayette (T)
Girasole/AC (T)
Giumarello's Rist. (T)
Goat Hollow (T)
Golden Pheasant (D,T)
Good N' Plenty/LB (T)
Gourley's (T)
Gourmet's Table (T)
Gracie's/LB (T)
Graziella's (T)
Green Cuisine/CM (T)
Gregory's/CM (T)
Gullifty's (T)
Gypsy Rose (T)
Hank's Place (T)
Hard Rock Cafe/AC (T)
Hardshell Cafe (T)
Harry's Savoy Grill/DE (T)
Hartefeld National (T)
Haute To Trot (D,T)
Havana (T)
Haydn Zug's/LB (T)
Herb Garden (T)
Historic Revere Tav./LB (T)
Hoss's Steak/LB (T)
Hot Tamales Cafe (T)
Hunt Room (T)
Il Portico (T)
Il Sol D'Italia (D,T)
Il Tartufo (T)
India Palace/DE (T)
Ingleneuk Tea Hse. (T)
Inn of the Hawke (T)
Iron Hill Brewery/DE (T)
Isaac Newton's (D,T)
Jackson Mountain/CM (T)
Jake & Oliver's (T)
Jake's (T)
Jamaican Jerk Hut (T)
Johnny Mott's (T)
Joseph's Italian (D,T)
Kaminski's (T)
Kansas City Prime (T)
Kaufman House (T)
Khajuraho (T)
King George II (T)
Knave of Hearts (T)
La Bonne Auberge (T)
La Campagne (T)
La Grolla (T)
Lamberti's Cucina (D,T)
Lambertville Station (T)
Landing, The (T)
La Padella (T)
La Terrasse (T)

La Tolteca/DE (D,T)
Lauren's (T)
Le Bus (T)
Liberties (T)
Little Brat's Haus/CM (T)
Little Fish (T)
Lobster House/CM (T)
Lobster Loft/CM (T)
London Grill (T)
Lone Star Steakhse. (T)
Loose Ends (D,T)
Los Amigos/AC (T)
Los Amigos' New Mexico (T)
L'Osteria Cucina/DE (T)
Luigi's Canal Hse. (T)
Luigi Vitrone's/DE (T)
Maccabeam (D,T)
Mac's/CM (T)
Mad Batter/CM (T)
Mademoiselle Paris (T)
Mad 4 Mex (T)
Maloney's Beef/CM (T)
Malvern Meeting Hse. (T)
Mama Rosa (T)
Ma Ma Yolanda's (T)
Mamma Maria (T)
Manayunk Brewing (T)
Marathon Grill (D,T)
Marbles (T)
Marco Polo (T)
Market Fare/LB (D,T)
Marshalton Inn (T)
Marsilio's (D,T)
Martine's (T)
Meil's (T)
Mexican Food (T)
Mexican Post (D,T)
Michele's/DE (T)
Minar Palace (D,T)
Mirna's Cafe (T)
Monk's Café (T)
Montserrat (T)
Moonstruck (D,T)
More Than Ice Cream (T)
Moriarty's (D,T)
Morton's of Chicago (T)
Mother's (T)
Mrs. London's Cafe (T)
Mrs. Robino's/DE (D,T)
Nav Jiwan Tea Rm./LB (T)
New Delhi (D,T)
New Orleans Cafe (T)
New Orleans Cafe II (T)
Nick's B&G (T)
Nonna's (D,T)

Norma's Middle Eastern (D,T)
North Star Bar (T)
Obadiah's/CM (T)
Olde Greenfield Inn/LB (D,T)
Old Guard House (T)
Old Original Book (T)
Old Waterway Inn/AC (T)
Opus 251 (T)
Ortlieb's Jazzhaus (T)
Otto's Brauhaus (T)
Outback Steakhse. (T)
Pacific Grille (T)
Painted Parrot (T)
Palace of Asia (D,T)
Pala's Cafe/DE (T)
Palladium (D,T)
Palm (T)
Pamplona (T)
Paradigm (T)
Passage to India (D,T)
Passerelle (D,T)
Pastavino Tratt. (D,T)
Peacock Parkwy. (T)
Penang (T)
Pepper's Cafe (T)
Persian Grill (T)
Piccolo Mondo/DE (T)
Pilot House/CM (T)
Pineville Tavern (T)
Pollo Rosso (T)
Pompano Grille (D,T)
Poor Henry's (T)
Prime Rib (T)
Provence (T)
Pub Rest. (T)
Purple Sage (T)
Rajbhog Indian (D,T)
Ram's Head Inn/CM (T)
Rangoon (T)
Red Caboose/LB (T)
Red Hot & Blue (T)
Rembrandt's (T)
Remi's Cafe (T)
Rib Crib (T)
Rio Station/CM (T)
Ristorante Alberto (T)
Ristorante Amalfi/DE (T)
Ristorante Attilio/DE (T)
Ristorante Gallo Nero (T)
Ristorante Laceno (T)
Ristorante Mediterraneo (T)
Ristorante Positano (T)
Ristorante Primavera (T)
Rock Lobster (T)
Roller's (T)

Ron's Ribs (T)
Roscoe's Kodiak (T)
Rose Tattoo Cafe (T)
Rose Tree Inn (T)
Rouge 98 (T)
Ruhling's Seafood (T)
Ruth's Chris (T)
Sal's/DE (T)
Samuel Adams Brew (T)
Sansom St. Oyster (T)
Santa Fe Burrito (D,T)
Saranac (T)
Savaradio/CM (T)
Savona (T)
Sawan's Med. Bistro (D,T)
Scampi Rist. (T)
Schooners & C.B.'s/CM (T)
Screnci's/CM (T)
Seafood Unlimited (D,T)
Sea Grill/CM (T)
Serrano (T)
Seven Stars (T)
Shank's & Evelyn's (T)
Ship Inn (D,T)
Shipley Grill/DE (T)
Sienna/DE (T)
Siggie's L'Auberge (T)
Silk Purse/DE (T)
Sitar India (D,T)
Smokin' Sam's (T)
Snockey's Oyster (T)
Society Hill Hotel (T)
Solaris Grille (T)
Sonoma (T)
Spiaggi/CM (T)
Spotted Hog (T)
State St. Cafe (T)
Stix (T)
Stockton Inn (T)
Stockyard Inn/LB (T)
Stoudt's Black Angus/LB (T)
Sugar Mom's (T)
Sutor's Owl Tree/CM (T)
Sweetwater Casino/CM (T)
Taj Mahal (T)
Tandoor India (D,T)
Taqueria Moroleon (T)
Tavern on Green (T)
Tavola Toscana/DE (T)
Taxi (T)
Tenth St. Pour Hse. (D,T)
Terrace at Greenhill/DE (T)
Tex Mex Connection (T)
Tierra Colombiana (T)
Toscana Cucina (T)

Totaro's Ristorante (T)
Trattoria San Nicola (T)
Tre Figlio/CM (T)
Triangle Tavern (T)
Tuckahoe Inn/CM (T)
Ugly Mug/CM (T)
United States Hotel (T)
Upstares at Varalli (T)
Urie's Waterfront/CM (T)
Valley Forge (T)
Valley Green Inn (T)
Valley Stream Inn (T)
Vega Grill (T)
Ventura Greenhse./CM (T)
Villa Di Roma (T)
Village Porch (D,T)
Waldorf Café (D,T)
Walter's Steakhse./DE (T)
Warmdaddy's (T)
Washington House (D,T)
Waterfront/CM (T)
Waters Edge/CM (T)
White House/AC (T)
Wild Onion Rest. (T)
Willow Valley Rst./LB (T)
Windmill/LB (T)
W.L. Goodfellows/CM (T)
Wolfgang's Cafe (T)
Wrap Planet (D,T)
Wycombe Inn (T)
Yellow Springs Inn (D,T)
Ye Olde Temp. (D,T)
Yesterday's/CM (D,T)
Zanzibar Blue (T)
Zocalo (T)
ZuZu (T)

Dining Alone

(Other than hotels, coffee shops, sushi bars and places with counter service)
Capriccio Cafe
Cassatt Tea Rm.
Jim's Steaks
Le Bus
Manayunk Farmer's Mkt.
Pat's King Steaks
Reading Terminal Mkt.
Samosa
Spiga D'Oro
30th St. Station
Tony Luke's

Fireplaces

Abbey Grill
Alberto's

Arroyo Grille
A Touch of Italy/CM
Axelsson's/CM
Azalea Room
Bay Pony Inn
Beau Monde
Beau Rivage
Big Fish
Big River Fish Co.
Black Bass
Blüe Ox Brauhaus
Braddock's Tavern
Brandywine Brewing/DE
Bridgid
Broad Axe Tavern
Buckley's Tavern/DE
Bugaboo Creek
Cafe Espresso
Cafe Flower Shop
Cafe Giuseppe
Cafe Zesty
Carversville Inn
Centre Bridge Inn
Chadds Ford Inn
Champps Amer.
Chateau Silvana
Chef Tell's
Cock 'n Bull
Columbus Inn/DE
Concordville Inn
Cousins Country/CM
Coventry Forge
Coyote Crossing
Crab Trap/CM
Cresheim Cottage
Crier in Country
Cuttalossa Inn
Cuvee Notredame
Dave & Buster's
David's Yellow Brick
Deauville Inn/CM
Deux Cheminées
Dickens Inn
D'Ignazio's
Dilworthtown Inn
Doc's Place/CM
Duling-Kurtz House
Ebenezer's
Epicurean, The
Evermay on Del.
Evviva
Fat Jack's
Filomena Cuc. Rustica
Finnigan's Wake
Fireside Room

Flowing Springs
Founders
Four Dogs Tavern
Frankie's Seafood
Frenchtown Inn
General Lafayette
General Warren
Girasole/AC
Girasole Rist.
Golden Pheasant
Gracie's/LB
Green Hills Inn/LB
Gregory's/CM
Harry's Savoy Grill/DE
Hartefeld National
Hatteras Coastal/CM
Havana
Herb Garden
Historic Revere Tav./LB
Hotel du Village
Inn at Phillips Mill
Inn at Sugar Hill/CM
Inn of the Hawke
Inn on Blueberry Hill
Inn Philadelphia
Italian Bistro
Jake & Oliver's
Jean Pierre's
Kaminski's
Katmandu
Kaufman House
Kennedy-Supplee
Kimberton Inn
King George II
Knave of Hearts
Krazy Kats/DE
La Bonne Auberge
La Campagne
La Casa Pasta/DE
La Familia Sonsini
Lambertville Station
Landing, The
La Veranda
Le Colonial
Lenape Inn
Little Saigon/AC
Lobster House/CM
Log Cabin/LB
Luigi's Canal Hse.
Mad Batter/CM
Mademoiselle Paris
Marker, The
Marshalton Inn
Martine's
McGillin's

Mendenhall Inn
Michael's Rist.
Miller's Smorgasbord/LB
Monte Carlo
Moselem Springs/LB
Odette's
Olde Greenfield Inn/LB
Old Guard House
Old Mill Inn
Otto's Brauhaus
Palace of Asia
Palladium
Passerelle
Peaches at Sunset/CM
Peter Shields/CM
Pietro's Pizzeria
Pilot House/CM
Pippo's Fantastico
Plain & Fancy/LB
Plough & the Stars
Plumsteadville Inn
Port Saloon
Pub Rest.
Ram's Head Inn/CM
Ristorante Fieni's
Ristorante Mediterraneo
Ritz-Carlton Grill
Rococo
Rose Tree Inn
Sal's/DE
Samuels
Sassafras Cafe
Schooners & C.B.'s/CM
Serrano
Seven Stars
Ship Inn
Sign of Sorrel Horse
Silk Purse/DE
Sonoma
Sow's Ear/DE
Stockton Inn
Sweetwater Casino/CM
Tira Misu Rist.
Tuckahoe Inn/CM
Union Park/CM
Valley Green Inn
Valley Stream Inn
Vickers Tavern
Villa Strafford
Vincent's
Washington Crossing
Washington Inn/CM
William Penn Inn
Willistown Grille
Willow Valley Rst./LB

Yellow Springs Inn
Ye Olde Temp.

Game In Season

Abilene
Acacia
Alisa Cafe
America B&G
Anton's at Swan
Assaggi Italiani
Axelsson's/CM
Back Burner/DE
Barrymore Room
Bay Pony Inn
Beaujolais
Beau Rivage
Black Bass
Black Walnut
Blüe Ox Brauhaus
Braddock's Tavern
Brandywine Brewing/DE
Brandywine Room/DE
Bravo Bistro
Buckley's Tavern/DE
Cafe Arielle
Cafe 8 South/CM
Cafe Noelle
Cafe Zesty
California Cafe
Carambola
Carman's Country Kit.
Carucci/DE
Carversville Inn
Catelli
Cent'Anni
Chadds Ford Inn
Chef Tell's
Church St. Bistro
Cibo
Ciboulette
City Tavern
Clayton's
Coco Pazzo
Columbus Inn/DE
Crier in Country
Cuttalossa Inn
Cuvee Notredame
D'Angelo's
David's Yellow Brick
Diamond's
Dickens Inn
Dilworthtown Inn
Dinon's
Dock Street
Ebbitt Room/CM

Epicurean, The
Evermay on Del.
Fireside Room
Foggia
Food for Thought
Forager
Fork's Inn/CM
Founders
Fountain Rest.
Fox Point Grill/DE
Frangelica
Frederick's
Garden, The
General Lafayette
Golden Pheasant
Gourmet's Table
Gracie's/LB
Grasshopper
Graziella's
Green Hills Inn/LB
Green Room/DE
Gregory's/CM
Gypsy Rose
Hamilton's Grill
Harry's Savoy Grill/DE
Hatteras Coastal/CM
Haute To Trot
Havana
Homestead Rest.
Il Portico
Inn at Sugar Hill/CM
Inn on Blueberry Hill
Inn Philadelphia
Isabella's
Jack's Firehouse
Jean Pierre's
Joseph Ambler
Joseph Poon
Joseph's Italian
Judy's Cafe
Kaminski's
Kansas City Prime
King George II
Krazy Kats/DE
La Bonne Auberge
La Campagne
La Collina
La Famiglia
La Fourchette
La Grolla
La Locanda
Lambertville Station
Landing, The
Lauren's
La Veranda

Le Bar Lyonnais
Le Bec-Fin
Liberties
Little Brat's Haus/CM
Log Cabin/LB
London Grill
Luigi Vitrone's/DE
Mainland Inn
Mama Mia/CM
Marabella's
Marco's Cafe
Marshalton Inn
Marsilio's
Martine's
Mendenhall Inn
Monk's Café
Moonstruck
Museum Rest.
Nais Cuisine
New Orleans Cafe
New Orleans Cafe II
New World Cafe
Odette's
Old Guard House
Old Mill Inn
Opus 251
Overtures
Pace One
Paradigm
Passerelle
Pattaya Grill
Piccolo Mondo/DE
Pilot House/CM
Pineville Tavern
Porcini
Portofino/AC
Positano Rist./DE
Provence
Ram's Head Inn/CM
Renault Winery/CM
Ristorante Gallo Nero
Ristorante Mediterraneo
Ristorante Positano
Rococo
Roller's
Roscoe's Kodiak
Rose Tree Inn
Russell's 96 West
Sal's/DE
Saranac
Savaradio/CM
Savona
Scampi Rist.
Scannicchio's/AC
Schooners & C.B.'s/CM

Ship Inn
Shipley Grill/DE
Siggie's L'Auberge
Silk Purse/DE
Siri's Thai French
Sonoma
Sow's Ear/DE
Spiaggi/CM
Spring Mill Café
Stockton Inn
Swann Lounge
Sweetwater Casino/CM
Taquet
Tavola Toscana/DE
Tira Misu Rist.
Tony Clark's
Union Park/CM
Valley Green Inn
Village Porch
Villa Strafford
Vincent's
Waldorf Café
Waters Edge/CM
White Dog Cafe
Wild Onion Rest.
William Penn Inn
Windmill/LB
Wolfgang's Cafe
Yellow Springs Inn
Yesterday's/CM

Health/Spa Menus

(Most places cook to order to
meet any dietary request;
call in advance to check;
almost all Chinese, Indian and
other ethnics have
health-conscious
meals, as do the following)
Allie's American
Arroyo Grille
Axelsson's/CM
Azalea Room
Barrymore Room
Between Friends
Black Bass
Bravo Bistro
Cafe 8 South/CM
Cafe Noelle
Carambola
Catelli
Church St. Bistro
Ciboulette
Clayton's
Coppermill Harvest

Crier in Country
Cuttalossa Inn
Edge
Emerald Fish
Epicurean, The
Fisher's Tudor Hse.
Foggia
Fountain Rest.
Garden, The
Golden Pheasant
Green Cuisine/CM
Lambertville Station
Lucy's Hat Shop
Mama Palma's
Montserrat
Nonna's
Paradigm
Passerelle
Provence
Roscoe's Kodiak
Rouge 98
Sansom St. Oyster
Santa Fe Burrito
Waters Edge/CM
William Penn Inn
Wolfgang's Cafe

Historic Interest

(Year opened; *building)
1681 King George II*
1700 Concordville Inn*
1700 Gypsy Rose*
1700 Mendenhall Inn*
1710 Stockton Inn*
1714 William Penn Inn*
1722 Yellow Springs Inn*
1736 Chadds Ford Inn*
1739 Lamb Tavern*
1740 Crier in Country*
1745 Black Bass*
1745 General Warren*
1748 Cresheim Cottage*
1750 La Bonne Auberge*
1751 Plumsteadville Inn*
1772 Ye Olde Temp.*
1773 Liberties*
1780 Olde Greenfield Inn/LB*
1796 Kimberton Inn*
1796 Ship Inn*
1798 Chateau Silvana*
1798 Old Mill Inn*
1800 Alois/LB*
1800 Bottling Works/LB*
1800 Catacombs/LB*
1813 Carversville Inn*

1814 Marshalton Inn*
1817 Washington Crossing*
1824 Inn Philadelphia*
1830 Bay Pony Inn*
1830 Duling-Kurtz House*
1836 Seven Stars*
1848 Cousins Country/CM*
1850 Kaufman House*
1852 Kennedy-Supplee*
1853 Moselem Springs/LB*
1857 Golden Pheasant*
1860 McGillin's
1865 Old Original Book*
1865 Valley Green Inn*
1880 Frescos/CM*
1880 Ristorante Gallo Nero*
1890 Historic Revere Tav./LB*
1892 Reading Terminal Mkt.*
1893 Bookbinders
1899 Wycombe Inn*
1900 Ralph's
1900 Stockyard Inn/LB
1903 United States Hotel*
1908 Gregory's/CM*
1910 Joe's Tomato Pies
1910 Victor Café
1911 Union Park/CM*
1912 Snockey's Oyster
1920 Flowing Springs
1927 Marra's
1930 Otto's Brauhaus
1932 Mayfair Diner
1933 Log Cabin/LB
1934 Old Guard House
1935 Angelo's Fairmount/AC
1935 Melrose Diner
1938 Joe Italiano's/Inn/CM
1939 Jim's Steaks
1945 Blue Bell Inn
1948 DeLorenzo's
1948 Tacconelli's Pizza
1950 Zinn's Diner/LB

Longevity

(20+ years; year opened)
1684 Broad Axe Tavern
1897 Dock's Oyster Hse./AC
1899 Dante & Luigi's
1913 Brandywine Room/DE
1913 Green Room/DE
1916 Ingleneuk Tea Hse.
1920 Ugly Mug/CM
1921 Chef Vola's/AC
1923 Famous 4th St. Deli
1930 Pat's King Steaks

1932 Ozzie's Tratt.
1933 Ron's Ribs
1938 DiNardo's/DE
1938 DiNardo's Seafood
1939 Cuttalossa Inn
1939 Miller's Smorgasbord/LB
1940 Mrs. Robino's/DE
1942 Charlie's Bar/CM
1942 Orsatti's/AC
1944 Pala's Cafe/DE
1944 Ram's Head Inn/CM
1945 Murray's Deli
1946 White House/AC
1951 Buckley's Tavern/DE
1951 China Castle
1951 Marsilio's
1951 Pub Rest.
1952 Mac's/CM
1953 Columbus Inn/DE
1954 Coventry Forge
1954 Lobster House/CM
1955 Hymie's
1956 Charcoal Pit/DE
1959 Plain & Fancy/LB
1960 Crier in Country
1960 Dalessandro's
1960 Frenchtown Inn
1960 Groff's Farm/LB
1960 Olga's Diner
1962 Cock 'n Bull
1962 Fisher's
1962 Stoudt's Black Angus/LB
1963 Cent'Anni
1963 Henny's/CM
1963 Shank's & Evelyn's
1963 Villa Di Roma
1965 Kaminski's
1965 Sabatini's/AC
1966 Tony's Balt. Grill/AC
1967 Saloon
1967 Willow Valley Rst./LB
1968 Crab Trap/CM
1968 Dave's Center Point Deli/CM
1968 Happy Rooster
1968 Jefferson House
1968 Red Caboose/LB
1968 Rib Crib
1968 Stoltzfus Farm/LB
1968 Yorktown Inn
1969 Good N' Plenty/LB
1970 Dickens Inn
1970 Le Bec-Fin
1970 Ravioli House/CM
1971 Haydn Zug's/LB
1971 Seafood Unlimited

1972 Green Hills Inn/LB	1978 Los Amigos/AC
1972 Taco House	1978 Pace One
1972 Vickers Tavern	1978 Scannicchio's/AC
1972 Village Porch	1978 Silk Purse/DE
1972 Windmill/LB	1978 Sow's Ear/DE
1973 Astral Plane	
1973 Bird-in-Hand/LB	**Hotel Dining**
1973 Dilworthtown Inn	Adam's Mark Hotel
1973 Friday, Sat., Sun.	Marker, The
1973 Jow's Garden	Bally's Park Place
1973 Portofino	Prime Place/AC
1974 Garden, The	Best Western Inn
1974 Inn at Phillips Mill	Palace of Asia
1974 La Cocotte	Black Bass Hotel
1974 Malvern Meeting Hse.	Black Bass
1974 Peking Rest.	Caesars
1974 Sagami	Planet Hollywood/AC
1974 Vincente's/DE	Primavera/AC
1975 Aleathea's/CM	Carrol Villa Hotel
1975 Gullifty's	Mad Batter/CM
1975 Knave of Hearts	Cherry Hill Hilton
1975 Mother's	Bentley's Five
1975 Ruhling's Seafood	Chestnut Hill Hotel
1975 Top of the Marq/CM	Chestnut Grill
1976 City Tavern	Convention Ctr. Marriott
1976 Downey's	Allie's American
1976 Judy's Cafe	Champion's
1976 Landing, The	JW's Steakhse.
1976 Mace's Crossing	Desmond Great Valley Hotel
1976 Mad Batter/CM	Hunt Room
1976 Sal's/DE	Doubletree Hotel
1976 Sassafras Cafe	Academy Cafe
1976 Yesterday's/CM	Four Seasons Hotel
1977 Axelsson's/CM	Fountain Rest.
1977 Copabanana	Swann Lounge
1977 Fisher's Tudor Hse.	Harrah's
1977 Hotel du Village	Andreotti's/AC
1977 Los Amigos' New Mexico	Fantasea Reef/AC
1977 Ma Ma Yolanda's	Steakhouse/AC
1977 Marrakesh	William Fisk/AC
1977 Moriarty's	Hilton Atlantic City
1977 Pilot House/CM	Caruso's/AC
1977 Saigon	Oaks, The/AC
1977 South St. Souvlaki	Peregrines/AC
1977 Washington Inn/CM	Holiday Inn Cherry Hill
1978 Alexander's Inn/CM	Red Hot & Blue
1978 Back Burner/DE	Holiday Inn Select
1978 Beau Rivage	Elephant & Castle
1978 Bridget Foy's	Hotel du Pont
1978 Chung Hing	Brandywine Room/DE
1978 David's Yellow Brick	Green Room/DE
1978 Havana	Hotel Macomber
1978 Johnny Mott's	Union Park/CM
1978 Kobe Japanese	Inn at Montchanin Village
1978 La Casa Pasta/DE	Krazy Kats/DE

Inn at Sugar Hill
   Inn at Sugar Hill/CM
Inn of Cape May
   Aleathea's/CM
Inn of the Hawke
   Inn of the Hawke
Marquis de Lafayette
   Top of the Marq/CM
Mendenhall Hotel
   Mendenhall Inn
Omni Hotel
   Azalea Room
Park Hyatt at the Bellevue
   Barrymore Room
   Founders
   Palm
   Zanzibar Blue
Park Ridge Hotel
   Coppermill Harvest
Penn's View Hotel
   Ristorante Panorama
Philadelphia Marriott West
   Regatta B&G
Radnor Hotel
   Abbey Grill
Resorts Casino Hotel
   California Pizza Kit./AC
   Camelot/AC
   Capriccio/AC
   Le Palais/AC
Rittenhouse Hotel
   Cassatt Tea Rm.
   Nicholas Nickolas
   Nick's B&G
   Treetops
Ritz-Carlton Hotel
   Ritz-Carlton Grill
Sands Hotel & Casino
   Brighton Steakhse./AC
   China Moon/AC
   Medici/AC
Sheraton Society Hill
   Hadley's Bistro
Showboat Hotel Casino
   Casa DiNapoli/AC
   Mississippi Steak/AC
Stockton Inn
   Stockton Inn
Tropicana
   A.C. Station/AC
   Il Verdi/AC
   Pier 7/AC
   Regent Court/AC

Trump Marina
   Portofino/AC
   Steak House/AC
Trump Plaza
   Fortune's/AC
   Max's Steak Hse./AC
   Roberto's/AC
Trump Taj Mahal
   Casa Nicola/AC
   Hard Rock Cafe/AC
   Official All Star/AC
   Safari Steakhse./AC
   Scheherazade/AC
Valley Forge Hilton
   Alexander's Cafe
   Kobe Japanese
Virginia Hotel
   Ebbitt Room/CM
Warwick Hotel
   Capriccio Cafe
   Mia's
   Prime Rib
Wayne Hotel
   Taquet
Wyndam Franklin Plaza
   Between Friends

"In" Places

Black Walnut
Blue in Green
Bonaparte
Brasserie Perrier
Coco Pazzo
Fork
La Terrasse
Latest Dish
Le Colonial
Morning Glory Diner
Nicholas Nickolas
Opus 251
Paradigm
Plough & the Stars
Rococo
Savona
Vega Grill

Jacket Required

Anton's at Swan
Azalea Room
Barrymore Room
Beau Rivage
Between Friends
Brasserie Perrier
Ciboulette
Coventry Forge
Cuttalossa Inn

Dilworthtown Inn
Duling-Kurtz House
Evermay on Del.
Evviva
Food for Thought
Founders
Fountain Rest.
Girasole/AC
Graziella's
Green Room/DE
Il Portico
Inn on Blueberry Hill
Jefferson House
Kennedy-Supplee
Krazy Kats/DE
La Bonne Auberge
La Collina
La Famiglia
La Fourchette
Le Bec-Fin
Lenape Inn
Le Palais/AC
Mendenhall Inn
Morton's of Chicago
Moshulu
Nicholas Nickolas
Passerelle
Positano Rist./DE
Prime Rib
Ram's Head Inn/CM
Ritz-Carlton Grill
Savona
Seven Stars
Sign of Sorrel Horse
Silk & Spice
Susanna Foo
Tira Misu Rist.
Vickers Tavern
William Penn Inn

Kaminski's (3)
Lee Ho Seafood (3)
Little Pete's (24 hrs.)
Los Amigos/AC (6)
McGillin's (1)
Melrose Diner (24 hrs.)
Monk's Café (1)
Moriarty's (1)
North Sea (3)
Official All Star/AC (2)
Olga's Diner (24 hrs.)
Pat's King Steaks (24 hrs.)
Planet Hollywood/AC (1)
Plough & the Stars (1)
Pompano Grille (2)
Ponzio's Kingsway (1)
Poor Henry's (2)
Rib Crib (1)
Sage Diner (1)
Sal's/DE (1)
Sugar Mom's (1:30)
Sutor's Owl Tree/CM (1)
Swann Lounge (1)
Tai Lake (2:30)
Tony's Balt. Grill/AC (3)
Xando Coffee (1)

Meet For A Drink
(Most top hotels and the
following standouts)
America B&G
Bistro St. Tropez
Brasserie Perrier
California Cafe
Caribou Cafe
Cary Restaurant
Champps Amer.
Coco Pazzo
Cutters
Dock Street
Happy Rooster
Iron Hill Brewery/DE
Italian Bistro
Jake & Oliver's
Le Bar Lyonnais
Mace's Crossing
Martini Café
Martini's Lounge
Rococo
Samuel Adams Brew
Samuels
Society Hill Hotel
Sonoma
Tony Clark's
United States Hotel

Late Late — After 12:30
(All hours are AM)
Abbey Grill (24 hrs.)
Alfe's/CM (2)
Angeloni's II/AC (1)
Champion's (2)
China Castle (2)
Copabanana (1)
Downey's (1)
East Side Mario's (1)
Elephant & Castle (1)
Geno's Steaks (24 hrs.)
Gregory's/CM (1)
House of Chen (5)
Jim's Steaks (1)

Xando Coffee
Ye Olde Temp.

Noteworthy Newcomers (44)

Abilene
A Ca Mia/CM
A Little Cafe
Beaujolais
Beau Monde
Big River Fish Co.
Brasserie Perrier
Casa Nicola/AC
Chestnut Grill
Cibo
Cotton Club
Dick Clark's
Edge
Filomena Cuc. Rustica
Fireside Room
Five Spot
Fork
Gourmet's Table
Hard Rock Cafe/AC
H.K. Golden Phoenix
Il Tartufo
John Harvard's
Joseph Poon
La Terrasse
Latest Dish
Le Colonial
Ly Michael's
Mademoiselle Paris
Nicholas Nickolas
Official All Star/AC
Opus 251
Paradigm
Penang
Pizzicato
Poor Henry's
Prime Rib
River City Diner
Rouge 98
Savona
Sienna/DE
Siggie's L'Auberge
Spiaggi/CM
Stix
Van Scoy's Bistro/CM

Noteworthy Closings (65)

Athen's West
A Work of Art
Bistro Bix

Brother's Bistro
Cafe Nola
Cafe on Quince
Cafe Sorella
Carlos & Co.
Carlucci's Gill n' Grille
Carolina's
Central Bar & Grill
Chez Orly Cafe
Ellen Rose
Family-Style/LB
Frisanco Ristorante/AC
Gargoyles
General Wayne Inn
Himalayan Exotic
Ivanka's/AC
Jam's Spirited Grille
Joseph's on the Avenue
Julia's Comet
Katie O'Brien's
King David Deli
La Serena
Lilies on 12th
Marabella's Italian/CM
Marabella's Seafood/CM
Marco Polo/AC
Maureen/CM
Melange
Middle East
Mirage/DE
My Huong
Napoleon
Noah's Riverboat Cafe
Ocean Harbor
Peking Duck House/AC
Picciotti's/DE
Porto Bello
Prickly Pear
River Deck Cafe
Rock-n-Roll Diner
Rodz
Rosebuds Cafe
Savoy, The/DE
Scarpinato's
Sergeantsville Inn
1700 Lombard Cafe
16th St. Bar & Grill
Solo Mio
South of Siam
Tavern Restaurant
Tierra
Tiffany Dining Place
Tiffin/DE
Topeka
Tsui Hang Chun

Tucci's Ristorante/AC
Under the Blue Moon
Vinh Hoa
Wazoo's
Widow Finney's/LB
Wildflower
Wild Orchid Cafe

Offbeat

Al Khimah
Astral Plane
Bitar's
Cafette
Carman's Country Kit.
Dahlak
Gracie's/LB
Jamaican Jerk Hut
Joseph Poon
Kabul
La Locanda
LionFish
Melting Pot
Michele's/DE
Ortlieb's Jazzhaus
Triangle Tavern

Outdoor Dining

(G=garden; P=patio;
S=sidewalk; T=terrace;
W=waterside; best of many)
A Ca Mia/CM (P,S)
Aleathea's/CM (P)
Alfe's/CM (P)
A Little Cafe (P)
America B&G (P)
Arpeggio (S)
Arroyo Grille (W)
Axelsson's/CM (G,W)
Barnacle Ben's West (P,W)
Bitar's (S)
Black Bass (P,W)
Black Walnut (G,P)
Blue Bell Inn (G,P,T)
Blüe Ox Brauhaus (G,S)
Braddock's Tavern (G)
Bravo Bistro (P,T,W)
Bridget Foy's (S,T)
Brittany Cafe/AC (S)
Buckley's Tavern/DE (T)
Cafe Flower Shop (P)
Cafe Gallery (G,T,W)
Cafe Preeya (P,S)
Cafette (G,S)
Caffé Aldo Lamberti (P)
Cary Restaurant (S)

Casa Nicola/AC (W)
Catelli (G,P)
Centre Bridge Inn (G,W)
Chart House (P,W)
Chateau Silvana (P)
Chestnut Grill (P,S)
Church St. Bistro (P)
Cibo (P)
City Tavern (G)
Coco Pazzo (P)
Columbus Inn/DE (P)
Concordville Inn (P)
Cotton Club (S)
Cousin's/CM (P)
Cousins Country/CM (W)
Crab Trap/CM (S,W)
Cresheim Cottage (P)
Crier in Country (G,T)
Cucina Rosa/CM (S)
Cutters (P)
Cuvee Notredame (T)
Dahlak (G,P)
Dave & Buster's (W)
David's Yellow Brick (P)
Deauville Inn/CM (T,W)
Dilworthtown Inn (G,P)
Doc's Place/CM (W)
Downey's (S)
Doylestown Inn (P)
Dry Dock Ice Cream/CM (S)
Ebenezer's (S)
Edge (P,W)
Effie's (G)
Engine 46 Steakhse. (P)
Evermay on Del. (W)
Filomena Cuc. Rustica (P)
Foggia (T)
Fork (S)
Fork's Inn/CM (P,W)
Fortune's/AC (W)
Four Dogs Tavern (T)
410 Bank St./CM (G,P,T)
Frenchtown Inn (W)
Frescos/CM (P)
Garden, The (G,P)
General Lafayette (P)
General Warren (G,P)
Geno's Steaks (S)
Girasole/AC (P)
Golden Inn/CM (W)
Golden Pheasant (T,W)
Gourley's (P,T)
Gourmet's Table (P,S)
Gracie's/LB (P)
Groff's Farm/LB (P)

Gypsy Rose (T,W)
Hamilton's Grill (G,T,W)
Hard Rock Cafe/AC (S,W)
Harry's Savoy Grill/DE (P)
Hartefeld National (P)
Hatteras Coastal/CM (P,W)
Haute To Trot (S)
Havana (G,P,S,T)
Herb Garden (P)
Hotel du Village (G)
Il Sol D'Italia (P)
Il Tartufo (S)
Inn at Phillips Mill (P)
Inn at Sugar Hill/CM (S,W)
Inn Philadelphia (G)
Iron Hill Brewery/DE (P)
Italian Bistro (S)
Jack's Firehouse (G,S)
Jackson Mountain/CM (P)
Jake & Oliver's (S)
Jamaican Jerk Hut (G)
Johan's/AC (S)
Joseph Ambler (T)
JW's Steakhse. (T)
Katmandu (P,W)
Kaufman House (P)
King George II (W)
La Campagne (T)
La Cipolla Torta (S)
La Familia Sonsini (P)
Lamberti's Cucina (T)
Lambertville Station (T,W)
Landing, The (G,P,W)
La Terrasse (P)
La Tolteca/DE (P)
Lauren's (T)
La Veranda (W)
La Vigna (P)
Le Bus (S)
Little Brat's Haus/CM (W)
Lobster House/CM (T,W)
Lobster Loft/CM (W)
London Grill (S)
Lucy's Hat Shop (S)
Luigi's Canal Hse. (G,W)
Mace's Crossing (T)
Mad Batter/CM (G,P,T)
Mad 4 Mex (P)
Main-ly Desserts (S)
Maloney's Beef/CM (P)
Manayunk Brewing (P,W)
Manayunk Farmer's Mkt. (P,W)
Marathon Grill (S)
Martine's (P,S,W)
Merion Inn/CM (P)

Mexican Food (P)
Monte Carlo (G,P,S)
Montserrat (S)
Morning Glory Diner (G)
Moshulu (W)
Mother's (G)
Nonna's (P,T)
Oceanfront/CM (P,W)
Odette's (W)
Official All Star/AC (P)
Olde Greenfield Inn/LB (G)
Old Waterway Inn/AC (P,W)
Opus 251 (G)
Pace One (G)
Palladium (T)
Passerelle (P,W)
Pat's King Steaks (S)
Peaches at Sunset/CM (P)
Peacock Parkwy. (P,S)
Pepper's Cafe (T)
Peter Shields/CM (P,W)
Philadelphia Fish (P,S)
Pompano Grille (S)
Portofino/AC (W)
Port Saloon (P,W)
Red Caboose/LB (P)
Remi's Cafe (S)
Renault Winery/CM (W)
Rest. at Doneckers/LB (S)
Ristorante Amalfi/DE (P)
Ristorante Fieni's (P)
Ristorante Gallo Nero (G,P)
River City Diner (P,W)
Roberto's/AC (W)
Rock Lobster (T,W)
Roller's (S)
Ron's Ribs (S)
Roselena's Coffee (S)
Rouge 98 (S)
Russell's 96 West (G,P)
Sal's/DE (G,P)
Samuels (P)
Savaradio/CM (S)
Siam Cuisine III (S)
Sign of Sorrel Horse (G,T,W)
Society Hill Hotel (S)
Solaris Grille (G,T)
Spring Mill Café (G,P,T)
Stockton Inn (G,P,T,W)
Sweetwater Casino/CM (T,W)
Taquet (T)
Tavern on Green (S)
Terrace at Greenhill/DE (P,T)
Tisha's Fine Din./CM (T,W)
Tomatoes/CM (S)

Tony Luke's (S)
Tuckahoe Inn/CM (W)
Ugly Mug/CM (P)
Urie's Waterfront/CM (T,W)
Valley Green Inn (P,W)
Valley Stream Inn (P)
Van Scoy's Bistro/CM (P)
Vega Grill (G,P,S)
Ventura Greenhse./CM (P,W)
Vickers Tavern (P)
Washington Crossing (G,P)
Washington Inn/CM (P)
Waterfront/CM (P,W)
Waters Edge/CM (P)
Waterworks Cafe/DE (P,W)
White Dog Cafe (P)
W.L. Goodfellows/CM (P)
Xando Coffee (S)
Yellow Springs Inn (P,T)

Outstanding Views

A.C. Station/AC
Aleathea's/CM
Arroyo Grille
Azalea Room
Black Bass
Bridget Foy's
Cafe Gallery
Chart House
Church St. Bistro
Cuttalossa Inn
Dave & Buster's
Doc's Place/CM
Edge
Evermay on Del.
Hamilton's Grill
Hartefeld National
Katmandu
Lambertville Station
Landing, The
La Veranda
Lenape Inn
Little Brat's Haus/CM
Mad Batter/CM
Manayunk Farmer's Mkt.
Meiji-En
Obadiah's/CM
Oceanfront/CM
Odette's
Old Waterway Inn/AC
Passerelle
Peter Shields/CM
Port Saloon
Rock Lobster
Spiaggi/CM

Top of the Marq/CM
Treetops
Tuckahoe Inn/CM
Upstares at Varalli
Valley Green Inn
Valley Stream Inn
Ventura Greenhse./CM
Waters Edge/CM
Waterworks Cafe/DE

Parking/Valet

(L=parking lot;
V=valet parking;
*=validated parking)
Abacus (L)
Abbey Grill (L)
Academy Cafe (L,V)
A.C. Station/AC (V)
Adobe Cafe (L)
Alaina's (L)
Alberto's (L)
Al Dar (L)
Aleathea's/CM (L,V)
Alexander's Cafe (L)
Alfe's/CM (L)
Alfio's (L)
Alisa Cafe (L)
A Little Cafe (L)
Al Khimah (L)
Allie's American (V)*
Alois/LB (L)
America B&G (L)
Andreotti's (L)
Andreotti's/AC (L,V)
Angeloni's II/AC (L)
Angelo's Fairmount/AC (L)
Anthony's (L)
Anton's at Swan (L)
Arpeggio (L)
Arroyo Grille (L)
Artful Dodger (L)*
Arugula! (L)
Asakura (L)
Assaggi Italiani (L)
Athena (L)
Athens Cafe (L)
A Touch of Italy/CM (L)
August Moon (L)
Axelsson's/CM (L)
Azalea Room (V)*
Back Burner/DE (L)
Bangkok City (L)
Bangkok House/DE (L)
Bards*
Barnacle Ben's (L)

Barnacle Ben's West (L)
Barrymore Room (L,V)*
Bay Pony Inn (L)
Beaujolais*
Beau Rivage (L,V)
Ben & Irv Deli (L)
Bentley's Five (L)
Bertolini's (L)
Bertucci's (L)
Best of British*
Between Friends (L,V)
Big Fish (L)
Big River Fish Co. (L)
Bird-in-Hand/LB (L)
Bistro Romano (V)*
Black Bass (L)
BLT's Cobblefish (V)
Blue Bell Inn (L)
Blüe Ox Brauhaus (L)
Bobby's Seafood (L)
Bonaparte (V)
Bookbinders*
Bottling Works/LB (L)
Braddock's Tavern (L)
Brandywine Brewing/DE (L)
Brandywine Room/DE (V)*
Brasserie Perrier (V)
Bravo Bistro (L)
Bridget Foy's (V)*
Brighton Steakhse./AC (L,V)
Broad Axe Tavern (L)
Buckley's Tavern/DE (L)
Bugaboo Creek (L)
Bunha Faun (L)
Busch's/CM (L)
Cafe Arielle (L)
Cafe 8 South/CM (L)
Cafe Espresso (L)
Cafe Giuseppe (L)
Cafe Michaelangelo (L)
Cafe Preeya (L)
Cafe Zesty (V)
Caffé Aldo Lamberti (L,V)
Caffe Bellissimo/DE (L)
California Cafe (L)
California Pizza Kit. (L)
Camelot/AC (L,V)
Capital Vietnam*
Capriccio/AC (L,V)
Carambola (L)
Caribou Cafe*
Carman's Country Kit. (L)
Carucci/DE (L)
Caruso's/AC (V)
Carversville Inn (L)

Cary Restaurant (V)*
Casa DiNapoli/AC (L,V)
Casa Nicola/AC (L)
Cassano Italian (L)
Cassatt Tea Rm. (V)
Casselli's Rist. (L)
Catacombs/LB (L)
Catelli (L)
Cedars*
Celebre's Pizzeria (L)
Cent'Anni (V)
Center Point Deli/AC (L)
Centre Bridge Inn (L,V)
Century House (L)
Chadds Ford Inn (L)
Chambers*
Champps Amer. (L)
Charcoal Pit/DE (L)
Charlie's Bar/CM (L)
Chart House (L,V)
Chateau Silvana (L)
Chef Tell's (L)
Cherry St. Chinese (L)
Chestnut Grill (L)
China Castle*
China Moon/AC (L,V)
Christopher's (L)
Chung Hing (L)
Ciboulette (L,V)
Circa (V)
Clayton's (L,V)
Cock 'n Bull (L)
Columbus Inn/DE (L,V)
Concordville Inn (L)
Coppermill Harvest (L)
Country Club (L)
Cousins Country/CM (L)
Coventry Forge (L)
Coyote Crossing (L)
Crab Trap/CM (L)
Cresheim Cottage (L)
Crier in Country (L)
Cuisines (L)
Cuttalossa Inn (L)
Cutters*
Cuvee Notredame (L)
Dahlak (L)
Dave & Buster's (L,V)
Dave's Center Point Deli/CM (L)
David's Yellow Brick (L)
Deauville Inn/CM (L,V)
Diamond's (L,V)*
Dick Clark's (L)
Dickens Inn*
D'Ignazio's (L)

DiNardo's/DE (L)
DiNardo's Seafood (L)
Dock's Oyster Hse./AC (L)
Doc's Place/CM (L)
Downey's*
Doylestown Inn*
Dry Dock Ice Cream/CM (L)
Duling-Kurtz House (V)
East Side Mario's (L)
Ebbitt Room/CM (V)
Ebenezer's (L)
Edge (V)
El Azteca (L)
Elena Wu (L)
El Mariachi (L)
El Sombrero (L)
Emerald Fish (L)
Engine 46 Steakhse. (L)
Epicurean, The (L)
Evermay on Del. (L)
Evviva (L,V)
Fantasea Reef/AC (L,V)
Fat Jack's (L)
Feby's Fishery/DE (L)
Felicia's (V)
Fergie's Pub (L)
Fez Moroccan*
Finnigan's Wake (L)
Fireside Room (L)
Fisher's (L)
Fisher's Tudor Hse. (L)
Five Spot*
Flowing Springs (L)
Flying Fish*
Foggia (L)
Food for Thought (V)*
Fork's Inn/CM (L)
Fortune's/AC (L,V)
Founders (V)*
Fountain Rest. (V)*
Four Dogs Tavern (L)
410 Bank St./CM*
Fox Point Grill/DE (L)
Frederick's (V)
Frenchtown Inn (L)
Frescos/CM (L)*
Fuji Mountain (L)
Garden, The (V)*
Garnian Wa (L)
General Lafayette (L)
General Warren (L)
Genji II (L)
Gianna's (L)
Girasole/AC (V)*
Giumarello's Rist. (L)

Golden Inn/CM (L)
Golden Pheasant (L)
Golden Pond*
Golden Sea (L)
Good N' Plenty/LB (L)
Gourmet's Table (L)
Gracie's/LB (L)
Grasshopper (L,V)
Graziella's (L)
Green Hills Inn/LB (L)
Green Room/DE (V)*
Groff's Farm/LB (L)
Gullifty's (L)
Gypsy Rose (L)
Hadley's Bistro (L)*
Happy Rooster (L)
Hard Rock Cafe/AC (L)
Hardshell Cafe (L)
Harry's Bar & Grill*
Hartefeld National (L,V)
Hatteras Coastal/CM (L)
Havana (L)
Haydn Zug's/LB (L)
Henny's/CM (L)
Herb Garden (L)
Hibachi Japanese/DE (L)
Historic Revere Tav./LB (L)
H.K. Golden Phoenix (L)
Hoss's Steak/LB (L)
Hotel du Village (L)
House of Chen*
Hunan Rest. (L)
Hunt Room (L)
Hymie's (L)
Il Portico (V)
Il Sol D'Italia (L)
Il Verdi/AC (V)
Imperial Inn*
India Palace/DE (L)
Inn at Phillips Mill (L)
Inn at Sugar Hill/CM (L)
Inn of the Hawke (L)
Inn on Blueberry Hill (L)
Inn Philadelphia*
Iron Hill Brewery/DE (L)*
Isaac Newton's (L)
Isaac's/LB (L)
Isabella's (L)
Italian Bistro (L)*
Jack's Firehouse (L)
Jake & Oliver's (L)
Jake's (V)
Jannie (L)
Jefferson House (L)
Jim's Steaks (L)

J.J.'s Grotto (L)
Joe Italiano's/Inn/CM (L)
Joe Italiano's/II/CM (L)
Joe's Peking (L)
Joe's Tomato Pies (L)
John Harvard's (L)
Johnny Mott's (L,V)
Joseph Ambler (L)
Joseph Poon*
Joseph's Italian (V)
Jow's Garden (L)
Joy Tsin Lau*
Judy's Cafe (L)
JW's Steakhse. (V)*
Kaminski's (L)
Kansas City Prime (V)
Katmandu (L,V)
Kaufman House (L)
Kawabata (L)
Kennedy-Supplee (V)
Khajuraho (L)
Kimberton Inn (L)
Kimono Sushi Bar (L)
Kim's (L)
Kingdom Vegetarians (V)
King George II (V)
Kobe Japanese (L)*
Krazy Kats/DE (L)
La Bonne Auberge (L)
La Campagne (L)
La Casa Pasta/DE (L)
La Cocotte (L)
La Collina (V)
La Famiglia (V)
La Familia Sonsini (L)
La Forno (L)
La Fourchette (L)
La Locanda (L)
Lamberti's Cucina (L)
Lambertville Station (L)
Lamb Tavern (L)
Landing, The (L)
La Paella Tio Pepe (L)
La Pergola (L)
La Terrasse (V)
La Tolteca/DE (L)
Lauren's (L)
La Veranda (V)
La Vigna (L)
Le Bec-Fin (L,V)
Le Colonial (V)
Lee Ho Seafood (L,V)*
Lee How Fook (L)
Lemon Grass/LB (L)
Lenape Inn (L)

Le Palais/AC (L,V)
Le Petit Cafe (L)
Little Brat's Haus/CM (L)
Little Fish (L)
Little Saigon/AC (L)
Lobster House/CM (L)
Lobster Loft/CM (L)
Log Cabin/LB (L)
London Grill (L)
Lone Star Steakhse. (L)
Los Amigos/AC (L)
Los Amigos' New Mexico*
L'Osteria Cucina/DE (L)
Luigi's Canal Hse. (V)
Maccabeam (L)
Mace's Crossing (L)
Mac's/CM (L)
Mad Batter/CM (L)
Mainland Inn (L)
Maloney's Beef/CM (V)
Mama Mia/CM (L)
Mama Rosa (L)
Ma Ma Yolanda's (L)
Mamma Maria (L)
Manayunk Brewing (L,V)*
Manayunk Farmer's Mkt. (L)
Mandarin Garden (L)
Marabella's (L,V)*
Marbles (L)
Marco Polo (L)
Margaret Kuo's (L)
Marker, The (L,V)
Market Fare/LB*
Marshalton Inn (L)
Marsilio's (L)
Martine's (L)
Max's Steak Hse./AC (L,V)
Mayfair Diner (L)
McGillin's*
Medici/AC (L,V)
Meiji-En (V)
Meil's (L)
Melrose Diner (L)
Mel's Italian (V)
Melting Pot (L)
Mendenhall Inn (L)
Merion Inn/CM (L,V)
Mexican Food (L)
Mexican Post (L)*
Mia's (L)
Michael's Family (L)
Michael's Rist. (V)
Michele's/DE (L)
Mikasa/DE (L)
Miller's Smorgasbord/LB (L)

Minar Palace (L)
Mirage, The/CM (L)
Mississippi Steak/AC (L,V)
Monte Carlo (V)
Montserrat*
Moonstruck (L)
Moriarty's (L)*
Morton's of Chicago (V)
Moselem Springs/LB (L)
Moshulu (V)
Mother's (L)
Mr. Martino's Tratt. (L)
Mrs. London's Cafe (L)
Murray's Deli (L)
Museum Rest. (L)
Nais Cuisine (L)
Nav Jiwan Tea Rm./LB (L)
New Delhi (L)
New World Cafe (L)
Nicholas Nickolas (V)
Nick's B&G (V)
Nifty Fifty's (L)
Nonna's (L)
Noodle Heaven (L,V)*
Norma's Middle Eastern (L)
North Sea*
North Star Bar (L)
Nul Bom (L)
Oaks, The/AC (V)
Obadiah's/CM (L)
Oceanfront/CM (L)*
Odette's (V)
Official All Star/AC (L)
Olde Greenfield Inn/LB (L)
Old Guard House (L)
Old Mill Inn (L)
Old Original Book (V)
Old Waterway Inn/AC (L)
Olga's Diner (L)
Opus 251 (V)
Orsatti's/AC*
Ortlieb's Jazzhaus (L)
Otto's Brauhaus (L)
Outback Steakhse. (L)
Overtures (L)
Ozzie's Tratt. (L)*
Pace One (L)
Palace of Asia (L)
Pala's Cafe/DE (L)
Palladium*
Palm (V)*
Paradigm (V)
Passage to India*
Passerelle (L)
Pastavino Tratt. (L)

Peaches at Sunset/CM (L)
Peacock Parkwy. (L)
Peking Rest. (L)
Pepper's Cafe (L)
Peregrines/AC (V)
Persian Grill (L)
Peter Shields/CM (L)
Philly Crab & Steak (L)
Pho 75 (L)
Pho Xe Lua*
Piccolo Mondo/DE (L)
Pier 7/AC (V)
Pietro's Pizzeria*
Pineville Tavern (L)
Pippo's Fantastico (L)
Plain & Fancy/LB (L)
Planet Hollywood/AC (L)
Plough & the Stars*
Plumsteadville Inn (L)
Pollo Rosso (L)
Pompano Grille (V)
Ponzio's Kingsway (L)
Poor Henry's (L)
Porcini*
Portofino*
Portofino/AC (L,V)
Port Saloon (V)
Positano Rist./DE (L)
Primavera/AC (L,V)
Primavera Pizza Kit. (L)
Prime Place/AC (L)
Prime Rib (V)
Provence (L)
Pub Rest. (L)
Ram's Head Inn/CM (L,V)*
Ravioli House/CM (L)
Red Caboose/LB (L)
Red Hot & Blue (L)
Regatta B&G (L,V)
Rembrandt's (L)
Renault Winery/CM (L)
Rest. at Doneckers/LB (L)
Rhapsody's (L)
Rio Station/CM (L)
Ristorante Alberto (L,V)
Ristorante Amalfi/DE (L)
Ristorante Fieni's (L)
Ristorante La Buca*
Ristorante Laceno (L)
Ristorante Mediterraneo (L)
Ristorante Ottimo*
Ristorante Panorama (V)*
Ristorante Positano (L)
Ristorante Primavera (L)
Ritz-Carlton Grill (V)

River City Diner (L)
Roberto's/AC (L,V)
Rock Lobster (L,V)
Rococo (V)
Roller's (L)*
Roscoe's Kodiak*
Roselena's Coffee (L)
Rose Tree Inn (L)
Ruby's (L)*
Ruhling's Seafood (L)
Russell's 96 West*
Ruth's Chris (V)
Sabatini's/AC*
Safari Steakhse./AC (L,V)
Sagami (L)
Sage Diner (L)
Sakura Spring (L)
Saloon (L)
Sal's/DE (L)
Samuel Adams Brew*
Samuels (L)
Sang Kee*
Sansom St. Oyster*
Savona (L,V)
Scampi Rist. (L)
Scannicchio's/AC*
Scheherazade/AC (L,V)
Schooners & C.B.'s/CM (L)
Scoogi's Classic (L)
Screnci's/CM (L)
Seafood Unlimited*
Sea Grill/CM (L)
Serrano*
Seven Stars (L)
Ship Inn (L)
Shiroi Hana*
Siam Cuisine I (L)
Siam Cuisine II (V)
Siam Cuisine III (V)
Sienna/DE (V)
Siggie's L'Auberge (V)
Sign of Sorrel Horse (L)
Silk & Spice (L)
Silk City (L)
Silk Purse/DE (L)
Singapore Kosher (V)
Siri's Thai French (L)
Sitar India (L)
Smokin' Sam's (L)
Society Hill Hotel*
Somsak Thai (L)
Sonoma (L,V)*
Spaghetti Warehse. (L)
Spotted Hog (L)
Spring Mill Café (L)

State St. Cafe*
Stazi Milano (L)
Steakhouse/AC (L,V)
Steak House/AC (L,V)
Stephen's (L)
Stockton Inn (L,V)
Stockyard Inn/LB (L)
Stoltzfus Farm/LB (L)
Stoudt's Black Angus/LB (L)
Striped Bass (V)*
Sullivan's Steakhse./DE (L,V)
Susanna Foo (V)
Sutor's Owl Tree/CM (L)
Swann Lounge (L)
Sweetwater Casino/CM (L)
Tacconelli's Pizza (L)
Tai Lake*
Taqueria Moroleon (L)
Taquet (L)
Tavola Toscana/DE (L)
Terrace at Greenhill/DE (L)
Tex Mex Connection (L)
Thai Pepper (L)
30th St. Station (L)
Thomas' (L)
Tira Misu Rist. (V)
Tomatoes/CM (L)
Tony Clark's (L,V)
Tony Luke's (L)
Tony's Balt. Grill/AC (L)
Top of the Marq/CM (L,V)
Toscana Cucina (L)
Totaro's Ristorante (L)
Treetops (L,V)*
Tre Scalini (L)
Trinacria (L)
Tuckahoe Inn/CM (L)
Tulipano Nero (L)
Ugly Mug/CM (L)
United States Hotel*
Upstares at Varalli*
Urie's Waterfront/CM (L)
Utage/DE (L)
Valley Forge (L)
Valley Green Inn (L)
Valley Stream Inn (L)
Ventura Greenhse./CM (L)
Vickers Tavern (V)
Villa Di Roma (L)
Village Porch (L)
Villa Strafford (V)
Vincente's/DE (L)
Vincent's (L)
Walter's Steakhse./DE (L)
Warmdaddy's (L)

Washington Crossing (L)
Washington House (L)
Washington Inn/CM (L)
Waterfront/CM (L)
Waterworks Cafe/DE (L)
White House/AC (L)
Wild Onion Rest. (L)
William Fisk/AC (L,V)
William Penn Inn (L)
Willistown Grille (L)
Willow Valley Rst./LB (L)
Windmill/LB (L)
W.L. Goodfellows/CM (L)
Wycombe Inn (L)
Yangming (L)
Yellow Springs Inn (L)
Yesterday's/CM (L)
Yorktown Inn (L)
Zanzibar Blue (V)*
Zinn's Diner/LB (L)
Zocalo (L)
ZuZu (L)

Parties & Private Rooms

(Any nightclub or restaurant
charges less at off-times;
* indicates private rooms
available; best of many)
Acacia
A.C. Station/AC
Alberto's*
Alexander's Inn/CM
Alfe's/CM*
Al Khimah
Alois/LB*
America B&G*
Andreotti's*
Angeloni's II/AC*
Angelo's Fairmount/AC*
Anton's at Swan*
Asakura*
A Touch of Italy/CM*
Audrey Claire*
Axelsson's/CM
Azafran
Azalea Room*
Bangkok House/DE
Bards
Barnacle Ben's West*
Barrymore Room*
Bay Pony Inn*
Beau Monde*
Beau Rivage*
Bentley's Five*
Berlengas Island*

Between Friends*
Big Fish*
Bird-in-Hand/LB*
Bistro Romano*
Bistro St. Tropez*
Black Bass*
Black Walnut*
BLT's Cobblefish
Blue Bell Inn*
Blüe Ox Brauhaus*
Bomb Bomb BBQ
Bonaparte*
Bookbinders*
Bottling Works/LB*
Braddock's Tavern*
Brandywine Brewing/DE
Brandywine Room/DE*
Brasil's*
Bravo Bistro
Bridget Foy's*
Buckley's Tavern/DE*
Busch's/CM
Cafe Arielle*
Cafe 8 South/CM
Cafe Gallery*
Cafe Noelle*
Cafe Preeya*
Caffé Aldo Lamberti*
Caffe Bellissimo/DE*
California Cafe*
Carambola
Caribou Cafe
Carucci/DE*
Carversville Inn
Cary Restaurant
Casa Nicola/AC*
Casselli's Rist.*
Catacombs/LB*
Catelli*
Cedars
Cent'Anni*
Centre Bridge Inn*
Century House*
Chadds Ford Inn*
Chanterelles
Charles Plaza*
Charlie's Bar/CM*
Chart House*
Chateau Silvana*
Cherry St. Chinese*
Cibo*
Ciboulette*
CinCin*
Circa*
City Tavern*

Clayton's*
Coco Pazzo*
Columbus Inn/DE*
Concordville Inn*
Continental
Coppermill Harvest*
Cotton Club*
Cousin's/CM
Cousins Country/CM*
Coventry Forge*
Crab Trap/CM*
Crier in Country*
Cucina Rosa/CM*
Cucina Rustica/CM
Cuisines*
Culinary Garden/CM
Cutters*
Cuvee Notredame*
Dahlak*
D'Angelo's*
Dante & Luigi's*
David's Yellow Brick*
Day by Day
Deauville Inn/CM
Deetrick's Cafe*
Deux Cheminées*
Diamond's*
DiLullo Centro*
Dilworthtown Inn*
DiNardo's Seafood
Dinon's*
Doc's Place/CM*
Ebbitt Room/CM*
Effie's
Elena Wu
El Mariachi*
Epicurean, The*
Evermay on Del.*
Evviva*
Fedeli's/CM
Felicia's*
Fez Moroccan*
Filomena Cuc. Rustica*
Fireside Room*
Five Spot*
Flying Fish*
Foggia*
Food for Thought*
Forager*
Fork's Inn/CM*
Founders*
Fountain Rest.*
Four Dogs Tavern*
410 Bank St./CM
Fox Point Grill/DE

Frangelica*
Frankie's at Night*
Frankie's Seafood*
Frederick's*
Frenchtown Inn*
Frescos/CM
Fuji Mountain*
Garden, The*
General Warren*
Girasole/AC
Girasole Rist.
Giumarello's Rist.
Goat Hollow*
Golden Inn/CM*
Golden Pheasant*
Golden Pond*
Good N' Plenty/LB*
Gourley's*
Gourmet Rest.*
Gourmet's Table
Gracie's/LB
Grasshopper*
Graziella's*
Green Hills Inn/LB*
Green Room/DE*
Gregory's/CM
Groff's Farm/LB*
Gypsy Rose*
Hadley's Bistro*
Hamilton's Grill*
Hard Rock Cafe*
Harmony Vegetarian*
Harry's Bar & Grill*
Harry's Savoy Grill/DE*
Hartefeld National*
Hatteras Coastal/CM*
Haute To Trot*
Haydn Zug's/LB*
Henny's/CM
Herb Garden*
Hibachi Japanese/DE*
Hikaru*
Historic Revere Tav./LB*
H.K. Golden Phoenix
Hotel du Village*
House of Chen*
Il Portico*
Il Sol D'Italia
Imperial Inn*
India Palace/DE*
Inn at Phillips Mill*
Inn of the Hawke*
Inn on Blueberry Hill*
Inn Philadelphia*
Io E Tu Rist.*

Iron Hill Brewery/DE*
Jack's Firehouse
Jannie
Jean Pierre's*
Jefferson House*
Joe's Bistro 614/LB*
Joe's Peking*
Joe's Tomato Pies*
Johan's/AC
Johnny Mott's*
Joseph Ambler*
Joseph's Italian*
Jow's Garden*
Joy Tsin Lau*
Judy's Cafe
JW's Steakhse.
Kansas City Prime*
Kaufman House*
Kawabata*
Kennedy-Supplee*
Khajuraho
Kimberton Inn*
Kingdom Vegetarians*
King George II*
Knave of Hearts*
Kobe Japanese
Krazy Kats/DE*
La Bonne Auberge*
La Campagna*
La Campagne*
La Casa Pasta/DE*
La Cipolla Torta*
La Cocotte*
La Collina*
La Famiglia*
La Familia Sonsini*
La Fourchette*
La Grolla*
Lamberti's Cucina*
Lambertville Station*
Landing, The
La Padella*
La Paella Tio Pepe
La Pergola
La Terrasse*
Latest Dish*
La Tolteca/DE
Lauren's*
La Veranda*
La Vigna*
Le Bar Lyonnais*
Le Bec-Fin*
Le Champignon*
Le Colonial*
Lee Ho Seafood*

Lee How Fook*
Lenape Inn*
Little Brat's Haus/CM*
Lobster House/CM*
Log Cabin/LB*
London Grill*
Loose Ends
Los Amigos' New Mexico*
Lucy's Hat Shop*
Luigi Vitrone's/DE*
Ly Michael's
Maccabeam
Mac's/CM*
Mad Batter/CM*
Mad 4 Mex*
Mainland Inn*
Mama Mia/CM*
Ma Ma Yolanda's*
Mamma Maria*
Mandarin Garden*
Manila Bay B&G*
Marco's Cafe
Margaret Kuo's*
Marker, The
Market Fare/LB*
Marrakesh*
Marra's*
Marshalton Inn*
Marsilio's*
Martine's
Martini's Lounge
Meiji-En*
Mendenhall Inn*
Merion Inn/CM
Mia's
Michael's Family*
Michael's Rist.*
Michele's/DE*
Minar Palace
Mirage, The/CM*
Monk's Café*
Monte Carlo*
Moonstruck*
Morton's of Chicago*
Moselem Springs/LB*
Mrs. London's Cafe*
Mrs. Robino's/DE*
Museum Rest.*
Mustard Greens*
My Thai*
Nav Jiwan Tea Rm./LB*
New World Cafe*
Nicholas Nickolas*
Nick's B&G*
Nonna's*

213

Norma's Middle Eastern
Nul Bom*
Obadiah's/CM*
Oceanfront/CM*
Odette's*
Official All Star/AC
Olde Greenfield Inn/LB*
Old Guard House*
Old Mill Inn*
Old Original Book*
Old Waterway Inn/AC
Opus 251*
Orsatti's/AC*
Otto's Brauhaus*
Ozzie's Tratt.*
Pace One*
Palace of Asia*
Palladium*
Palm*
Pamplona
Paradigm
Passage to India*
Passerelle*
Pastaria Franco & Luigi's
Pastavino Tratt.*
Pattaya Grill*
Peacock Parkwy.
Peking Rest.*
Pepper's Cafe
Peter Shields/CM*
Pho Xe Lua*
Piccolo Mondo/DE*
Pilot House/CM
Pizzicato
Plain & Fancy/LB*
Plumsteadville Inn*
Pompano Grille
Poor Henry's*
Portofino*
Portofino/AC*
Port Saloon*
Positano Rist./DE
Primavera Pizza Kit.*
Prime Rib*
Pub Rest.*
Purple Sage*
Rajbhog Indian*
Ralph's
Ram's Head Inn/CM*
Ravioli House/CM
Red Caboose/LB*
Rembrandt's
Remi's Cafe*
Renault Winery/CM*
Rest. at Donreckers/LB*

Rhapsody's*
Rio Station/CM*
Ristorante Alberto*
Ristorante Amalfi/DE*
Ristorante Fieni's*
Ristorante Gallo Nero*
Ristorante La Buca*
Ristorante Laceno*
Ristorante Mediterraneo*
Ristorante Panorama*
Ristorante Positano*
Ristorante Primavera*
Rococo*
Roscoe's Kodiak
Rose Tattoo Cafe*
Rose Tree Inn*
Ruhling's Seafood*
Russell's 96 West*
Sabatini's/AC*
Saffron*
Saigon
Sakura Spring*
Saloon*
Sal's/DE*
Samuels*
Santa Fe Burrito
Saranac
Savona*
Schooners & C.B.'s/CM*
Serrano
Seven Stars*
Shipley Grill/DE*
Sienna/DE*
Siggie's L'Auberge
Sign of Sorrel Horse*
Silk Purse/DE*
Siri's Thai French*
Solaris Grille*
Sonoma*
Sow's Ear/DE*
Spring Mill Café*
Stazi Milano*
Steak House/AC*
Stephen's*
Stockton Inn*
Stockyard Inn/LB*
Sullivan's Steakhse./DE*
Susanna Foo*
Sweetwater Casino/CM*
Taquet*
Tavola Toscana/DE*
Taxi*
Terrace at Greenhill/DE*
Thai Garden*
Thomas'

Tierra Colombiana*
Tira Misu Rist.*
Tony Clark's
Toscana Cucina
Totaro's Ristorante*
Trinacria*
Tuckahoe Inn/CM*
Union Park/CM*
Upstares at Varalli*
Urie's Waterfront/CM*
Utage/DE*
Valley Green Inn
Vega Grill*
Ventura Greenhse./CM
Vickers Tavern*
Victor Café
Villa Di Roma*
Villa Strafford*
Vincente's/DE*
Walter's Steakhse./DE*
Warmdaddy's*
Washington Crossing*
Washington House*
Washington Inn/CM*
Waterfront/CM*
Waters Edge/CM
Waterworks Cafe/DE*
White Dog Cafe*
William Penn Inn*
Willow Valley Rst./LB*
W.L. Goodfellows/CM*
Wycombe Inn*
Yangming*
Yellow Springs Inn*
Yesterday's/CM*
Zanzibar Blue
Zocalo*

Murray's Deli
New Corned Beef
Old City Coffee
Old Original Book
Palm
Pompano Grille
Reading Terminal Mkt.
Rococo
Savona
Shank's & Evelyn's
Sonoma
Spiaggi/CM
Taquet
Tony Clark's
Triangle Tavern
Vega Grill
Warmdaddy's
White Dog Cafe
White House/AC
Xando Coffee
Zanzibar Blue

Power Scenes
Brasserie Perrier
Cary Restaurant
Coco Pazzo
Fountain Rest.
Green Room/DE
Harry's Bar & Grill
Le Bec-Fin
Morton's of Chicago
New Corned Beef
Palm
Ritz-Carlton Grill
Saloon
Shipley Grill/DE
Striped Bass
Susanna Foo

People-Watching
Al Dar
Bonaparte
Brasserie Perrier
Circa
Continental
Copabanana
Famous 4th St. Deli
Five Spot
Fork
Geno's Steaks
Hymie's
Joe's Peking
La Terrasse
Latest Dish
Mad Batter/CM
Montserrat

Pre-Theater Dining
(Call to check prices,
days and times)
Academy Cafe
A Ca Mia/CM
Adobe Cafe
Aleathea's/CM
Alfe's/CM
Alfio's
A Little Cafe
Andreotti's
Arroyo Grille
Arugula!
A Touch of Italy/CM
Barnacle Ben's
Barnacle Ben's West

Bay Pony Inn
Big Fish
Blue Bell Inn
Bookbinders
Brandywine Room/DE
Busch's/CM
Cafe 8 South/CM
Cafe Zesty
Caffe Bellissimo/DE
Cary Restaurant
Century House
Charlie's Bar/CM
Cibo
Ciboulette
Coco Pazzo
Columbus Inn/DE
Concordville Inn
Country Club
Cousin's/CM
Cousins Country/CM
Culinary Garden/CM
Cutters
David's Yellow Brick
Deauville Inn/CM
D'Ignazio's
DiLullo Centro
DiNardo's Seafood
Doc's Place/CM
Fireside Room
Five Spot
Foggia
Founders
Frankie's Seafood
Garden, The
General Lafayette
Gianna's
Girasole Rist.
Gourley's
Gregory's/CM
Harry's Savoy Grill/DE
Henny's/CM
Hunt Room
Inn at Sugar Hill/CM
Inn Philadelphia
Johnny Mott's
Kaufman House
King George II
Lamberti's Cucina
La Paella Tio Pepe
Lobster Loft/CM
Merion Inn/CM
Olde Greenfield Inn/LB
Old Mill Inn
Opus 251
Orfèo

Otto's Brauhaus
Pattaya Grill
Peaches at Sunset/CM
Peacock Parkwy.
Plumsteadville Inn
Rest. at Doneckers/LB
Rio Station/CM
Ruhling's Seafood
Sabatini's/AC
Scampi Rist.
Scannicchio's/AC
Schooners & C.B.'s/CM
Screnci's/CM
Ship Inn
Stockton Inn
Sweetwater Casino/CM
Tavern on Green
Top of the Marq/CM
Tuckahoe Inn/CM
Washington House
William Penn Inn
Yesterday's/CM
Zanzibar Blue

Post-Theater Dining

(Call to check prices,
days and times)
Academy Cafe
America B&G
Andreotti's
Aoi
Arroyo Grille
Azalea Room
Beaujolais
Big River Fish Co.
Black Bass
Bobby's Seafood
Bonaparte
Bookbinders
Brandywine Room/DE
Cafe Zesty
Cary Restaurant
Charlie's Bar/CM
Cibo
Coco Pazzo
Columbus Inn/DE
Deauville Inn/CM
Deetrick's Cafe
Diamond's
D'Ignazio's
DiLullo Centro
Dock Street
Edge
Epicurean, The
General Lafayette

216

Goat Hollow
Golden Pheasant
Gullifty's
Harry's Savoy Grill/DE
Havana
Il Sol D'Italia
Inn of the Hawke
Iron Hill Brewery/DE
Joseph Poon
Latest Dish
Liberties
Los Amigos' New Mexico
Lucy's Hat Shop
Mad 4 Mex
Margaret Kuo's
Martini's Lounge
Monk's Café
Montserrat
Moselem Springs/LB
Nicholas Nickolas
North Star Bar
Opus 251
Pamplona
Plough & the Stars
Poor Henry's
Provence
Rouge 98
Ruth's Chris
Sabatini's/AC
Sal's/DE
Shipley Grill/DE
Solaris Grille
Upstares at Varalli
Van Scoy's Bistro/CM
Ventura Greenhse./CM
Wild Onion Rest.
Yesterday's/CM
Zanzibar Blue

Prix Fixe Menus

(Call to check prices,
days and times)
Academy Cafe
A Ca Mia/CM
Alexander's Inn/CM
Alois/LB
Andreotti's
Anton's at Swan
Aoi
Asakura
Astral Plane
Azalea Room
Barrymore Room
Bay Pony Inn
Bistro St. Tropez

Blue Bell Inn
Bobby's Seafood
Bonaparte
Bookbinders
Bottling Works/LB
Brewery Inn/LB
Caruso's/AC
Catacombs/LB
Centre Bridge Inn
Chanterelles
Chart House
Ciboulette
CinCin
Coco Pazzo
Concordville Inn
Cousins Country/CM
Coventry Forge
Crier in Country
David's Yellow Brick
Deauville Inn/CM
Deetrick's Cafe
Deux Cheminées
Dickens Inn
DiLullo Centro
DiNardo's/DE
Evermay on Del.
Fantasea Reef/AC
Foggia
Founders
Fountain Rest.
Frenchtown Inn
Gary's Little Rock/CM
General Lafayette
Gourmet's Table
Graziella's
Green Hills Inn/LB
Gypsy Rose
Hatteras Coastal/CM
Haute To Trot
Inn Philadelphia
Jack's Firehouse
Jean Pierre's
La Bonne Auberge
La Terrasse
La Veranda
Le Bec-Fin
Le Champignon
Le Colonial
Lemon Grass
Mainland Inn
Mandarin Garden
Marrakesh
Martini's Lounge
Meiji-En
Merion Inn/CM

Miller's Smorgasbord/LB
Monte Carlo
My Thai
Nan
Nicholas Nickolas
Olde Greenfield Inn/LB
Opus 251
Orfèo
Painted Parrot
Passerelle
Pattaya Grill
Peacock Parkwy.
Plain & Fancy/LB
Poor Henry's
Prime Place/AC
Regatta B&G
Regent Court/AC
Renault Winery/CM
Rest. at Doneckers/LB
Ruhling's Seafood
Russell's 96 West
Sala Thai
Samosa
Sansom St. Oyster
Savaradio/CM
Savona
Serrano
Ship Inn
Sutor's Owl Tree/CM
Swann Lounge
Taquet
Treetops
Tre Figlio/CM
Valley Green Inn
Willow Valley Rst./LB
Yangming
Zanzibar Blue

McGillin's
Moriarty's
Otto's Brauhaus
Pala's Cafe/DE
Pilot House/CM
Poor Henry's
Samuel Adams Brew
Society Hill Hotel
Valley Forge

Quiet Conversation

Astral Plane
Chanterelles
Ciboulette
Coventry Forge
Deux Cheminées
DiLullo Centro
Dilworthtown Inn
Duling-Kurtz House
Ebbitt Room/CM
Evermay on Del.
Founders
Fountain Rest.
Frenchtown Inn
Friday, Sat., Sun.
Garden, The
Harmony Vegetarian
Inn at Phillips Mill
Inn Philadelphia
Jean Pierre's
Jefferson House
Kennedy-Supplee
Knave of Hearts
La Campagne
La Grolla
Le Bar Lyonnais
Le Bec-Fin
Old Guard House
Ristorante Panorama
Roselena's Coffee
Susanna Foo
Swann Lounge
Treetops
Vickers Tavern
William Penn Inn
Yangming

Pubs/Bars/ Microbreweries

Artful Dodger
Bottling Works/LB
Brandywine Brewing/DE
Cedar Creek/CM
Champion's
Champps Amer.
Copa-Too!
Dickens Inn
Dock Street
Elephant & Castle
Fergie's Pub
Finnigan's Wake
John Harvard's
Maloney's Beef/CM
Manayunk Brewing

Raw Bars

Alberto's
Andreotti's
Axelsson's/CM
Azalea Room
Barnacle Ben's
Berlengas Island
Big River Fish Co.
BLT's Cobblefish

Bobby's Seafood
Bookbinders
Cafe Arielle
Casa Nicola/AC
Chart House
Cock 'n Bull
Crab Trap/CM
Dock's Oyster Hse./AC
Downey's
Feby's Fishery/DE
Frankie's Seafood
Garden, The
Girasole/AC
Golden Inn/CM
Hardshell Cafe
Harry's Bar & Grill
La Veranda
Lobster House/CM
Mamma Maria
Market Fare/LB
Meiji-En
Old Original Book
Pace One
Paradigm
Philadelphia Fish
Rock Lobster
Sagami
Sansom St. Oyster
Savona
Seafood Unlimited
Ship Inn
Snockey's Oyster
Striped Bass
Tuckahoe Inn/CM
United States Hotel
Utage/DE
Ventura Greenhse./CM
William Penn Inn

Reservations Essential

Adobe Cafe
Alaina's
Alberto's
Alexander's Cafe
Alfio's
Alisa Cafe
A Little Cafe
Al Khimah
Alois/LB
Amara Cafe
Andreotti's/AC
Anton's at Swan
Aoi
Arroyo Grille
Azalea Room

Back Burner/DE
Barrymore Room
Bay Pony Inn
Bella Trattoria
Between Friends
Big Fish
Black Bass
Black Walnut
Bobby's Seafood
Bottling Works/LB
Brandywine Room/DE
Brasil's
Bravo Bistro
Brewery Inn/LB
Brighton Steakhse./AC
Cafe Arielle
Cafe Gallery
Cafe Preeya
Cafe Zesty
California Cafe
Carucci/DE
Caruso's/AC
Carversville Inn
Casa Nicola/AC
Catelli
Century House
Chambers
Charles Plaza
Chateau Silvana
Chef Charin
Chef Vola's/AC
Ciboulette
Circa
City Tavern
Clayton's
Coco Pazzo
Cousin's/CM
Crier in Country
Cucina Rosa/CM
Cucina Rustica/CM
Cuisines
Deauville Inn/CM
Dilworthtown Inn
Doc's Place/CM
El Mariachi
Evermay on Del.
Evviva
Fedeli's/CM
Felicia's
Fez Moroccan
Food for Thought
Fork's Inn/CM
Founders
Frankie's at Night
Frankie's Seafood

Freda's Cafe/CM
Frederick's
Friday, Sat., Sun.
Gary's Little Rock/CM
Girasole/AC
Giumarello's Rist.
Golden Inn/CM
Golden Pheasant
Gracie's/LB
Graziella's
Green Room/DE
Gypsy Rose
Happy Rooster
Hatteras Coastal/CM
Il Tartufo
Il Verdi/AC
Inn at Phillips Mill
Inn on Blueberry Hill
Io E Tu Rist.
Italian Bistro
Jean Pierre's
Jefferson House
Johan's/AC
Joy Tsin Lau
JW's Steakhse.
Kingdom Vegetarians
Kobe Japanese
Krazy Kats/DE
La Bonne Auberge
La Casa Pasta/DE
La Famiglia
La Familia Sonsini
La Fourchette
Lai Lai
La Paella Tio Pepe
La Veranda
Le Bec-Fin
Little Saigon/AC
Log Cabin/LB
L'Osteria Cucina/DE
Mainland Inn
Marrakesh
Meiji-En
Mendenhall Inn
Moshulu
Mr. Martino's Tratt.
Nais Cuisine
Nicholas Nickolas
Norma's Middle Eastern
Opus 251
Overtures
Pace One
Paradigm
Peregrines/AC
Peter Shields/CM

Philadelphia Fish
Piccolo Mondo/DE
Pier 7/AC
Pippo's Fantastico
Plough & the Stars
Portofino/CM
Positano Rist./DE
Primavera/AC
Prime Place/AC
Provence
Purple Sage
Regent Court/AC
Remi's Cafe
Renault Winery/CM
Ristorante Amalfi/DE
Ristorante Fieni's
Ristorante Laceno
Ristorante Mediterraneo
Ristorante Positano
Ritz-Carlton Grill
Roscoe's Kodiak
Rose Tree Inn
Ruhling's Seafood
Russell's 96 West
Ruth's Chris
Saloon
Savona
Scheherazade/AC
Screnci's/CM
Serrano
Seven Stars
Siggie's L'Auberge
Sign of Sorrel Horse
Silk & Spice
Silk Cuisine
Spiga D'Oro
State St. Cafe
Steakhouse/AC
Steak House/AC
Stoudt's Black Angus/LB
Striped Bass
Sullivan's Steakhse./DE
Susanna Foo
Taquet
Tavola Toscana/DE
Tira Misu Rist.
Tomatoes/CM
Tony Clark's
Totaro's Ristorante
Tre Figlio/CM
Tre Scalini
Tulipano Nero
Umbria
Utage/DE
Victor Café

Villa Strafford
Vincente's/DE
Warmdaddy's
Waterfront/CM
Waterworks Cafe/DE
White Dog Cafe
William Fisk/AC
William Penn Inn
Wolfgang's Cafe
Wycombe Inn
Yellow Springs Inn

Romantic Spots

Alexander's Inn/CM
Amara Cafe
Cafe Flower Shop
Ciboulette
Deux Cheminées
Duling-Kurtz House
Evermay on Del.
Inn at Phillips Mill
Inn Philadelphia
Knave of Hearts
La Campagne
La Paella Tio Pepe
Le Bar Lyonnais
Monte Carlo
Mr. Martino's Tratt.
Pink Rose Pastry
Ram's Head Inn/CM
Rembrandt's
Roselena's Coffee
Rose Tattoo Cafe
Spring Mill Café
Valley Green Inn
Yellow Springs Inn
Zanzibar Blue

Saturday – Best Bets

(B=brunch; L=lunch;
best of many)
A Ca Mia/CM (L)
Alaina's (L)
Alberto's (L)
Alexander's Cafe (B,L)
Alfe's/CM (L)
Al Khimah (L)
Amara Cafe (L)
America B&G (L)
Andreotti's (B,L)
Arpeggio (L)
Athens Cafe (L)
August Moon (L)
Azalea Room (L)
Back Burner/DE (L)

Bards (L)
Barrymore Room (B,L)
Bay Pony Inn (L)
Bentley's Five (L)
Berlengas Island (L)
Black Bass (L)
Blue Bell Inn (L)
Blue in Green (B,L)
Bridget Foy's (L)
Bridgid (B,L)
Brittany Cafe/AC (L)
Buckley's Tavern/DE (L)
Cafe Gallery (L)
Cafe Michaelangelo (L)
Cafe Zesty (L)
Caffé Aldo Lamberti (L)
California Cafe (L)
Capriccio Cafe (L)
Caribou Cafe (L)
Carman's Country Kit. (B)
Carversville Inn (L)
Cary Restaurant (L)
Cedar Creek/CM (L)
Cedars (L)
Chadds Ford Inn (L)
Charcoal Pit/DE (L)
Charlie's Bar/CM (L)
Chef Tell's (L)
Church St. Bistro (L)
CinCin (L)
City Tavern (L)
Clayton's (L)
Concordville Inn (L)
Coppermill Harvest (L)
Crab Trap/CM (L)
Cuvee Notredame (L)
Dante & Luigi's (L)
David's Yellow Brick (L)
Deauville Inn/CM (L)
DiNardo's/DE (L)
Doc's Place/CM (B,L)
Elena Wu (L)
Epicurean, The (L)
Fantasea Reef/AC (L)
Fat Jack's (L)
1521 Café (L)
Fireside Room (L)
Flowing Springs (L)
Flying Fish (L)
Food for Thought (L)
Forager (L)
Fork (L)
Fork's Inn/CM (L)
Founders (L)
Fountain Rest. (L)

Frangelica (L)
Freda's Cafe/CM (L)
Frenchtown Inn (L)
Full Moon (L)
Goat Hollow (L)
Good N' Plenty/LB (L)
Gourmet's Table (L)
Green Cuisine/CM (L)
Green Room/DE (L)
Gregory's/CM (L)
Gypsy Rose (L)
Hadley's Bistro (B,L)
Hank's Place (L)
Happy Rooster (L)
Hartefeld National (L)
Henny's/CM (L)
Herb Garden (L)
Historic Revere Tav./LB (L)
Hoss's Steak/LB (L)
Hot Tamales Cafe (L)
Il Tartufo (L)
Inn of the Hawke (L)
Iron Hill Brewery/DE (L)
Jack's Firehouse (L)
Jake's (L)
Jamaican Jerk Hut (L)
Jannie (L)
Jefferson House (L)
Joe's Bistro 614/LB (L)
King George II (L)
La Casa Pasta/DE (L)
La Cipolla Torta (L)
Lambertville Station (L)
Lamb Tavern (L)
Landing, The (L)
La Pergola (L)
Latest Dish (L)
La Tolteca/DE (L)
La Veranda (L)
Le Bus (B,L)
Le Colonial (L)
Lenape Inn (L)
Little Brat's Haus/CM (L)
Lobster House/CM (L)
Lobster Loft/CM (L)
Los Amigos/AC (L)
Luigi's Canal Hse. (L)
Mad Batter/CM (L)
Main-ly Desserts (L)
Maloney's Beef/CM (L)
Mama Mia/CM (L)
Mama Rosa (L)
Marathon Grill (B,L)
Marco Polo (L)
Market Fare/LB (L)

Marra's (L)
Martine's (L)
Meil's (L)
Mendenhall Inn (L)
Mexican Food (L)
Mia's (L)
Michael's Family (L)
Mikasa/DE (L)
Minar Palace (L)
Monk's Café (L)
Moselem Springs/LB (L)
Mrs. London's Cafe (L)
Museum Rest. (L)
Nav Jiwan Tea Rm./LB (L)
New Delhi (L)
Norma's Middle Eastern (L)
Oceanfront/CM (L)
Odette's (L)
Olde Greenfield Inn/LB (B,L)
Opus 251 (L)
Otto's Brauhaus (L)
Paganini (L)
Palace of Asia (B,L)
Paradigm (L)
Passage to India (L)
Pastavino Tratt. (L)
Pattaya Grill (L)
Philadelphia Fish (L)
Philly Crab & Steak (L)
Pilot House/CM (L)
Plough & the Stars (B,L)
Poor Henry's (L)
Primavera Pizza Kit. (L)
Provence (L)
Rangoon (L)
Rembrandt's (L)
Remi's Cafe (L)
Rest. at Doneckers/LB (L)
Rhapsody's (L)
Rib Crib (L)
Rio Station/CM (L)
Ristorante Attilio/DE (L)
Ristorante Laceno (L)
Ristorante Mediterraneo (L)
Ritz-Carlton Grill (L)
Rizzo's (L)
Roller's (L)
Rose Tree Inn (L)
Ruhling's Seafood (L)
Samuels (L)
Sansom St. Oyster (L)
Santa Fe Burrito (L)
Sassafras Cafe (L)
Savaradio/CM (B)
Sawan's Med. Bistro (L)

Schooners & C.B.'s/CM (L)
Scoogi's Classic (L)
Seafood Unlimited (L)
Shank's & Evelyn's (L)
Siri's Thai French (L)
Smokin' Sam's (L)
Sonoma (L)
South St. Souvlaki (L)
Spaghetti Warehse. (L)
Spring Mill Café (B,L)
State St. Cafe (L)
Stockton Inn (L)
Stoltzfus Farm/LB (L)
Stoudt's Black Angus/LB (L)
Sutor's Owl Tree/CM (L)
Swann Lounge (L)
Taqueria Moroleon (L)
Taquet (L)
Tavern on Green (L)
Terrace at Greenhill/DE (L)
Tex Mex Connection (L)
Thomas' (B,L)
Tierra Colombiana (L)
Tomatoes/CM (B)
Tony Clark's (L)
Tony's Balt. Grill/AC (L)
Treetops (L)
Tuckahoe Inn/CM (L)
Upstares at Varalli (L)
Valley Green Inn (L)
Valley Stream Inn (L)
Van Scoy's Bistro/CM (L)
Ventura Greenhse./CM (L)
Villa Di Roma (L)
Vincente's/DE (L)
Warsaw Cafe (L)
Washington Crossing (L)
Washington Inn/CM (L)
White Dog Cafe (B,L)
William Penn Inn (L)
Windmill/LB (L)
Yangming (L)
Yesterday's/CM (L)

Sunday Dining – Best Bets
(B=brunch; L=lunch;
D=dinner; plus all hotels
and most Asians)
A Ca Mia/CM (L,D)
Adobe Cafe (D)
Alaina's (D)
Alberto's (B,D)
Al Dar (L,D)
Aleathea's/CM (D)
Alexander's Inn/CM (B,D)

Alfe's/CM (D)
Alfio's (D)
A Little Cafe (D)
Al Khimah (L,D)
Alois/LB (D)
Alyan's (L,D)
Amara Cafe (D)
America B&G (B,L,D)
Andreotti's (L,D)
Angeloni's II/AC (D)
Angelo's Fairmount/AC (D)
Anton's at Swan (D)
Arpeggio (L,D)
Arroyo Grille (B,L,D)
Assaggi Italiani (D)
Astral Plane (B,D)
Athens Cafe (L,D)
A Touch of Italy/CM (D)
Audrey Claire (D)
Axelsson's/CM (D)
Back Burner/DE (B)
Bards (B,L,D)
Barnacle Ben's (D)
Barnacle Ben's West (D)
Bay Pony Inn (B,D)
Beau Rivage (D)
Bella Trattoria (B,L,D)
Benkady (L,D)
Berlengas Island (L,D)
Bertolini's (L,D)
Best of British (D)
Between Friends (B)
Big Fish (L,D)
Big River Fish Co. (D)
Bistro Romano (D)
Black Bass (B,L,D)
Black Walnut (D)
BLT's Cobblefish (D)
Blue in Green (L)
Blüe Ox Brauhaus (B,D)
Bonaparte (D)
Bookbinders (D)
Bottling Works/LB (D)
Braddock's Tavern (B,D)
Brasil's (D)
Brasserie Perrier (D)
Bridget Foy's (B,L,D)
Bridgid (L,D)
Brighton Steakhse./AC (B,D)
Brittany Cafe/AC (L,D)
Broad Axe Tavern (L,D)
Buckley's Tavern/DE (B,L,D)
Cafe Arielle (D)
Cafe 8 South/CM (D)
Cafe Flower Shop (B,D)

Cafe Gallery (B,D)
Cafe Giuseppe (D)
Cafe Michaelangelo (D)
Cafe Preeya (D)
Cafe Zesty (L,D)
Caffé Aldo Lamberti (L,D)
Caffe Bellissimo/DE (L,D)
Caffe La Bella (B,D)
California Cafe (B,L,D)
Carambola (D)
Caribou Cafe (B,L,D)
Carversville Inn (B,D)
Cassano Italian (D)
Catacombs/LB (D)
Catelli (D)
Cedar Creek/CM (L,D)
Cedars (L,D)
Celebre's Pizzeria (L,D)
Cent'Anni (D)
Centre Bridge Inn (B,D)
Century House (D)
Chadds Ford Inn (B,D)
Charcoal Pit/DE (L,D)
Charles Plaza (D)
Charlie's Bar/CM (L,D)
Chart House (B,D)
Chateau Silvana (B,D)
Chef Charin (D)
Chef Tell's (B,D)
Chef Vola's/AC (D)
Christopher's (D)
Church St. Bistro (L,D)
Circa (D)
City Tavern (L,D)
Clayton's (B,L)
Columbus Inn/DE (B,D)
Concordville Inn (D)
Continental (D)
Cousin's/CM (D)
Cousins Country/CM (B,D)
Coyote Crossing (D)
Crab Trap/CM (L,D)
Cresheim Cottage (B,D)
Crier in Country (B,D)
Cucina Rosa/CM (D)
Cuvee Notredame (L,D)
Dahlak (B,D)
Dante & Luigi's (L,D)
David's Yellow Brick (B,D)
Deetrick's Cafe (B)
DeLorenzo's (D)
Diamond's (D)
Dilworthtown Inn (D)
DiNardo's/DE (D)
DiNardo's Seafood (D)

Dmitri's (D)
Dock's Oyster Hse./AC (D)
Doc's Place/CM (L,D)
Downey's (B,D)
Doylestown Inn (B,L,D)
Duling-Kurtz House (D)
Effie's (D)
El Azteca (L,D)
El Mariachi (D)
El Sombrero (D)
Epicurean, The (B,L)
Evermay on Del. (D)
Famous 4th St. Deli (L)
Fantasea Reef/AC (L,D)
Fat Jack's (L,D)
Felicia's (D)
Fergie's Pub (D)
Fez Moroccan (D)
1521 Café (B)
Filomena Cuc. Rustica (D)
Fireside Room (B,L,D)
Five Spot (D)
Flowing Springs (D)
Forager (L,D)
Fork (L,D)
Fork's Inn/CM (B,L,D)
410 Bank St./CM (D)
Frangelica (L,D)
Frankie's at Night (D)
Frankie's Seafood (D)
Freda's Cafe/CM (L,D)
Frederick's (D)
Frenchtown Inn (B,D)
Frescos/CM (D)
Friday, Sat., Sun. (D)
Full Moon (B)
Gary's Little Rock/CM (D)
General Lafayette (D)
Gianna's (D)
Girasole/AC (D)
Girasole Rist. (D)
Goat Hollow (B,L,D)
Golden Pheasant (B,D)
Gourmet's Table (B)
Graziella's (D)
Green Cuisine/CM (L,D)
Groff's Farm/LB (B)
Hadley's Bistro (L,D)
Hamilton's Grill (D)
Hank's Place (L)
Harry's Savoy Grill/DE (B,D)
Hartefeld National (B,L,D)
Hatteras Coastal/CM (B,D)
Henny's/CM (L,D)
Historic Revere Tav./LB (L,D)

Hoss's Steak/LB (L,D)
Hotel du Village (D)
Hymie's (L,D)
Il Giardino (D)
Il Portico (D)
Il Tartufo (L,D)
India Palace/DE (L,D)
Inn at Phillips Mill (D)
Inn at Sugar Hill/CM (D)
Inn on Blueberry Hill (D)
Inn Philadelphia (B,D)
Io E Tu Rist. (D)
Iron Hill Brewery/DE (B,L,D)
Isaac's/LB (B,L,D)
Isabella's (D)
Italian Bistro (L,D)
Jack's Firehouse (L,D)
Jake's (B,L,D)
Jamaican Jerk Hut (L,D)
Jean Pierre's (B)
Jefferson House (D)
Joe Italiano's/Inn/CM (L,D)
Joe Italiano's/II/CM (D)
Joe's Tomato Pies (D)
Johnny Mott's (D)
Joseph Ambler (D)
Joseph's Italian (D)
Judy's Cafe (B,D)
JW's Steakhse. (D)
Kansas City Prime (D)
Kaufman House (D)
Kimberton Inn (B,D)
Kingdom Vegetarians (L,D)
King George II (L,D)
Knave of Hearts (B,D)
La Bonne Auberge (D)
La Campagna (D)
La Campagne (B,D)
La Casa Pasta/DE (L,D)
La Cipolla Torta (L,D)
La Cocotte (D)
La Collina (D)
La Famiglia (D)
La Familia Sonsini (B,D)
La Fourchette (B,D)
La Locanda (D)
Lambertville Station (B,L,D)
Lamb Tavern (D)
Landing, The (L,D)
La Padella (D)
La Pergola (D)
La Terrasse (B,D)
Latest Dish (B,D)
La Veranda (D)
La Vigna (D)

Le Bus (B,L,D)
Lee Ho Seafood (D)
Lenape Inn (D)
Le Petit Cafe (D)
Little Brat's Haus/CM (L,D)
Little Fish (D)
Lobster House/CM (D)
Log Cabin/LB (D)
London Grill (B,D)
Los Amigos' New Mexico (L,D)
Luigi's Canal Hse. (L,D)
Luigi Vitrone's/DE
Mac's/CM (D)
Mainland Inn (D)
Main-ly Desserts (L)
Mama Mia/CM (L,D)
Mama Rosa (L,D)
Ma Ma Yolanda's (D)
Marathon Grill (L,D)
Marco's Cafe (D)
Market Fare/LB (B,D)
Marrakesh (D)
Marra's (D)
Marshalton Inn (D)
Martine's (L,D)
Mayfair Diner (L,D)
Meil's (L,D)
Melissa's Bistro/CM (D)
Mexican Food (L,D)
Michael's Family (L,D)
Michael's Rist. (D)
Miller's Smorgasbord/LB (D)
Mirna's Cafe (D)
Mississippi Steak/AC (D)
Monk's Café (B,L,D)
Monte Carlo (D)
Moonstruck (D)
Morton's of Chicago (D)
Moselem Springs/LB (D)
Mother's (L,D)
Mr. Martino's Tratt. (D)
Mrs. London's Cafe (D)
Mrs. Robino's/DE (L,D)
Museum Rest. (B)
Nais Cuisine (D)
New Delhi (L,D)
New Orleans Cafe (B,D)
New Orleans Cafe II (D)
Nonna's (D)
Nul Bom (D)
Oceanfront/CM (B,L,D)
Odette's (B,D)
Old Original Book (D)
Old Waterway Inn/AC (D)
Opus 251 (B,L,D)

Otto's Brauhaus (L,D)
Overtures (D)
Ozzie's Tratt. (D)
Pace One (B,D)
Pacific Grille (D)
Paganini (L,D)
Painted Parrot (D)
Pamplona (D)
Paradigm (L,D)
Passage to India (L,D)
Pastavino Tratt. (L,D)
Persian Grill (L,D)
Peter Shields/CM (B,D)
Philadelphia Fish (D)
Philly Crab & Steak (D)
Pilot House/CM (L,D)
Plain & Fancy/LB (D)
Plough & the Stars (L,D)
Plumsteadville Inn (B,D)
Pollo Rosso (D)
Pompano Grille (D)
Poor Henry's (L,D)
Primavera Pizza Kit. (L,D)
Provence (B,L,D)
Pub Rest. (D)
Purple Sage (B,D)
Ralph's (D)
Ram's Head Inn/CM (D)
Ravioli House/CM (D)
Regent Court/AC (B)
Rembrandt's (B,D)
Renault Winery/CM (B,D)
Ristorante Alberto (D)
Ristorante Attilio/DE (L,D)
Ristorante Fieni's (D)
Ristorante Gallo Nero (D)
Ristorante Laceno (L,D)
Ristorante Mediterraneo (L,D)
Ristorante Positano (D)
Ristorante Primavera (D)
Ristorante San Carlo (D)
Rizzo's (L,D)
Rococo (D)
Roller's (B,D)
Ron's Ribs (L,D)
Ruhling's Seafood (L,D)
Ruth's Chris (D)
Sabatini's/AC (D)
Sage Diner (L,D)
Samosa (L,D)
Samuels (B,D)
Santa Fe Burrito (L,D)
Sassafras Cafe (D)
Savaradio/CM (D)
Savona (D)

Sawan's Med. Bistro (D)
Scampi Rist. (D)
Scannicchio's/AC (D)
Scheherazade/AC (D)
Schooners & C.B.'s/CM (L,D)
Sea Grill/CM (D)
Serrano (D)
Seven Stars (D)
Shipley Grill/DE (D)
Sign of Sorrel Horse (D)
Silk City (L,D)
Sitar India (L,D)
Smokin' Sam's (L,D)
Sonoma (B,L,D)
South St. Souvlaki (L,D)
Sow's Ear/DE (D)
Spaghetti Warehse. (B,L,D)
Spiaggi/CM (D)
Spiga D'Oro (D)
State St. Cafe (B)
Stazi Milano (D)
Stix (D)
Stoudt's Black Angus/LB (L,D)
Striped Bass (D)
Sutor's Owl Tree/CM (B,L,D)
Tacconelli's Pizza (D)
Tandoor India (L,D)
Taqueria Moroleon (L,D)
Tavern on Green (B,D)
Tavola Toscana/DE (B,D)
Terrace at Greenhill/DE (B,D)
Tex Mex Connection (L,D)
Thai Singha Hse. (D)
Thomas' (L,D)
Tierra Colombiana (L,D)
Tira Misu Rist. (D)
Tomatoes/CM (D)
Tony Clark's (D)
Tony's Balt. Grill/AC (L,D)
Top of the Marq/CM (D)
Toscana Cucina (D)
Tre Figlio/CM (D)
Tre Scalini (D)
Tuckahoe Inn/CM (L,D)
Tulipano Nero (D)
Umbria (D)
Upstares at Varalli (D)
Valley Green Inn (B,D)
Valley Stream Inn (B,D)
Vega Grill (D)
Ventura Greenhse./CM (L,D)
Victor Café (D)
Villa Di Roma (D)
Walter's Steakhse./DE (D)

Warmdaddy's (B,D)
Washington Crossing (B,L,D)
Washington Inn/CM (L)
Waters Edge/CM (D)
White Dog Cafe (L,D)
Wild Onion Rest. (D)
William Penn Inn (B,L,D)
Windmill/LB (L,D)
Wycombe Inn (B,L,D)
Yellow Springs Inn (B,D)
Ye Olde Temp. (B,D)
Yesterday's/CM (L,D)
Zinn's Diner/LB (L,D)
Zocalo (D)

Senior Appeal
Abacus
A Ca Mia/CM
Adobe Cafe
Aleathea's/CM
Alfe's/CM
Alfio's
Al Khimah
Allie's American
Andreotti's
Arroyo Grille
Arugula!
A Touch of Italy/CM
Barnacle Ben's
Barnacle Ben's West
Barrymore Room
Bay Pony Inn
Ben & Irv Deli
Blue Bell Inn
Bobby's Seafood
Bookbinders
Cafe 8 South/CM
Cafe Preeya
Cafe Zesty
Caffe Bellissimo/DE
Century House
Charlie's Bar/CM
Columbus Inn/DE
Concordville Inn
Country Club
Cousin's/CM
Cousins Country/CM
Cutters
David's Yellow Brick
Deauville Inn/CM
D'Ignazio's
DiNardo's Seafood
Doc's Place/CM
Duling-Kurtz House
Fireside Room

Frankie's Seafood
General Lafayette
Gianna's
Gregory's/CM
Henny's/CM
Hunt Room
Il Giardino
Ingleneuk Tea Hse.
Inn at Sugar Hill/CM
Inn Philadelphia
Johnny Mott's
Kaufman House
King George II
Lamberti's Cucina
La Paella Tio Pepe
Lobster Loft/CM
Old Mill Inn
Olga's Diner
Opus 251
Otto's Brauhaus
Pattaya Grill
Ponzio's Kingsway
River City Diner
Ruhling's Seafood
Ship Inn
Sweetwater Casino/CM
Tavern on Green
Top of the Marq/CM
Tuckahoe Inn/CM
Washington Crossing
William Penn Inn
Windmill/LB
Yesterday's/CM

Singles Scenes
Bards
Continental
Copa-Too!
Fergie's Pub
Finnigan's Wake
Five Spot
Jake & Oliver's
Katmandu
Latest Dish
LionFish
North Star Bar
Samuel Adams Brew
Silk City
Sugar Mom's
Valley Forge
Xando Coffee

Sleepers

(Good to excellent food, but little known)

A Ca Mia/CM
Aleathea's/CM
Alexander's Inn/CM
Alfe's/CM
Andreotti's/AC
Bangkok City
Bonaparte
Brewery Inn/LB
Brittany Cafe/AC
Cafe 8 South/CM
Cafe Espresso
Carambola
Caruso's/AC
Casa DiNapoli/AC
Cedar Creek/CM
China Moon/AC
Church St. Bistro
Cucina Rosa/CM
Cuisines
Dinon's
Filomena Cuc. Rustica
Fireside Room
Fortune's/AC
Fox Point Grill/DE
Freda's Cafe/CM
Golden Sea
Gracie's/LB
Green Cuisine/CM
Groff's Farm/LB
Hartefeld National
Haydn Zug's/LB
Il Verdi/AC
India Palace/DE
Iron Hill Brewery/DE
Isaac's/LB
Jannie
Joe's Tomato Pies
Johan's/AC
Jow's Garden
JW's Steakhse.
Kim's
Kobe Japanese
La Campagna
La Casa Pasta/DE
Le Colonial
Lee Ho Seafood
Log Cabin/LB
L'Osteria Cucina/DE
Mama Mia/CM
Mama Rosa
Marco's Cafe
Market Fare/LB

Marsilio's
Martine's
Max's Steak Hse./AC
Medici/AC
Michele's/DE
Mikasa/DE
Mississippi Steak/AC
Morning Glory Diner
Nav Jiwan Tea Rm./LB
New Orleans Cafe
New Orleans Cafe II
Norma's Middle Eastern
North Sea
Oaks, The/AC
Olde Greenfield Inn/LB
Ozzie's Tratt.
Pastaria Franco & Luigi's
Peregrines/AC
Philly Crab & Steak
Pho Xe Lua
Piccolo Mondo/DE
Pier 7/AC
Portofino/AC
Positano Rist./DE
Primavera/AC
Prime Place/AC
Ravioli House/CM
Regent Court/AC
Rhapsody's
Rib Crib
Ristorante Amalfi/DE
Ristorante Fieni's
Ristorante Laceno
Roberto's/AC
Russell's 96 West
Safari Steakhse./AC
Sal's/DE
Scheherazade/AC
Schooners & C.B.'s/CM
Silk Purse/DE
Sow's Ear/DE
Steakhouse/AC
Steak House/AC
Stockyard Inn/LB
Stoltzfus Farm/LB
Sullivan's Steakhse./DE
Taqueria Moroleon
Tierra Colombiana
Trinacria
Union Park/CM
Utage/DE
Van Scoy's Bistro/CM
Vincente's/DE
Vincent's

Walter's Steakhse./DE
Windmill/LB

Teflons

(Get lots of business, despite
so-so food, i.e. they have
other attractions that prevent
criticism from sticking)
Abbey Grill
Artful Dodger
Copabanana
Dave & Buster's
Dick Clark's
East Side Mario's
Elephant & Castle
Engine 46 Steakhse.
Fisher's
Gullifty's
Jake & Oliver's
Little Pete's
Lone Star Steakhse.
Marbles
Mel's Italian
Montserrat
Olga's Diner
River City Diner
Rock Lobster
Ruby's
Society Hill Hotel
Spaghetti Warehse.
Tavern on Green
Valley Forge
Yorktown Inn

Tasting Menus

Alois/LB
America B&G
Azalea Room
Barrymore Room
BLT's Cobblefish
Bottling Works/LB
Chanterelles
Ciboulette
Dilworthtown Inn
Dock Street
Fez Moroccan
Founders
Frenchtown Inn
La Campagne
La Terrasse
La Vigna
Marco Polo
Marrakesh
Nonna's
Paradigm
Passerelle

Peregrines/AC
Provence
Sal's/DE
Sign of Sorrel Horse
Taquet
Trinacria
Ye Olde Temp.

Teas

Abbey Grill
Barrymore Room
Best of British
Cassatt Tea Rm.
Clayton's
Evermay on Del.
Founders
Green Room/DE
La Fourchette
Mademoiselle Paris
Mia's
Passerelle
Plough & the Stars
Rhapsody's
Spring Mill Café

Teenagers & Other
Youthful Spirits

A Touch of Italy/CM
Bugaboo Creek
Champps Amer.
Charcoal Pit/DE
Dalessandro's
Dave & Buster's
DeLorenzo's
East Side Mario's
Fat Jack's
Hard Rock Cafe/AC
Jim's Steaks
Le Bus
Nifty Fifty's
Pietro's Pizzeria
Rizzo's
White House/AC

Visitors on Expense
Accounts

Azalea Room
Brasserie Perrier
Deux Cheminées
Founders
Fountain Rest.
Il Portico
Kansas City Prime
Le Bec-Fin
Morton's of Chicago
Nicholas Nickolas

Old Original Book
Palm
Ruth's Chris
Saloon
Striped Bass
Susanna Foo
Tony Clark's
Treetops

Wheelchair Access
(Most places now have
wheelchair access; call in
advance to check)

Wine/Beer Only
Bangkok House/DE
California Pizza Kit.
Capital Vietnam
Celebre's Pizzeria
Charles Plaza
Chung Hing
Fuji Mountain
India Palace/DE
Jim's Steaks
Kimono Sushi Bar
Kim's
Kingdom Vegetarians
Le Bus
Mikasa/DE
Overtures
Pamplona
Rangoon
Ravioli House/CM
Rizzo's
Saigon
Sang Kee
Siri's Thai French
30th St. Station
Valley Forge

Winning Wine Lists
Angeloni's II/AC
Back Burner/DE
Beau Rivage
Blue Bell Inn
Brandywine Room/DE
Brasserie Perrier
Caribou Cafe
Casa Nicola/AC
Chanterelles
Chef Tell's
Deux Cheminées
Diamond's
Dilworthtown Inn
Ebbitt Room/CM
Fountain Rest.

Frenchtown Inn
Green Room/DE
Harry's Savoy Grill/DE
Haydn Zug's/LB
Jake's
Jean Pierre's
Jefferson House
La Fourchette
Le Bar Lyonnais
Le Bec-Fin
Le Palais/AC
Mainland Inn
Michele's/DE
Monte Carlo
Morton's of Chicago
Nicholas Nickolas
Ram's Head Inn/CM
Ristorante La Buca
Ristorante Panorama
Ristorante Positano
Savona
Shipley Grill/DE
Taquet
Tavola Toscana/DE
Toscana Cucina
Washington Inn/CM

Worth a Trip
PENNSYLVANIA
Carversville
 Carversville Inn
Chadds Ford
 Chadds Ford Inn
Chester Springs
 Yellow Springs Inn
Coventryville
 Coventry Forge
Denver
 Zinn's Diner/LB
Doylestown
 Doylestown Inn
 Russell's 96 West
 Sign of Sorrel Horse
East Petersburg
 Haydn Zug's/LB
Erwinna
 Evermay on Del.
 Golden Pheasant
Exton
 Duling-Kurtz House
 Vickers Tavern
Fort Washington
 Palace of Asia
Glen Mills
 Crier in Country

Kimberton
  Kimberton Inn
Lamberville
  Black Bass
  Cuttalossa Inn
Leola
  Log Cabin/LB
Mainland
  Mainland Inn
Mt. Joy
  Alois/LB
  Bottling Works/LB
  Catacombs/LB
  Groff's Farm/LB
New Hope
  Centre Bridge Inn
  Forager
  Hotel du Village
  Inn at Phillips Mill
  La Bonne Auberge
Newtown
  Jean Pierre's
Norristown
  Jefferson House
Paradise
  Historic Revere Tav./LB
Pine Forge
  Gracie's/LB
Reading
  Green Hills Inn/LB
West Chester
  Dilworthtown Inn
  Marshalton Inn
NEW JERSEY
Atlantic City
  Angeloni's II/AC
Burlington
  Cafe Gallery
Cape May
  410 Bank St./CM
  Ebbitt Room/CM
  Freda's Cafe/CM
  Peter Shields/CM
  Washington Inn/CM
  Waters Edge/CM
Cherry Hill
  La Campagne
  Siri's Thai French
Collingswood
  Sagami
Frenchtown
  Frenchtown Inn
Somer's Point
  Beau Rivage
  Chateau Silvana

Stockton
  Stockton Inn
Trenton
  DeLorenzo's
  Diamond's
  Joe's Tomato Pies
DELAWARE
Hockessin
  Back Burner/DE
Wilmington
  Brandywine Room/DE
  Green Room/DE
  Michele's/DE
  Positano Rist./DE
  Ristorante Amalfi/DE
  Shipley Grill/DE
  Silk Purse/DE
  Sow's Ear/DE
  Tavola Toscana/DE

Young Children
(Besides the normal fast-food
places; * indicates children's
menu available)
Abbey Grill*
Abilene*
Academy Cafe
A Ca Mia/CM*
Adobe Cafe*
Alaina's*
Alberto's*
Al Dar*
Aleathea's/CM*
Alexander's Cafe*
Alfe's/CM*
Alfio's*
A Little Cafe*
Al Khimah*
Allie's American*
America B&G*
Angeloni's II/AC*
Angelo's Fairmount/AC*
Arroyo Grille*
Arugula!*
A Touch of Italy/CM*
Axelsson's/CM*
Barnacle Ben's*
Barnacle Ben's West*
Barrymore Room*
Bay Pony Inn
Bella Trattoria*
Ben & Irv Deli*
Bentley's Five*
Bertucci's*
Big Fish*

Big River Fish Co.*
Bird-in-Hand/LB*
Bistro Romano*
Blue in Green*
Blüe Ox Brauhaus*
Bobby's Seafood*
Bomb Bomb BBQ*
Bookbinders*
Braddock's Tavern*
Brandywine Brewing/DE*
Bravo Bistro*
Broad Axe Tavern*
Buckley's Tavern/DE*
Bugaboo Creek*
Busch's/CM*
Cafe Michaelangelo*
Cafe Noelle*
Cafette*
Cafe Zesty*
Caffe Bellissimo/DE*
Caffe La Bella*
California Cafe*
California Pizza Kit.*
Carambola*
Cedar Creek/CM*
Cent'Anni*
Century House*
Chambers*
Champps Amer.*
Charcoal Pit/DE*
Charlie's Bar/CM*
Chart House*
Chef Tell's*
Chestnut Grill*
Christopher's*
City Tavern*
Clayton's*
Cock 'n Bull*
Columbus Inn/DE
Concordville Inn*
Coppermill Harvest*
Country Club*
Cousin's/CM*
Cousins Country/CM*
Cresheim Cottage*
Crier in Country*
Cucina Rosa/CM*
Culinary Garden/CM*
Cutters*
Dahlak*
Dalessandro's
Dave's Center Point Deli/CM*
David's Yellow Brick*
Deauville Inn/CM*
DeLorenzo's

Dick Clark's*
D'Ignazio's*
DiNardo's/DE*
DiNardo's Seafood*
Dock Street*
Downey's*
Down Home Diner
Doylestown Inn*
East Side Mario's*
Ebenezer's*
El Azteca*
Elephant & Castle*
El Mariachi*
El Sombrero*
Engine 46 Steakhse.*
Epicurean, The*
Evermay on Del.
Famous 4th St. Deli*
Fat Jack's*
Feby's Fishery/DE*
Filomena Cuc. Italiana*
Filomena Cuc. Rustica*
Fireside Room
Fisher's*
Fisher's Tudor Hse.*
Flowing Springs*
Fork's Inn/CM*
Founders*
Fountain Rest.*
Four Dogs Tavern*
Fox Point Grill/DE*
Freda's Cafe/CM*
General Lafayette*
Goat Hollow*
Golden Inn/CM*
Golden Pheasant*
Good N' Plenty/LB*
Gourley's*
Gourmet's Table*
Green Cuisine/CM*
Green Room/DE*
Gregory's/CM*
Groff's Farm/LB*
Gullifty's*
Gypsy Rose*
Hadley's Bistro*
Hard Rock Cafe*
Hard Rock Cafe/AC*
Hardshell Cafe*
Harry's Savoy Grill/DE*
Hartefeld National*
Havana*
Haydn Zug's/LB*
Henny's/CM*
Hibachi Japanese/DE*

Historic Revere Tav./LB*
Hoss's Steak/LB*
Hunt Room
Hymie's*
Il Sol D'Italia*
Ingleneuk Tea Hse.*
Inn at Sugar Hill/CM*
Inn of the Hawke*
Iron Hill Brewery/DE*
Isaac's/LB*
Italian Bistro*
Jake & Oliver's*
Jim's Steaks
Joe Italiano's/Inn/CM*
Joe Italiano's/II/CM*
Joe's Tomato Pies*
John Harvard's*
Joseph Poon*
Joy Tsin Lau*
Kaminski's*
Katmandu*
Kaufman House*
Kim's*
Kobe Japanese*
La Campagne*
La Casa Pasta/DE*
La Forno*
Lamberti's Cucina*
Lambertville Station*
Lamb Tavern*
La Tolteca/DE*
Le Bus*
Liberties*
Little Brat's Haus/CM*
Lobster House/CM*
Lobster Loft/CM*
Log Cabin/LB*
London Grill*
Lone Star Steakhse.*
Los Amigos/AC*
Los Amigos' New Mexico*
Mac's/CM*
Mad Batter/CM*
Mad 4 Mex*
Malvern Meeting Hse.*
Mama Mia/CM*
Manayunk Brewing*
Manayunk Farmer's Mkt.
Marabella's*
Market Fare/LB*
Marrakesh*
Marra's
Mayfair Diner*
McGillin's*
Melrose Diner

Mendenhall Inn*
Merion Inn/CM*
Michael's Family*
Mikasa/DE*
Mirage, The/CM*
Montserrat*
Moonstruck*
More Than Ice Cream*
Moriarty's*
Moselem Springs/LB*
Mrs. Robino's/DE*
Nifty Fifty's*
Nonna's*
Obadiah's/CM*
Odette's*
Olde Greenfield Inn/LB*
Old Guard House*
Old Mill Inn*
Old Original Book*
Old Waterway Inn/AC*
Olga's Diner*
Otto's Brauhaus*
Outback Steakhse.*
Ozzie's Tratt.*
Passerelle*
Pastavino Tratt.*
Philadelphia Fish*
Philly Crab & Steak*
Pietro's Pizzeria
Pilot House/CM*
Pippo's Fantastico*
Plain & Fancy/LB
Planet Hollywood/AC*
Plough & the Stars*
Plumsteadville Inn*
Ponzio's Kingsway*
Poor Henry's*
Pub Rest.*
Purple Sage
Rajbhog Indian*
Ram's Head Inn/CM*
Ravioli House/CM*
Reading Terminal Mkt.
Red Caboose/LB*
Red Hot & Blue*
Regatta B&G*
Remi's Cafe*
Renault Winery/CM*
Rest. at Doneckers/LB*
Rio Station/CM*
Ritz-Carlton Grill*
River City Diner*
Rizzo's*
Rock Lobster*
Ruby's*

Ruhling's Seafood*
Sage Diner*
Sala Thai*
Santa Fe Burrito*
Scannicchio's/AC*
Schooners & C.B.'s/CM*
Scoogi's Classic*
Screnci's/CM*
Seafood Unlimited*
Sea Grill/CM*
Seven Stars*
Ship Inn*
Silk City*
Sonoma*
Spaghetti Warehse.*
Spotted Hog*
Stazi Milano*
Stix*
Stockyard Inn/LB*
Stoltzfus Farm/LB*
Stoudt's Black Angus/LB*
Sutor's Owl Tree/CM*
Swann Lounge*
Tacconelli's Pizza
Teresa's Cafe*
Terrace at Greenhill/DE*
Tex Mex Connection*
30th St. Station*

Thomas'*
Tony's Balt. Grill/AC*
Top of the Marq/CM*
Treetops*
Tuckahoe Inn/CM*
Ugly Mug/CM*
Urie's Waterfront/CM*
Valley Forge*
Valley Green Inn*
Ventura Greenhse./CM*
Village Porch*
Washington Crossing*
Washington House*
Waterfront/CM*
Waters Edge/CM*
White Dog Cafe*
White House/AC
Wild Onion Rest.*
William Penn Inn*
Willow Valley Rst./LB*
Windmill/LB*
W.L. Goodfellows/CM*
Wolfgang's Cafe*
Wrap Planet*
Yesterday's/CM*
Zinn's Diner/LB*
Zocalo*
ZuZu*

NOTES

Wine Vintage Chart 1985-1997

This chart is designed to help you select wine to go with your meal. It is based on the same 0 to 30 scale used throughout this *Survey*. The ratings (prepared by our friend **Howard Stravitz**, a law professor at the University of South Carolina) reflect both the quality of the vintage and the wine's readiness for present consumption. Thus, if a wine is not fully mature or is over the hill, its rating has been reduced. We do not include 1987 or 1991 vintages because, with the exception of cabernets and '91 Northern Rhônes, those vintages are not especially recommended.

	'85	'86	'88	'89	'90	'92	'93	'94	'95	'96	'97
WHITES											
French:											
Burgundy	24	25	20	29	24	24	–	23	28	27	26
Loire Valley	–	–	–	26	25	19	22	23	24	25	23
Champagne	28	25	24	26	28	–	24	–	25	26	–
Sauternes	22	28	29	25	26	–	–	18	22	24	23
California:											
Chardonnay	–	–	–	–	25	24	23	26	23	22	
REDS											
French:											
Bordeaux	26	27	25	28	29	19	22	24	25	24	22
Burgundy	25	–	24	27	29	23	25	22	24	25	24
Rhône	26	20	26	28	27	16	23*	23	24	22	–
Beaujolais	–	–	–	–	–	–	20	21	24	22	23
California:											
Cab./Merlot	26	26	–	21	28	26	25	27	23	24	22
Zinfandel	–	–	–	–	–	21	21	23	20	21	23
Italian:											
Tuscany	27	16	24	–	26	–	21	20	25	19	–
Piedmont	26	–	25	27	27	–	19	–	24	25	–

*Rating is only for Southern Rhône wine.

Bargain sippers take note: Some wines are reliable year in, year out, and are reasonably priced as well. These wines are best bought in the most recent vintages. They include: Alsatian Pinot Blancs, Côtes du Rhône, Muscadet, Bardolino, Valpolicella and inexpensive Spanish Rioja and California Zinfandel.